BODY BY DESIGN

*From the
Digestive
System to
the Skeleton*

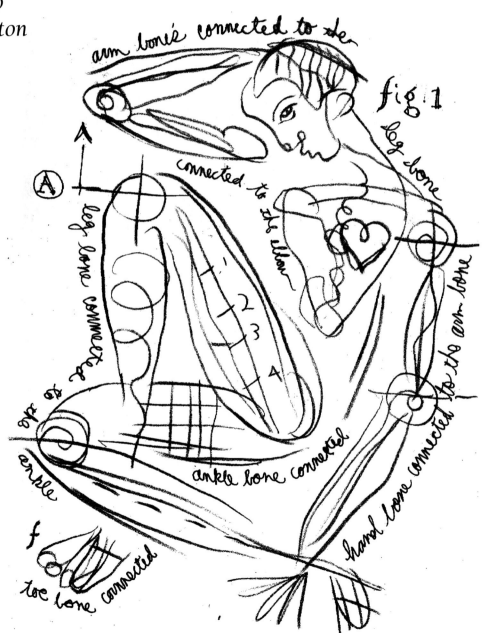

BODY BY DESIGN

*From the
Digestive
System to
the Skeleton*

volume

1

cardiovascular system
digestive system
endocrine system
integumentary system
lymphatic system
muscular system

Rob Nagel • **Betz Des Chenes, Editor**

AN IMPRINT OF THE GALE GROUP
DETROIT · SAN FRANCISCO · LONDON
BOSTON · WOODBRIDGE, CT

Body by Design
From the Digestive System to the Skeleton

Rob Nagel

STAFF

Elizabeth A. Des Chenes, *U•X•L Senior Editor*
Thomas L. Romig, *U•X•L Publisher*

Margaret A. Chamberlain, *Permissions Specialist (Pictures)*

Rita Wimberley, *Senior Buyer*
Evi Seoud, *Assistant Production Manager*
Dorothy Maki, *Manufacturing Manager*
Mary Beth Trimper, *Production Director*

Michelle Di Mercurio, *Senior Art Director*
Cynthia Baldwin, *Product Design Manager*

GGS Information Services, Inc., *Typesetting*

Cover illustration by Kevin Ewing Illustrations.

Library of Congress Cataloging-in-Publication Data.
Nagel, Rob.
       Body by Design: from the digestive system to the skeleton/Rob Nagel.
          p. cm.
       Includes bibliographical references and index.
Contents: v. 1. The cardiovascular system. The digestive system.
The endocrine system. The integumentary system. The lymphatic
system. The muscular system. v.2. The nervous system. The
reproductive system. The respiratory system. The skeletal system.
The urinary system. The special senses.
   ISBN 0-7876-3897-8 (set). -ISBN 0-7876-3898-6 (v.1). -ISBN 0-7876-3899-4 (v.2.)
   1. Human physiology Juvenile literature. [1. Body. Human. 1.
Human physiology. 3. Human anatomy.] I. Title.
QP36.N33 1999
612-dc21
                                                  99-14642

Printed in United States of America
10 9 8 7 6 5 4 3

To the memory of
Michael D. Merker
(1961–1999)

Contents

Reader's Guide

Body by Design: From the Digestive System to the Skeleton presents the anatomy (structure) and physiology (function) of the human body in twelve chapters spread over two volumes. Each chapter is devoted to one of the eleven organ systems that make up the body. The last chapter focuses on the special senses, which allow humans to connect with the real world.

Each chapter begins with a paragraph overview of that particular organ system (or the special senses) and its function or role in the body. The remaining information in the chapter is broken into four sections, each labeled by a particular subhead:

- The material under the subhead **Design** comprises the anatomy section of each chapter. It is a detailed presentation of the organs and any associated structures that compose that particular organ system or the special senses. Weight, size, color, position, and composition of the organs and their structures are given, where applicable, in this section.

- The material under the subhead **Workings** comprises the physiology section of each chapter. It is a step-by-step exploration of the functions of the organs and any associated structures that compose that particular organ system or the special senses. The mechanics of muscle contraction, the transmission of nerve impulses, the actions of swallowing and breathing, and numerous other physiological processes are all examined in depth in this section.

- The material under the subhead **Ailments** is a presentation of some of the many diseases and disorders that can target the organs or associated structures in that particular organ system or the special senses. Most of the ailments presented are well known, but a few are not. For each ailment, the number of people generally affected, causes, symptoms, and treatments are all covered.

- The material under the subhead **Taking care** is a presentation of ways an individual can keep a particular system healthy. Because of the connectedness of the organ systems, forming the human body as a whole, steps to keep a system healthy are often steps to keep the body healthy. Many of these steps are general (some would say common sense) approaches.

Each chapter also contains illustrations or photos (many in color) of the particular organs and any associated structures. Where applicable, photos depicting specific ailments have also been included. Historical discoveries, recent medical advances, short biographies of scientists, and other interesting facts relating to that particular system are presented in sidebar boxes sprinkled throughout each chapter.

A "Words to Know" box included at the beginning of each chapter provides pronunciations and definitions of words and terms used in that chapter. Another "Words to Know" box later in each chapter is devoted to system ailments. At the end of each chapter, under the heading "For More Information," appears a list of books and annotated web sites that provide students with further information about that particular system.

Each volume of *Body by Design* includes an overview essay, "How Systems and Other Structures Form the Living Body," followed by a comprehensive glossary collected from all the "Words to Know" boxes in the twelve chapters.

Each volume ends with a general bibliography section. The offerings in this section, twenty books and fifteen annotated web sites, are not system specific, but explore the human body as a whole. A cumulative index providing access to all major terms and topics covered throughout *Body by Design* concludes each volume.

Related Reference Sources

Body by Design is only one component of the three-part U•X•L Complete Health Resource. Other titles in this library include:

- *Sick! Diseases and Disorders, Injuries and Infections:* This four-volume set contains 140 alphabetically arranged entries on diseases, disorders, and injuries, including information on their causes, symptoms, diagnoses, tests and treatments, and prognoses. Each entry, four to seven pages long, includes sidebars on related people and topics, as well as a list of sources for further research. Each volume contains a 16-page color insert. *Sick* also features more than 240 black-and-white photographs and a cumulative subject index.

- *Healthy Living:* This three-volume set examines fitness, nutrition, and other lifestyle issues across fifteen subject chapters. Topics covered include hygiene, mental health, preventive care, alternative medicine, and careers in health care. Sidebar boxes within entries provide information on related issues, while over 150 black-and-white illustrations help illuminate the text. *Healthy Living* also features a cumulative index.

Acknowledgments

A note of appreciation is extended to the *Body by Design* advisors, who provided invaluable suggestions when this work was in its formative stages:

Carole Branson
Seminar Science Teacher
Wilson Middle School
San Diego, California

Bonnie L. Raasch
Media Specialist
Vernon Middle School
Marion, Iowa

Doris J. Ranke
Science Teacher
West Bloomfield High School
West Bloomfield, Michigan

I would like to express my deep appreciation to occupational therapist Diane Collins for her close reading of the material and her insightful comments and suggestions.

Thanks are also extended to Tom Romig, U•X•L Publisher, for giving me words of encouragement at a crucial point during the project. Finally, my debts on this project are great, but none is greater than to my editor, Elizabeth Des Chenes. Without her unflagging support and guidance, this work would not have come to fruition. It has been a collaborative effort, and I proudly share the cover with her.

Comments and Suggestions

We welcome your comments on *Body by Design: From the Digestive System to the Skeleton.* Please write: Editors, *Body by Design,* U•X•L, 27500 Drake Rd., Farmington Hills, Michigan, 48331–3535; call toll free: 1–800–877–4253; fax: 248–414–5043; or send e-mail via http://www.galegroup.com.

Please Read: Important Information

Body by Design is a medical reference product designed to inform and educate readers about the human body. U•X•L believes this product to be comprehensive, but not necessarily definitive. While U•X•L has made substantial efforts to provide information that is accurate and up to date, U•X•L makes no representations or warranties of any kind, including without limitation, warranties of merchantability or fitness for a particular purpose, nor does it guarantee the accuracy, comprehensiveness, or timeliness of the information contained in this product.

Readers should be aware that the universe of medical knowledge is constantly growing and changing, and that differences of medical opinion exist among authorities. They are also advised to seek professional diagnosis and treatment for any medical condition, and to discuss information obtained from this book with their health care provider.

Overview: How Systems and Other Structures Form the Living Body

The human body is composed of eleven organ systems. An organ is any part of the body formed of two or more tissues that performs a specialized function. Examples of organs are the brain, heart, kidneys, liver, lungs, and stomach. An organ system is a group of organs whose combined workings contribute to a particular function for the body as a whole.

All systems have important functions they alone perform. The cardio-vascular system—composed of the heart, blood, and blood vessels—transports nutrients, dissolved gases, and hormones to cells throughout the body. No other system in the body carries out this vital work.

But the cardiovascular system, like all other systems, cannot function alone. Indeed, to perform its work, it must interact with other systems. The red blood cells in the blood it transports are formed in the red bone marrow of certain bones (skeletal system). The nutrients it carries come from the breakdown of food by the organs of the digestive system. Oxygen and carbon dioxide, the dissolved gases that pass between the blood and cells of the body, are exchanged with the surrounding air through the work of the lungs and the passageways that carry air to them (respiratory system). Hormones, chemical messengers that maintain and regulate basic bodily functions, are produced by the glands of the endocrine system.

Although all organ systems are connected, certain systems combine with certain others to produce specific actions. The cardiovascular and lymphatic systems transport fluids through the body and provide defense against diseases and foreign substances. The nervous and endocrine systems regulate and coordinate the body's internal operations. The integumentary, muscular, and skeletal systems provide body support and movement. The digestive, respiratory, and urinary systems interact with the outside environment, exchanging material.

The human body is a well-designed and well-built machine. When its perfectly fitting parts are operating normally, the body runs smoothly and efficiently. When any part breaks down, however, so does the body. Indeed, the loss of just one system would result in death. All organ systems are necessary for survival. Thus, it is of vital importance to keep the body systems healthy, since all the systems work together.

Words to Know

A

Accommodation (ah-kah-mah-DAY-shun): Process of changing the shape of the lens of the eye to keep an image focused on the retina.

Acetylcholine (ah-see-til-KOE-leen): Neurotransmitter chemical released at the neuromuscular junction by motor nerves that translates messages from the brain to muscle fibers.

Acne (AK-nee): Disorder in which hair follicles of the skin become clogged and infected, often forming pimples as a result.

Acromegaly (ak-ro-MEG-ah-lee): Disorder in which the anterior pituitary overproduces growth hormone, resulting in abnormal enlargement of the extremities—nose, jaw, fingers, and toes; in children, the disorder produces gigantism.

Addison's disease (ADD-i-sonz): Disorder in which the adrenal cortex underproduces cortisol and aldosterone, resulting in the disruption of numerous bodily functions.

Adenosine triphosphate (ah-DEN-o-seen try-FOS-fate): High-energy molecule found in every cell in the body.

Adrenal cortex (ah-DREE-nul KOR-tex): Outer layer of the adrenal glands, which secretes cortisol and aldosterone.

Adrenal glands (ah-DREE-nul): Glands located on top of each kidney consisting of an outer layer (adrenal cortex) and an inner layer (adrenal medulla).

Adrenal medulla (ah-DREE-nul muh-DUH-luh): Inner layer of the adrenal glands, which secretes epinephrine and norepinephrine.

Adrenocorticotropic hormone (ah-dree-no-kor-ti-koh-TROH-pik): Hormone secreted by the anterior pituitary that stimulates the adrenal cortex to secrete cortisol.

Aerobic metabolism (air-ROH-bic muh-TAB-uh-lizm): Chemical reactions that require oxygen in order to create adenosine triphosphate.

Agglutination (ah-glue-ti-NA-shun): Clumping of blood cells brought about by the mixing of blood types.

AIDS: Acquired immune deficiency syndrome, a disorder caused by a virus (HIV) that infects helper T cells and weakens immune responses.

Aldosterone (al-DOS-te-rone): Hormone secreted by the adrenal cortex that controls the salt and water balance in the body.

Alimentary canal (al-i-MEN-tah-ree ka-NAL): Also known as the digestive tract, the series of muscular structures through which food passes while being converted to nutrients and waste products; includes the oral cavity, pharynx, esophagus, stomach, large intestine, and small intestine.

Allergen (AL-er-jen): Substance that causes an allergy.

Allergy (AL-er-jee): An abnormal immune reaction to an otherwise harmless substance.

Alveoli (al-VEE-oh-lie): Air sacs of the lungs.

Alzheimer's disease (ALTS-hi-merz): Disease of the nervous system marked by a deterioration of memory, thinking, and reasoning.

Amylase (am-i-LACE): Any of various digestive enzymes that convert starches to sugars.

Amyotrophic lateral sclerosis (a-me-o-TROW-fik LA-ter-al skle-ROW-sis): Also known as Lou Gehrig's disease, a disease that breaks down motor neurons, resulting in the loss of the ability to move any of the muscles in the body.

Androgens (AN-dro-jens): Hormones that control male secondary sex characteristics.

Anemia (ah-NEE-me-yah): Diseased condition in which there is a deficiency of red blood cells or hemoglobin.

Anorexia nervosa (an-ah-REK-see-ah ner-VO-sa): Eating disorder usually occurring in young women that is characterized by an abnormal fear of becoming obese, a persistent aversion to food, and severe weight loss.

Antagonist (an-TAG-o-nist): Muscle that acts in opposition to a prime mover.

Antibody (AN-ti-bod-ee): Specialized substance produced by the body that can provide immunity against a specific antigen.

Antibody-mediated immunity (AN-ti-bod-ee MEE-dee-a-ted i-MYOO-ni-tee): Immune response involving B cells and their production of antibodies.

Antidiuretic hormone (an-tee-die-yu-REH-tik HOR-mone): Hormone produced by the hypothalamus and stored in the posterior pituitary that increases the absorption of water by the kidneys.

Antigen (AN-ti-jen): Any substance that, when introduced to the body, is recognized as foreign and activates an immune response.

Aorta (ay-OR-ta): Main artery of the body.

Apocrine sweat glands (AP-oh-krin): Sweat glands located primarily in the armpit and genital areas.

Appendicitis (ah-pen-di-SIGH-tis): Inflammation of the appendix.

Appendix (ah-PEN-dix): Small, apparently useless organ extending from the cecum.

Aqueous humor (AYE-kwee-us HYOO-mer): Tissue fluid filling the cavity of the eye between the cornea and the lens.

Arachnoid (ah-RAK-noid): Weblike middle layer of the three meninges covering the brain and spinal cord.

Arrector pili muscle (ah-REK-tor PIE-lie): Smooth muscle attached to a hair follicle that, when stimulated, pulls on the follicle, causing the hair shaft to stand upright.

Arteriole (ar-TEER-e-ohl): Small artery.

Arteriosclerosis (ar-tir-ee-o-skle-ROW-sis): Diseased condition in which the walls of arteries become thickened and hard, interfering with the circulation of blood.

Artery (AR-te-ree): Vessel that carries blood away from the heart.

Asthma (AZ-ma): Respiratory disease often caused by an allergy that is marked by tightness in the chest and difficulty in breathing.

Astigmatism (ah-STIG-mah-tiz-um): Incorrect shaping of the cornea that results in an incorrect focusing of light on the retina.

Atherosclerosis (ath-a-row-skle-ROW-sis): Diseased condition in which fatty material accumulates on the interior walls of arteries, making them narrower.

Athlete's foot: Common fungus infection in which the skin between the toes becomes itchy and sore, cracking and peeling away.

Atria (AY-tree-a): Upper chambers of the heart that receive blood from the veins.

Atrioventricular (AV) node (a-tree-oh-ven-TRICK-u-lar): Node of specialized tissue lying near the bottom of the right atrium that fires an electrical impulse across the ventricles, causing them to contract.

Atrioventricular (AV) valves: Valves located between the atria and ventricles.

Autoimmune disease (au-toe-i-MYOON): Condition in which the body produces antibodies that attack and destroy the body's own tissues.

Autonomic nervous system (aw-toh-NOM-ik NERV-us SIS-tem): Part of the peripheral nervous system that controls involuntary actions, such as the heartbeat, gland secretions, and digestion.

Axon (AK-son): Taillike projection extending out a neuron that carries impulses away from the cell body.

B

B cell: Also called B lymphocyte, a type of lymphocyte that originates from the bone marrow and that changes into antibody-producing plasma cells.

Basal cell carcinoma (BAY-sal CELL car-si-NO-ma): Skin cancer that affects the basal cells in the epidermis.

Basal ganglia (BAY-zul GANG-lee-ah): Paired masses of gray matter within the white matter of the cerebrum that help coordinate subconscious skeletal muscular movement.

Bile: Greenish yellow liquid produced by the liver that neutralizes acids and emulsifies fats in the duodenum.

Biliary atresia (BILL-ee-a-ree ah-TREE-zee-ah): Condition in which ducts to transport bile from the liver to the duodenum fail to develop in a fetus.

Binocular vision (by-NOK-yoo-lur VI-zhun): Ability of the brain to create one image from the slightly different images received from each eye.

Blood pressure: Pressure or force the blood exerts against the inner walls of the blood vessels.

Bolus (BO-lus): Rounded mass of food prepared by the mouth for swallowing.

Botulism (BOCH-a-liz-em): Form of food poisoning in which a bacterial toxin prevents the release of acetylcholine at neuromuscular junctions, resulting in paralysis.

Bowman's capsule (BOW-manz KAP-sul): Cup-shaped end of a nephron that encloses a glomerulus.

Brain: Central controlling and coordinating organ of the nervous system.

Breathing (BREETH-ing): Process of inhaling and exhaling air.

Bronchi (BRONG-kie): Largest branch of the bronchial tree between the trachea and bronchioles.

Bronchial tree (BRONG-key-uhl TREE): Entire system of air passageways within the lungs formed by the branching of bronchial tubes.

Bronchioles (BRONG-key-ohls): Smallest of the air passageways within the lungs.

Bronchitis (bron-KIE-tis): Inflammation of the mucous membrane of the bronchial tubes.

Bulimia (boo-LEE-me-ah): Eating disorder characterized by eating binges followed by self-induced vomiting or laxative abuse.

C

Calcitonin (kal-si-TOE-nin): Hormone secreted by the thyroid gland that decreases calcium levels in the blood.

Calyces (KAY-li-seez): Cup-shaped extensions of the renal pelvis that enclose the tips of the renal pyramids and collect urine.

Capillary (CAP-i-lair-ee): Minute blood vessel that connects arterioles with venules.

Carcinoma (car-si-NO-ma): Cancerous tumor of the skin, mucous membrane, or similar tissue of the body.

Cardiac cycle (CAR-dee-ack): Series of events that occur in the heart during one complete heartbeat.

Carpal tunnel syndrome (CAR-pal TUN-nel SIN-drome): Disorder caused by the compression at the wrist of the median nerve supplying the hand, causing numbness and tingling.

Cataract (KAT-ah-rakt): Condition in which the lens of the eye turns cloudy, causing partial or total blindness.

Cauda equina (KAW-da ee-KWHY-nah): Spinal nerves that hang below the end of the spinal cord.

Cecum (SEE-kum): Blind pouch at the beginning of the large intestine.

Cell-mediated immunity (CELL MEE-dee-a-ted i-MYOO-ni-tee): Immune response led by T cells that does not involve the production of antibodies.

Central nervous system: Part of the nervous system consisting of the brain and spinal cord.

Cerebral cortex (se-REE-bral KOR-tex): Outermost layer of the cerebrum made entirely of gray matter.

Cerebrum (se-REE-brum): Largest part of the brain, involved with conscious perception, voluntary actions, memory, thought, and personality.

Cholesterol (ko-LESS-ter-ol): Fatlike substance produced by the liver that is an essential part of cell membranes and body chemicals; when present in excess in the body, cholesterol can accumulate on the inside walls of arteries and block blood flow.

Ceruminous glands (suh-ROO-mi-nus GLANDZ): Exocrine glands in the skin of the auditory canal of the ear that secrete earwax or cerumen.

Chemoreceptors (kee-moe-re-SEP-terz): Receptors sensitive to various chemicals substances.

Choroid (KOR-oid): Middle, pigmented layer of the eye.

Chyle (KILE): Thick, whitish liquid consisting of lymph and tiny fat globules absorbed from the small intestine during digestion.

Chyme (KIME): Soupylike mixture of partially digested food and stomach secretions.

Ciliary body (SIL-ee-air-ee BAH-dee): Circular muscle that surrounds the edge of the lens of the eye and changes the shape of the lens.

Cirrhosis (si-ROW-sis): Chronic disease of the liver in which normal liver cells are damaged and then replaced by scar tissue.

Cochlea (KOK-lee-ah): Spiral-shaped cavity in the inner ear that contains the receptors for hearing in the organ of Corti.

Colon (KOH-lun): Largest region of the large intestine, divided into four sections: ascending, transverse, descending, and sigmoid (the term "colon" is sometimes used to describe the entire large intestine).

Colostomy (kuh-LAS-tuh-mee): Surgical procedure where a portion of the large intestine is brought through the abdominal wall and attached to a bag to collect feces.

Cones: Photoreceptors in the retina of the eye that detect colors.

Conjunctiva (kon-junk-TIE-vah): Mucous membrane lining the eyelids and covering the front surface of the eyeball.

Conjunctivitis (kon-junk-ti-VIE-tis): Inflammation of the conjunctiva of the eye.

Cornea (KOR-nee-ah): Transparent front portion of the sclera of the eye.

Corpus callosum (KOR-pus ka-LOW-sum): Large band of neurons connecting the two cerebral hemispheres.

Cortisol (KOR-ti-sol): Hormone secreted by the adrenal cortex that promotes the body's efficient use of nutrients during stressful situations.

Cramp: Prolonged muscle spasm.

Creatinine (kree-AT-i-neen): Waste product in urine produced by the breakdown of creatine.

Crohn's disease (CRONES di-ZEEZ): Disorder that causes inflammation and ulceration of all the layers of the intestinal wall, particularly in the small intestine.

Cushing's syndrome (KU-shingz SIN-drome): Disorder caused by an overproduction of steroids (mostly cortisol) by the adrenal cortex, resulting in obesity and muscular weakness.

Cystic fibrosis (SIS-tik fie-BRO-sis): Genetic disease in which, among other things, the mucous membranes of the respiratory tract produce a thick, sticky mucus that clogs airways.

Cystitis (sis-TIE-tis): Inflammation of the urinary bladder caused by a bacterial infection.

D

Defecation (def-e-KAY-shun): Elimination of feces from the large intestine through the anus.

Dendrites (DEN-drites): Branchlike extensions of neurons that carry impulses toward the cell body.

Dentin (DEN-tin): Bonelike material underneath the enamel of teeth, forming the main part.

Dermal papillae (DER-mal pah-PILL-ee): Fingerlike projections extending upward from the dermis containing blood capillaries, which provide nutrients for the lower layer of the epidermis; also form the characteristic ridges on the skin surface of the hands (fingerprints) and feet.

Dermatitis (der-ma-TIE-tis): Any inflammation of the skin.

Dermis (DER-miss): Thick, inner layer of the skin.

Diabetes mellitus (die-ah-BEE-teez MUL-le-tus): Disorder in which the body's cells cannot absorb glucose, either because the pancreas does not produce enough insulin or the cells do not respond to the effects of insulin that is produced.

Diaphragm (DIE-ah-fram): Membrane of muscle separating the chest cavity from the abdominal cavity.

Diastole (die-ASS-te-lee): Period of relaxation and expansion of the heart when its chambers fill with blood.

Diencephalon (die-en-SEF-ah-lon): Rear part of the forebrain that connects the midbrain to the cerebrum and that contains the thalamus and hypothalamus.

Diffusion (dif-FEW-shun): Movement of molecules from an area of greater concentration to an area of lesser concentration.

Diverticulosis (di-ver-ti-cue-LOW-sis): Condition in which the inner lining of the large intestine bulges out through its muscular wall; if the bulges become infected, the condition is called diverticulitis.

Duodenum (doo-o-DEE-num or doo-AH-de-num): First section of the small intestine.

Dura mater (DUR-ah MAY-tur): Outermost and toughest of the three meninges covering the brain and spinal cord.

E

Eardrum (EER-drum): Thin membrane at the end of the outer ear that vibrates when sound waves strike it.

Eccrine sweat glands (ECK-rin): Body's most numerous sweat glands, which produce watery sweat to maintain normal body temperature.

Edema (i-DEE-mah): Condition in which excessive fluid collects in bodily tissue and causes swelling.

Emphysema (em-feh-ZEE-mah): Respiratory disease marked by breathlessness that is brought on by the enlargement of the alveoli in the lungs.

Emulsify (e-MULL-si-fie): To break down large fat globules into smaller droplets that stay suspended in water.

Enamel (e-NAM-el): Whitish, hard, glossy outer layer of teeth.

Endocardium (en-doe-CAR-dee-um): Thin membrane lining the interior of the heart.

Enzymes (EN-zimes): Proteins that speed up the rate of chemical reactions.

Epicardium (ep-i-CAR-dee-um): Lubricating outer layer of the heart wall and part of the pericardium.

Epidermis (ep-i-DER-miss): Thin, outer layer of the skin.

Epiglottis (ep-i-GLAH-tis): Flaplike piece of tissue at the top of the larynx that covers its opening when swallowing is occurring.

Epilepsy (EP-eh-lep-see): Disorder of the nervous system marked by seizures that often involve convulsions or the loss of consciousness.

Epinephrine (ep-i-NEFF-rin): Also called adrenaline, a hormone secreted by the adrenal medulla that stimulates the body to react to stressful situations.

Epithelial tissue (ep-i-THEE-lee-al): Tissue that covers the internal and external surfaces of the body and also forms glandular organs.

Erythrocyte (e-RITH-re-site): Red blood cell.

Esophagus (i-SOF-ah-gus): Muscular tube connecting the pharynx and stomach.

Estrogens (ES-tro-jenz): Female steroid hormones secreted by the ovaries that bring about the secondary sex characteristics and regulate the female reproductive cycle.

Eustachian tube (yoo-STAY-she-an TOOB): Slender air passage between the middle ear cavity and the pharynx, which equalizes air pressure on the two sides of the eardrum.

Exhalation (ex-ha-LAY-shun): Also known as expiration, the movement of air out of the lungs.

External auditory canal (ex-TER-nal AW-di-tor-ee ka-NAL): Also called the ear canal, the tunnel in the ear between the pinna and eardrum.

F

Farsightedness: Known formally as hyperopia, the condition of the eye where incoming rays of light reach the retina before they converge to form a focused image.

Fascicle (FA-si-kul): Bundle of myofibrils wrapped together by connective tissue.

Feces (FEE-seez): Solid body wastes formed in the large intestine.

Fever: Abnormally high body temperature brought about as a response to infection or severe physical injury.

Filtration (fill-TRAY-shun): Movement of water and dissolved materials through a membrane from an area of higher pressure to an area of lower pressure.

Flatus (FLAY-tus): Gas generated by bacteria in the large intestine.

Follicle-stimulating hormone (FAH-lik-uhl STIM-yoo-lay-ting HOR-mone): Gonadotropic hormone produced by the anterior pituitary gland that stimulates the development of follicles in the ovaries of females and sperm in the testes of males.

G

Gallstones (GAUL-stones): Solid crystal deposits that form in the gall bladder.

Ganglion (GANG-glee-on): Any collection of nerve cell bodies forming a nerve center in the peripheral nervous system.

Gastric juice (GAS-trick JOOSE): Secretion of the gastric glands of the stomach, containing hydrochloric acid, pepsin, and mucus.

Gigantism (jie-GAN-tizm): Disorder in children in which the anterior pituitary overproduces growth hormone, resulting in abnormal enlargement of the extremities (nose, jaw, fingers, and toes) and the long bones, causing unusual height.

Gland: Any organ that secretes or excretes substances for further use in the body or for elimination.

Glaucoma (glaw-KOE-mah): Eye disorder caused by a buildup of aqueous humor that results in high pressure in the eyeball, often damaging the optic nerve and eventually leading to blindness.

Glomerulonephritis (glah-mer-u-lo-ne-FRY-tis): Inflammation of the glomeruli in the renal corpuscles of the kidneys.

Glomerulus (glow-MER-yoo-lus): Network of capillaries enclosed by a Bowman's capsule.

Glottis (GLAH-tis): Opening of the larynx between the vocal cords.

Glucagon (GLUE-ka-gon): Hormone secreted by the islets of Langerhans that raises the level of sugar in the blood.

Gonad (GO-nad): Sex organ in which reproductive cells develop.

Gonadotropic hormones (gon-ah-do-TROP-ik): Hormones secreted by the anterior pituitary that affect or stimulate the growth or activity of the gonads.

Graves' disease: Disorder in which an antibody binds to specific cells in the thyroid gland, forcing them to secrete excess thyroid hormone.

Gray matter: Grayish nerve tissue of the central nervous system containing neuron cell bodies, neuroglia cells, and unmyelinated axons.

Gustation (gus-TAY-shun): The sense of taste.

Gustatory cells (GUS-ta-tor-ee CELLS): Chemoreceptors located within taste buds.

Gyri (JYE-rye): Outward folds on the surface of the cerebral cortex.

H

Hemoglobin (HEE-muh-glow-bin): Iron-containing protein pigment in red blood cells that can combine with oxygen and carbon dioxide.

Hemophilia (hee-muh-FILL-ee-ah): Inherited blood disease in which the blood lacks one or more of the clotting factors, making it difficult to stop bleeding.

Henle's loop (HEN-leez LOOP): Looped portion of a renal tubule.

Hepatic portal circulation (heh-PAT-ick POR-tal): System of blood vessels that transports blood from the digestive organs and the spleen through the liver before returning it to the heart.

Hepatitis (hep-a-TIE-tis): Inflammation of the liver that is caused mainly by a virus.

Hilus (HIGH-lus): Indentation or depression on the surface of an organ such as a kidney.

Hippocampus (hip-ah-CAM-pes): Structure in the limbic system necessary for the formation of long-term memory.

Histamine (HISS-ta-mean): Chemical compound released by injured cells that causes local blood vessels to enlarge.

HIV: Human immunodeficiency virus, which infects helper T cells and weakens immune responses, leading to the severe AIDS disorder.

Homeostasis (hoe-me-o-STAY-sis): Ability of the body or a cell to maintain the internal balance of its functions, such as steady temperature, regardless of outside conditions.

Huntington's disease: Inherited, progressive disease causing uncontrollable physical movements and mental deterioration.

Hypertension (hi-per-TEN-shun): High blood pressure.

Hyperthyroidism (hi-per-THIGH-roy-dizm): Disorder in which an overactive thyroid produces too much thyroxine.

Hypothalamus (hi-po-THAL-ah-mus): Region of the brain containing many control centers for body functions and emotions; also regulates the pituitary gland's secretions.

Hypothyroidism (hi-po-THIGH-roy-dizm): Disorder in which an underactive thyroid produces too little thyroxine.

I

Ileocecal valve (ill-ee-oh-SEE-kal VALV): Sphincter or ring of muscular that controls the flow of chyme from the ileum to the large intestine.

Ileum (ILL-ee-um): Final section of the small intestine.

Immunity (i-MYOO-ni-tee): Body's ability to defend itself against pathogens or other foreign material.

Inflammation (in-flah-MAY-shun): Response to injury or infection of body tissues, marked by redness, heat, swelling, and pain.

Inhalation (in-ha-LAY-shun): Also known as inspiration, the movement of air into the lungs.

Insulin (IN-suh-lin): Hormone secreted by the islets of Langerhans that regulates the amount of sugar in the blood.

Integument (in-TEG-ye-ment): In animals and plants, any natural outer covering, such as skin, shell, membrane, or husk.

Interferon (in-ter-FIR-on): Protein compound released by cells infected with a virus to prevent that virus from reproducing in nearby normal cells.

Interstitial fluid (in-ter-STI-shul): Fluid found in the spaces between cells.

Iris (EYE-ris): Pigmented (colored) part of the eye between the cornea and lens made of two sets of smooth muscle fibers.

Islets of Langerhans (EYE-lets of LAHNG-er-hanz): Endocrine cells of the pancreas that secrete insulin and glucagon.

J

Jejunum (je-JOO-num): Middle section of the small intestine.

K

Keratin (KER-ah-tin): Tough, fibrous, water-resistant protein that forms the outer layers of hair, calluses, and nails and coats the surface of the skin.

Kidney stones: Large accumulations of calcium salt crystals from urine that may form in the kidneys.

L

Lacrimal gland (LAK-ri-muhl GLAND): Gland located at the upper, outer corner of each eyeball that secretes tears.

Lacteals (LAK-tee-als): Specialized lymph capillaries in the villi of the small intestine.

Lactic acid (LAK-tik ASS-id): Chemical waste product created when muscle fibers break down glucose without the proper amount of oxygen.

Lactose intolerance (LAK-tose in-TOL-er-ance): Inability of the body to digest significant amounts of lactose, the predominant sugar in milk.

Larynx (LAR-ingks): Organ between the pharynx and trachea that contains the vocal cords.

Lens: Clear, oval, flexible structure behind the pupil in the eye that changes shape for the focusing of light rays.

Leukemia (loo-KEE-mee-ah): Type of cancer that affects the blood-forming tissues and organs, causing them to flood the bloodstream and lymphatic system with immature and abnormal white blood cells.

Leukocyte (LUKE-oh-site): White blood cell.

Limbic system (LIM-bik SIS-tem): Group of structures in the cerebrum and diencephalon that are involved with emotional states and memory.

Lipase (LIE-pace): Digestive enzyme that converts lipids (fats) into fatty acids.

Lower esophageal sphincter (LOW-er i-sof-ah-GEE-al SFINGK-ter): Strong ring of muscle at the base of the esophagus that contracts to prevent stomach contents from moving back into the esophagus.

Lungs: Paired breathing organs.

Lunula (LOO-noo-la): White, crescent-shaped area of the nail bed near the nail root.

Luteinizing hormone (loo-tee-in-EYE-zing): Gonadotropic hormone secreted by the anterior pituitary that stimulates, in women, ovulation and the release of estrogens and progesterone by the ovaries and, in men, the secretion of testosterone by the testes.

Lymph (LIMF): Slightly yellowish but clear fluid found within lymph vessels.

Lymphadenitis (lim-fad-e-NIE-tis): Inflammation of lymph nodes.

Lymphangitis (lim-fan-JIE-tis): Inflammation of lymphatic vessels.

Lymph node: Small mass of lymphatic tissue located along the pathway of a lymph vessel that filters out harmful microorganisms.

Lymphocyte (LIM-foe-site): Type of white blood cell produced in lymph nodes, bone marrow, and the spleen that defends the body against infection by producing antibodies.

Lymphoma (lim-FOE-mah): General term applied to cancers of the lymphatic system, which include Hodgkin's lymphoma and non-Hodgkin's lymphomas.

M

Macrophage (MACK-row-fage): Large white blood cell that engulfs and destroys bacteria, viruses, and other foreign substances in the lymph.

Malignant melanoma (ma-LIG-nant mel-ah-NO-ma): Cancer of melanocytes; the most serious type of skin cancer.

Mechanoreceptors (mek-ah-no-re-SEP-terz): Receptors sensitive to mechanical or physical pressures such as sound and touch.

Medulla oblongata (mi-DUL-ah ob-long-GAH-tah): Part of the brain located at the top end of the spinal cord that controls breathing and other involuntary functions.

Megakaryocyte (meg-ah-CARE-ee-oh-site): Large cell in the red bone marrow that breaks up into small fragments that become platelets.

Melanocyte (MEL-ah-no-site): Cell found in the lower epidermis that produces the protein pigment melanin.

Melatonin (mel-a-TOE-nin): Hormone secreted by the pineal gland that helps set the body's twenty-four-hour clock and plays a role in the timing of puberty and sexual development.

Meniere's disease (men-ee-AIRZ): Ear disorder characterized by recurring dizziness, hearing loss, and a buzzing or ringing sound in the ears.

Meninges (meh-NIN-jeez): Membranes that cover the brain and spinal cord.

Metabolism (muh-TAB-uh-lizm): Sum of all the physiological processes by which an organism maintains life.

Micturition (mik-tu-RISH-un): Urination, or the elimination or voiding of urine from the urinary bladder.

Midbrain: Part of the brain between the hypothalamus and the pons that regulates visual, auditory, and rightening reflexes.

Migraine (MY-grain): A particularly intense form of headache.

Multiple sclerosis (skle-ROW-sis): Disorder in which immune cells attack and destroy the insulation covering nerve fibers in the central nervous system, causing muscular weakness and loss of coordination.

Muscle tone: Sustained partial contraction of certain muscle fibers in all muscles.

Muscular dystrophy (MUS-kyu-lar DIS-tro-fee): One of several inherited muscular diseases in which a person's muscles gradually and irreversibly deteriorate, causing weakness and eventually complete disability.

Myasthenia gravis (my-ass-THEH-nee-ah GRA-vis): Autoimmune disease in which antibodies attack acetylcholine, blocking the transmission of nerve impulses to muscle fibers.

Myelin (MY-ah-lin): Soft, white, fatty material that forms a sheath around the axons of most neurons.

Myocardium (my-oh-CAR-dee-um): Cardiac muscle layer of the heart wall.

Myofibrils (my-o-FIE-brilz): cylindrical structures lying within skeletal muscle fibers that are composed of repeating structural units called sarcomeres.

Myofilament (my-o-FILL-ah-ment): Protein filament composing the myofibrils; can be either thick (composed of myosin) or thin (composed of actin).

N

Nasal cavity (NAY-zul KAV-i-tee): Air cavity in the skull through which air passes from the nostrils to the upper part of the pharynx.

Nasal conchae (NAY-zul KAHN-kee): Flat, spongy plates that project toward the nasal septum from the sides of the nasal cavity.

Nasal septum (NAY-zul SEP-tum): Vertical plate made of bone and cartilage that divides the nasal cavity.

Natural killer cell: Also known as an NK cell, a type of lymphocyte that patrols the body and destroys foreign or abnormal cells.

Nearsightedness: Known formally as myopia, the condition of the eye where incoming rays of light are bent too much and converge to form a focused image in front of the retina.

Negative feedback: Control system in which a stimulus initiates a response that reduces the stimulus, thereby stopping the response.

Nephrons (NEFF-ronz): Urine-forming structures in the kidneys.

Nerve: Bundle of axons in the peripheral nervous system.

Neuroglia (new-ROGUE-lee-ah): Also known as glial cells, these cells support and protect neurons in the central nervous system.

Neuromuscular junction (nu-row-MUSS-ku-lar JUNK-shun): Region where a motor neuron comes into close contact with a muscle fiber.

Neuron (NUR-on): Nerve cell.

Neurotransmitter (nur-oh-TRANS-mi-ter): Chemical released by the axon of a neuron that travels across a synapse and binds to receptors on the dendrites of other neurons or body cells.

Node of Ranvier (NODE OF rahn-VEEAY): Small area between Schwann cells on an axon that is unmyelinated or uncovered.

Norepinephrine (nor-ep-i-NEFF-rin): Also called noradrenaline, a hormone secreted by the adrenal medulla that raises blood pressure during stressful situations.

Nose: Part of the human face that contains the nostrils and organs of smell and forms the beginning of the respiratory tract.

Nostril (NOS-tril): Either of the two external openings of the nose.

O

Olfaction (ol-FAK-shun): The sense of smell.

Olfactory epithelium (ol-FAK-ter-ee ep-e-THEE-lee-um): Section of mucous membrane in the roof of the nasal cavity that contains odor-sensitive olfactory nerve cells.

Oligodendrocyte (o-li-go-DEN-dro-site): Cell that produces the myelin sheath around the axons of neurons in the central nervous system.

Organ (OR-gan): Any part of the body formed of two or more tissues that performs a specialized function.

Organ of Corti (OR-gan of KOR-tee): Structure in the cochlea of the inner ear that contains the receptors for hearing.

Osmosis (oz-MOE-sis): Diffusion of water through a semipermeable membrane.

Ossicles (OS-si-kuls): Three bones of the middle ear: hammer, anvil, and stirrup.

Otitis media (oh-TIE-tis ME-dee-ah): Infection of the middle ear.

Ovaries (O-var-eez): Female gonads in which ova (eggs) are produced and that secrete estrogens and progesterone.

Oxytocin (ahk-si-TOE-sin): Hormone produced by the hypothalamus and stored in the posterior pituitary that stimulates contraction of the uterus during childbirth and secretion of milk during nursing.

P

Palate (PAL-uht): Roof of the mouth, divided into hard and soft portions, that separates the mouth from the nasal cavities.

Papillae (pah-PILL-ee): Small projections on the upper surface of the tongue that contain taste buds.

Paranasal sinuses (pair-a-NAY-sal SIGH-nus-ez): Air-filled chambers in the bones of the skull that open into the nasal cavity.

Parasympathetic nervous system (pair-ah-sim-puh-THET-ik NERV-us SIS-tem): Division of the autonomic nervous system that controls involuntary activities that keep the body running smoothly under normal, everyday conditions.

Parathyroid glands (pair-ah-THIGH-roid): Four small glands located on the posterior surface of the thyroid gland that regulate calcium levels in the blood.

Parkinson's disease: Progressive disease in which cells in one of the movement-control centers of the brain begin to die, resulting in a loss of control over speech and head and body movements.

Pericardium (pair-i-CAR-dee-um): Tough, fibrous, two-layered membrane sac that surrounds, protects, and anchors the heart.

Peripheral nervous system (peh-RIFF-uh-ruhl NERV-us SIS-tem): Part of the nervous system consisting of the cranial and spinal nerves.

Peristalsis (per-i-STALL-sis): Series of wavelike muscular contractions that move material in one direction through a hollow organ.

Peyer's patches (PIE-erz): Masses of lymphatic tissue located in the villi of the small intestine.

Phagocyte (FAG-oh-site): Type of white blood cell capable of engulfing and digesting particles or cells harmful to the body.

Phagocytosis (fag-oh-sigh-TOE-sis): Process by which a phagocyte engulfs and destroys particles or cells harmful to the body.

Pharynx (FAR-inks): Short, muscular tube extending from the mouth and nasal cavities to the trachea and esophagus.

Photoreceptors (fo-to-re-SEP-terz): Receptors sensitive to light.

Pinna (PIN-nah): Commonly referred to as the ear, the outer, flaplike portion of the ear.

Pia mater (PIE-ah MAY-tur): Delicate innermost layer of the three meninges covering the brain and spinal cord.

Pineal gland (PIN-ee-al): Gland located deep in the rear portion of the brain that helps establish the body's day-night cycle.

Pituitary gland (pi-TOO-i-tair-ee): Gland located below the hypothalamus that controls and coordinates the secretions of other endocrine glands.

Plaque (PLACK): Sticky, whitish film on teeth formed by a protein in saliva and sugary substances in the mouth.

Plasma (PLAZ-muh): Fluid portion of blood.

Platelets (PLATE-lets): Irregular cell fragments in blood that are involved in the process of blood clotting.

Pleura (PLOOR-ah): Membrane sac covering and protecting each lung.

Pneumonia (noo-MOE-nya): Disease of the lungs marked by inflammation and caused by bacteria or viruses.

Poliomyelitis (po-lee-o-my-eh-LIE-tis; often referred to simply as polio): Contagious viral disease that can cause damage to the central nervous system, resulting in paralysis and loss of muscle tissue.

Pons: Part of the brain connecting the medulla oblongata with the midbrain.

Prime mover: Muscle whose contractions are chiefly responsible for producing a particular movement.

Progesterone (pro-JESS-te-rone): Female steroid hormone secreted by the ovaries that makes the uterus more ready to receive a fertilized ovum or egg.

Prolactin (pro-LAK-tin): Gonadotropic hormone secreted by the anterior pituitary that stimulates the mammary glands to produce milk.

Psoriasis (so-RYE-ah-sis): Chronic skin disease characterized by reddened lesions covered with dry, silvery scales.

Pulmonary circulation (PULL-mo-nair-ee): System of blood vessels that transports blood between the heart and lungs.

Pulmonary surfactant (PULL-mo-nair-ee sir-FAK-tent): Oily substance secreted by the alveoli to prevent their walls from sticking together.

Pupil (PYOO-pil): Opening in the center of the iris though which light passes.

Purkinje fibers (purr-KIN-gee): Specialized cardiac muscle fibers that conduct nerve impulses through the heart.

Pyelonephritis (pie-e-low-ne-FRY-tis): Inflammation of the kidneys caused by a bacterial infection.

Pyloric sphincter (pie-LOR-ick SFINGK-ter): Strong ring of muscle at the junction of the stomach and the small intestine that regulates the flow of material between them.

R

Receptors (re-SEP-terz): Specialized peripheral nerve endings or nerve cells that respond to a particular stimulus such as light, sound, heat, touch, or pressure.

Red blood cells: Most numerous blood cells in the blood, they carry oxygen bonded to the hemoglobin within them.

Reflex (REE-flex): Involuntary and rapid response to a stimulus.

Renal corpuscle (REE-nul KOR-pus-el): Part of a nephron that consists of a glomerulus enclosed by a Bowman's capsule.

Renal cortex (REE-nul KOR-tex): Outermost layer of the kidney.

Renal filtrate (REE-nul FILL-trait): Fluid formed in a Bowman's capsule from blood plasma by the process of filtration in the renal corpuscle.

Renal medulla (REE-nul muh-DUH-luh): Middle layer of a kidney.

Renal pelvis (REE-nul PELL-vis): A cavity at the innermost area of a kidney that connects to the ureter.

Renal pyramids (REE-nul PEER-ah-mids): Triangular or pie-shaped segments of the renal medulla in which urine production occurs.

Renal tubule (REE-nal TOO-byool): Twisting, narrow tube leading from the Bowman's capsule in a nephron.

Renin (REE-nin): Enzyme secreted by the cells of renal tubules that helps to raise blood pressure.

Respiration (res-pe-RAY-shun): Exchange of gases (oxygen and carbon dioxide) between living cells and the environment.

Retina (RET-i-nah): Innermost layer of the eyeball that contains the photoreceptors—the rods and cones.

Rigor mortis (RIG-er MOR-tis): Rigid state of the body after death due to irreversible muscle contractions.

Rods: Photoreceptors in the retina of the eye that detect the presence of light.

Rugae (ROO-jee): Folds of the inner mucous membrane of organs, such as the stomach, that allow those organs to expand.

S

Saccule (SAC-yool): Membranous sac in the vestibule of the inner ear that contains receptors for the sense of balance.

Sarcomere (SAR-koh-meer): Unit of contraction in a skeletal muscle fiber containing a precise arrangement of thick and thin myofilaments.

Schwann cell (SHWAHN SELL): Cell that forms the myelin sheath around axons of neurons in the peripheral nervous system.

Sclera (SKLER-ah): Outermost layer of the eyeball, made of connective tissue.

Sebaceous gland (suh-BAY-shus): Exocrine gland in the dermis that produces sebum.

Seborrheic dermatitis (seh-beh-REE-ik der-ma-TIE-tis): Commonly called seborrhea, a disease of the skin characterized by scaly lesions that usually appear on the scalp, hairline, and face.

Sebum (SEE-bum): Mixture of oily substances and fragmented cells secreted by sebaceous glands.

Semicircular canals (sem-eye-SIR-cue-lar ka-NALZ): Three oval canals in the inner ear that help to maintain balance.

Semilunar valves (sem-eye-LU-nar): Valves located between the ventricles and the major arteries into which they pump blood.

Serous fluid (SIR-us): Clear, watery, lubricating fluid produced by serous membranes, which line body cavities and cover internal organs.

Sickle cell anemia (SICK-el cell ah-NEE-me-yah): Inherited blood disorder in which red blood cells are sickle-shaped instead of round because of defective hemoglobin molecules.

Sinoatrial (SA) node (sigh-no-A-tree-al): Node of specialized tissue lying in the upper area of the right atrium that fires an electrical impulse across the atria, causing them to contract.

Sinusoids (SIGH-nuh-soids): Larger than normal capillaries whose walls are also more permeable, allowing proteins and blood cells to enter or leave easily.

Somatic nervous system (so-MAT-ik NERV-us SIS-tem): Part of the peripheral nervous system that controls the voluntary movements of the skeletal muscles.

Spasm: Sudden, involuntary muscle contraction.

Sphygmomanometer (sfig-moe-ma-NOM-i-tur): Instrument used to measure blood pressure.

Spinal cord: Long cord of nerve tissue running through the spine or backbone that transmits impulses to and from the brain and controls some reflex actions.

Spleen: Lymphoid organ located in the upper left part of the abdomen that stores blood, destroys old red blood cells, and filters pathogens from the blood.

Squamous cell carcinoma (SKWA-mus CELL car-si-NO-ma): Skin cancer affecting the cells of the second deepest layer of the epidermis.

Squamous cells (SKWA-mus): Cells that are flat and scalelike.

Strain: Slight tear in a muscle; also called a pulled muscle.

Subcutaneous (sub-kew-TAY-nee-us): Tissues between the dermis and the muscles.

Sulci (SUL-sye): Shallow grooves on the surface of the cerebral cortex.

Sympathetic nervous system (sim-puh-THET-ik NERV-us SIS-tem): Division of the autonomic nervous system that controls involuntary activities that help the body respond to stressful situations.

Synapse (SIN-aps): Small space or gap where a nerve impulse passes between the axon of one neuron and a dendrite of the next neuron.

Synergist (SIN-er-jist): Muscle that cooperates with another to produce a particular movement.

Systemic circulation (sis-TEM-ick): System of blood vessels that transports blood between the heart and all parts of the body other than the lungs.

Systemic lupus erythematosus (sis-TEM-ick LOU-pus er-i-the-mah-TOE-sis): Also called lupus or SLE, a disorder in which antibodies attack the body's own tissues as if they were foreign.

Systole (SIS-te-lee): Rhythmic contraction of the heart.

T

T cell: Also known as T lymphocyte, a type of lymphocyte that matures in the thymus and that attacks any foreign substance in the body.

Taste buds: Structures on the papillae of the tongue that contain chemoreceptors that respond to chemicals dissolved in saliva.

Tendon (TEN-den): Tough, white, cordlike tissue that attaches muscle to bone.

Testes (TESS-teez): Male gonads that produce sperm cells and secrete testosterone.

Testosterone (tess-TAHS-ter-ohn): Hormone secreted by the testes that spurs the growth of the male reproductive organs and secondary sex characteristics.

Tetanus (TET-n-es): Bacterial disease in which a bacterial toxin causes the repetitive stimulation of muscle fibers, resulting in convulsive muscle spasms and rigidity.

Thalamus (THAL-ah-mus): Part of the brain behind the hypothalamus that acts as the brain's main relay station, sending information to the cerebral cortex and other parts of the brain.

Thoracic duct (tho-RAS-ik): Main lymph vessel in the body, which transports lymph from the lower half and upper left part of the body.

Thrombocyte (THROM-bow-site): Platelet.

Thymosin (thigh-MOE-sin): Hormone secreted by the thymus that changes a certain group of lymphocytes into germ-fighting T cells.

Thymus (THIGH-mus): Glandular organ consisting of lymphoid tissue located behind the top of the breastbone that produces specialized lymphocytes; reaches maximum development in early childhood and is almost absent in adults.

Thyroid gland (THIGH-roid): Gland wrapped around the front and sides of the trachea at the base of the throat just below the larynx that affects growth and metabolism.

Thyroxine (thigh-ROK-seen): Hormone secreted by the thyroid gland that regulates the rate of metabolism and, in children, affects growth.

Tonsillitis (tahn-si-LIE-tis): Infection and swelling of the tonsils.

Tonsils (TAHN-sills): Three pairs of small, oval masses of lymphatic tissue located on either side of the inner wall of the throat, near the rear openings of the nasal cavity, and near the base of the tongue.

Trachea (TRAY-key-ah): Also known as the windpipe, the respiratory tube extending from the larynx to the bronchi.

Trypsin (TRIP-sin): Digestive enzyme that converts proteins into amino acids; inactive form is trypsinogen.

Tuberculosis (too-burr-cue-LOW-sis): Infectious, inflammatory disease of the lungs caused by a bacteria that leads to tissue damage.

U

Ulcer (digestive) (UL-sir): Any sore that develops in the lining of the lower esophagus, stomach, or duodenum.

Ulcerative colitis (UL-sir-a-tiv ko-LIE-tis): Disorder that causes inflammation and ulceration of the inner lining of the large intestine and rectum.

Urea (yoo-REE-ah): Main nitrogen-containing waste excreted in the urine, produced when the liver combines ammonia and carbon dioxide.

Ureter (you-REE-ter): Muscular tube that carries urine from the renal pelvis in a kidney to the urinary bladder.

Urethra (yoo-REE-thrah): Thin-walled tube that carries urine from the urinary bladder to the outside of the body.

Urethritis (yer-i-THRY-tis): Inflammation of the urethra caused by a bacterial infection.

Uric acid (YUR-ik AS-id): Waste product in urine formed by the breakdown of nucleic acids.

Urinary bladder (YER-i-nair-ee BLA-der) Hollow, collapsible, muscular sac that stores urine temporarily.

Urinary incontinence (YER-i-nair-ee in-KON-ti-nence): Involuntary and unintentional passage or urine.

Urine (YUR-in): Fluid formed by the kidneys from blood plasma.

Utricle (YOO-tri-kuhl): Membranous sac in the vestibule of the inner ear that contains receptors for the sense of balance.

Uvula (U-vue-lah): Fleshy projection hanging from the soft palate that raises to close off the nasal passages during swallowing.

V

Vaccine (vack-SEEN): Substance made of weakened or killed bacteria or viruses injected (or taken orally) into the body to stimulate the production of antibodies specific to that particular infectious disease.

Vein (VAIN): Vessel that carries blood to the heart.

Vena cava (VEE-na KAY-va): Either of two large veins that return blood to the right atrium of the heart.

Ventricles (VEN-tri-kuls): Lower chambers of the heart that contract to pump blood into the arteries.

Venule (VEN-yool): Small vein.

Vestibule (VES-ti-byool): Bony chamber of the inner ear that contains the utricle and the saccule.

Vestigial organ (ves-TIJ-ee-al OR-gan): Organ that is reduced in size and function when compared with that of its evolutionary ancestors.

Villi (VILL-eye): Tiny, fingerlike projections on the inner lining of the small intestine that increase the rate of nutrient absorption by greatly increasing the intestine's surface area.

Vitiligo (vit-i-LIE-go): Skin disorder in which the loss of melanocytes results in patches of smooth, milky white skin.

Vitreous humor (VIT-ree-us HYOO-mer): Transparent, gellike substance that fills the cavity of the eye behind the lens.

W

Warts: Small growths caused by a viral infection of the skin or mucous membrane.

White blood cells: Cells in blood that defend the body against viruses, bacteria, and other invading microorganisms.

White matter: Whitish nerve tissue of the central nervous system containing bundles of myelinated axons.

BODY BY DESIGN

From the Digestive System to the Skeleton

volume

1

nervous system
reproductive system
respiratory system
skeletal system
urinary system
special senses

Rob Nagel • **Betz Des Chenes, Editor**

AN IMPRINT OF THE GALE GROUP

DETROIT · SAN FRANCISCO · LONDON
BOSTON · WOODBRIDGE, CT

1

The Cardiovascular System

The cardiovascular system and the lymphatic system form what is collectively called the circulatory system. Together, these systems transport oxygen, nutrients, cell wastes, hormones, and many other substances to and from all cells in the body. The trillions of cells in the human body take up nutrients and excrete wastes every minute of every day. Although the pace of this exchange may increase with activity or slow with rest, it happens continuously. If it stops, so does life. Of the two systems, the cardiovascular system is the primary transport operator; the lymphatic system aids it in its function.

DESIGN: PARTS OF THE CARDIOVASCULAR SYSTEM

Cardiovascular comes from the Greek word *cardia,* meaning "heart," and the Latin *vasculum,* meaning "small vessel." The basic components of the cardiovascular system are the heart, the blood vessels, and the blood. The system can be compared to a large muscular pump (the heart) that sends a fluid (blood) through a series of large and small tubes (blood vessels). As blood circulates through the increasingly intricate system of vessels, it picks up oxygen from the lungs, nutrients from the small intestine, and hormones from the endocrine glands. It delivers these to the cells, picking up carbon dioxide (formed when cells use sugars or fats to produce energy) and other wastes in return. The blood then takes these waste products to the lungs and kidneys, where they are excreted.

The heart

The heart is a hollow, cone-shaped muscular organ located behind and slightly to the left of the sternum or breastbone. Nestled between the lungs, the heart sits within a protective, bony cage formed by the sternum, ribs, and spine. The lower tip of the heart, called the apex, points toward the left hip and rests on the diaphragm (a membrane of muscle separating the chest cavity from the abdominal cavity). The upper portion of the heart, called the base, points toward the right shoulder and lies beneath the second rib. It is from the base that the major blood vessels of the body emerge.

The heart is about the size of a clenched fist. At birth, an infant's heart and fist are about the same size. As a human body develops, the heart and fist grow at about the same rate. In adults, an average heart weighs between 9 and 11 ounces (255 and 310 grams). It is slightly larger in males than in females.

The pericardium is a tough, fibrous membrane sac that surrounds, protects, and anchors the heart. It is composed of three layers. The thin inner

WORDS TO KNOW

Agglutination (ah-glue-ti-NA-shun): Clumping of blood cells brought about by the mixing of blood types.

Alveoli (al-VEE-oh-lie): Air sacs of the lungs.

Antibody (AN-ti-bod-ee): Specialized substance produced by the body that can provide immunity against a specific antigen.

Antigen (AN-ti-jen): Any substance that, when introduced to the body, is recognized as foreign and activates an immune response.

Aorta (ay-OR-ta): Main artery of the body.

Arteriole (ar-TEER-e-ohl): Small artery.

Artery (AR-te-ree): Vessel that carries blood away from the heart.

Atria (AY-tree-a): Upper chambers of the heart that receive blood from the veins.

Atrioventricular (AV) node (a-tree-oh-ven-TRICK-u-lar): Node of specialized tissue lying near the bottom of the right atrium that fires an electrical impulse across the ventricles, causing them to contract.

Atrioventricular (AV) valves: Valves located between the atria and ventricles.

Blood pressure: Pressure or force the blood exerts against the inner walls of the blood vessels.

Capillary (CAP-i-lair-ee): Minute blood vessel that connects arterioles with venules.

Cardiac cycle (CAR-dee-ack): Series of events that occur in the heart during one complete heartbeat.

Cholesterol (ko-LESS-ter-ol): Fatlike substance produced by the liver that is an essential part of cell membranes and body chemicals; when present in excess in the body, it can accumulate on the inside walls of arteries and block blood flow.

Diaphragm (DIE-ah-fram): Membrane of muscle separating the chest cavity from the abdominal cavity.

Diastole (die-ASS-te-lee): Period of relaxation and expansion of the heart when its chambers fill with blood.

Diffusion (dif-FEW-shun): Movement of molecules from an area of greater concentration to an area of lesser concentration.

Endocardium (en-doe-CAR-dee-um): Thin membrane lining the interior of the heart.

Epicardium (ep-i-CAR-dee-um): Lubricating outer layer of the heart wall and part of the pericardium.

Erythrocyte (e-RITH-re-site): Red blood cell.

Filtration (fill-TRAY-shun): Movement of water and dissolved materials through a membrane from an area of higher pressure to an area of lower pressure.

Hemoglobin (HEE-muh-glow-bin): Iron-containing protein pigment in red blood cells that can combine with oxygen and carbon dioxide.

Hepatic portal circulation (heh-PAT-ick POR-tal): System of blood vessels that transports blood from the digestive organs and the spleen through the liver before returning it to the heart.

layer tightly hugs the outer surface of the heart and is actually a part of the heart wall. The fibrous outer layer protects the heart and anchors it to surrounding structures such as the sternum and diaphragm. The inner portion of this outer layer is lined by another layer, which produces serous fluid. This watery lubricant between the inner and outer layers of the pericardium allows the layers to slide smoothly across each other, reducing friction when the heart beats.

The heart wall is made up of three layers: the epicardium, the myocardium, and the endocardium. The outer layer, the epicardium, is actually

Interstitial fluid (in-ter-STI-shul): Fluid found in the spaces between cells.

Leukocyte (LUKE-oh-site): White blood cell.

Megakaryocyte (meg-ah-CARE-ee-oh-site): Large cell in the red bone marrow that breaks up into small fragments that become platelets.

Myocardium (my-oh-CAR-dee-um): Cardiac muscle layer of the heart wall.

Osmosis (oz-MOE-sis): Diffusion of water through a semipermeable membrane.

Pericardium (pair-i-CAR-dee-um): Tough, fibrous, two-layered membrane sac that surrounds, protects, and anchors the heart.

Plasma (PLAZ-muh): Fluid portion of blood.

Platelets (PLATE-lets): Irregular cell fragments in blood that are involved in the process of blood clotting.

Pulmonary circulation (PULL-mo-nair-ee): System of blood vessels that transports blood between the heart and lungs.

Purkinje fibers (purr-KIN-gee): Specialized cardiac muscle fibers that conduct nerve impulses through the heart.

Red blood cells: Most numerous blood cells in the blood, they carry oxygen bonded to the hemoglobin within them.

Semilunar valves (sem-eye-LOO-nar): Valves located between the ventricles and the major arteries into which they pump blood.

Serous fluid (SIR-us): Clear, watery, lubricating fluid produced by serous membranes, which line body cavities and cover internal organs.

Sinoatrial (SA) node (sigh-no-A-tree-al): Node of specialized tissue lying in the upper area of the right atrium that fires an electrical impulse across the atria, causing them to contract.

Sinusoids (SIGH-nuh-soids): Larger than normal capillaries whose walls are also more permeable, allowing proteins and blood cells to enter or leave easily.

Sphygmomanometer (sfig-moe-ma-NOM-i-tur): Instrument used to measure blood pressure.

Systemic circulation (sis-TEM-ick): System of blood vessels that transports blood between the heart and all parts of the body other than the lungs.

Systole (SIS-te-lee): Rhythmic contraction of the heart.

Thrombocyte (THROM-bow-site): Platelet.

Vein (VAIN): Vessel that carries blood to the heart.

Vena cava (VEE-na KAY-va): Either of two large veins that return blood to the right atrium of the heart.

Ventricles (VEN-tri-kuls): Lower chambers of the heart that contract to pump blood into the arteries.

Venule (VEN-yool): Small vein.

White blood cells: Cells in blood that defend the body against viruses, bacteria, and other invading microorganisms.

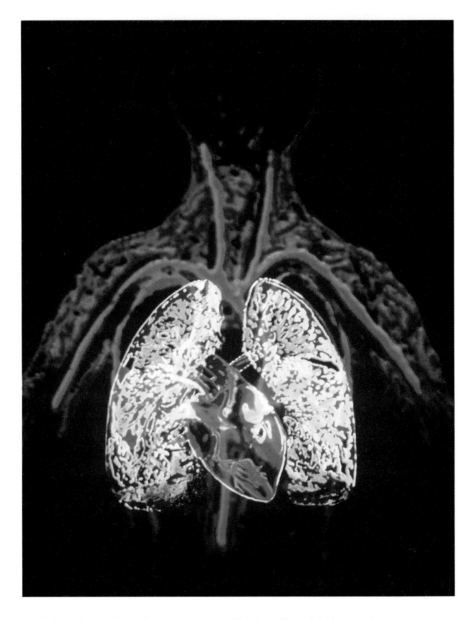

A colorized image of the circulatory system. The heart (in red) is located between the lungs (in yellow). (Photograph by Howard Sochurek. Reproduced by permission of The Stock Market.)

the thin inner layer of the pericardium. The middle layer, the myocardium, is a thick layer of cardiac muscle that contracts to force blood out of the heart. The inner layer, the endocardium, is a thin, glistening membrane that allows blood to flow smoothly through the chambers of the heart.

HEART CHAMBERS. The heart is divided into four chambers. A muscular septum or partition divides it into a left and right side. Each side is further divided into an upper and lower chamber. The upper chambers, the atria (singular atrium), are thin-walled. They are the receiving chambers of the heart. Blood flows into them from the body, which they then pump to the ventricles, the lower heart chambers. The ventricles are the discharging chambers of the heart. Their walls are thicker and contain more cardiac muscle than the walls of the atria. This enables the ventricles to contract and pump blood out of the heart to the lungs and the rest of the body.

As blood flows from one chamber to the next, one-way valves prevent the blood from flowing backward. The valves located between the atria and ventricles are called atrioventricular or AV valves. The left AV valve (between the left ventricle and left atrium) is the mitral or bicuspid valve. The right AV valve (between the right atrium and right ventricle) is the tricuspid valve. The valves located between the ventricles and the major arteries into which they pump blood are called semilunar valves. The pulmonary semilunar valve is located between the right ventricle and the pulmonary trunk. The aortic semilunar valve is located between the left ventricle and the aorta.

The valves open and close in response to pressure changes in the heart. Each set operates at a different time. The AV valves are open when the heart is relaxed and closed when the ventricles contract. The semilunar valves are closed when the heart is relaxed and forced open when the ventricles contract. The closing of the heart valves generates the "lub-dup" sounds that a physician hears through a stethoscope. The AV valves produce the "lub" sound; the semilunar valves produce the "dup" sound.

The heart is equipped with its own nervous system that controls its beating activity. This system, called the intrinsic conduction system, is located within the heart tissue. Nerve impulses sent out through the system cause parts of the heart to contract at various times. A small node of specialized muscle tissue located in the upper area of the right atrium is called the sinoatrial or SA node. Because it initiates the impulse, the SA node is known as the pacemaker. The system includes another node, the atrioventricular or AV node, located near the bottom of the right atrium just above the ventricles. The atrioventricular or AV bundle (also known as the bundle of His) is located in the upper portion of the septum between the ventricles. Two main branches leading from this bundle (called bundle branches) divide further into small fibers that spread out within the cardiac muscle of the ventricle walls. These are known as Purkinje fibers.

THE HEART IS EQUIPPED WITH ITS OWN NERVOUS SYSTEM THAT CONTROLS ITS BEATING ACTIVITY.

Blood vessels

The blood vessels form a closed transport system of tubes measuring about 60,000 miles (96,500 kilometers) in length—more than twice the distance

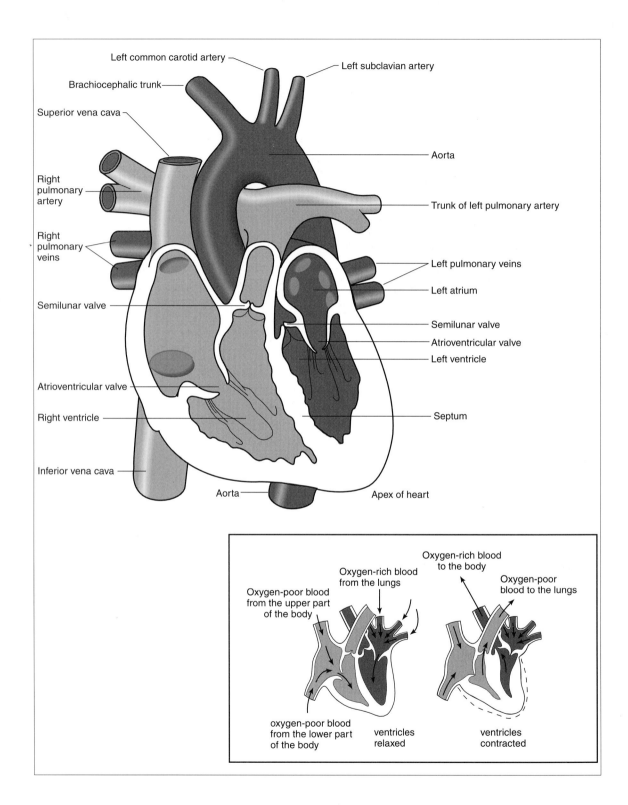

Left common carotid artery

Left subclavian artery

Brachiocephalic trunk

Superior vena cava

Aorta

Right pulmonary artery

Trunk of left pulmonary artery

Right pulmonary veins

Left pulmonary veins

Left atrium

Semilunar valve

Semilunar valve

Atrioventricular valve

Left ventricle

Atrioventricular valve

Right ventricle

Septum

Inferior vena cava

Aorta

Apex of heart

Oxygen-rich blood to the body

Oxygen-rich blood from the lungs

Oxygen-poor blood to the lungs

Oxygen-poor blood from the upper part of the body

oxygen-poor blood from the lower part of the body

ventricles relaxed

ventricles contracted

William Harvey. (Reproduced by permission of the Library of Congress.)

BLOOD AS AN OCEAN IN THE BODY?

Up until only about 350 years ago, people believed blood in the body flowed back and forth like ocean tides. The ancient Greeks were the first to put forth this theory. They believed blood moved away from the heart, then ebbed back to it carrying impurities in the same vessels. This theory remained unchallenged for 1,400 years.

In 1628, English physician William Harvey (1578–1657) published a new concept of blood circulation. He maintained that there was a constant flow of blood through the arteries that returned to the heart through the veins. This formed a continuing circular flow of blood through the body.

Harvey's theory was immediately scorned, as it contradicted the basis of medical knowledge at the time. Some thirty years later, however, his idea was validated by the discovery of capillaries. Because of his pioneering work, Harvey is considered by many to be the father of modern medicine.

around the equator of Earth. The entire blood vessel system can be thought of as a series of connected roads and highways. Blood leaves the heart through large vessels (highways) that travel forth into the body. At various points, these large vessels divide to become smaller vessels (secondary roads). In turn, these vessels continue to divide into smaller and smaller vessels (one-lane roads). On its return trip, the blood travels through increasingly larger and larger vessels (one-lane roads merging into secondary roads merging into highways) before eventually reaching the heart.

Arteries, capillaries, and veins are the main parts of this transport system. Arteries are the vessels that carry blood away from the heart. Large arteries leave the heart and then branch into smaller ones that reach out to various parts of the body. These divide even further into smaller vessels called arterioles. Within the tissues, arterioles divide into microscopic vessels called capillaries. The exchange of materials between the blood and the cells occurs through the walls of the capillaries. Before leaving the tissues, capillaries merge to form venules, which are small veins. As these vessels move closer to the heart, they merge to form larger and larger veins.

OPPOSITE: A cutaway view of the anatomy of the heart (top left). The smaller boxed diagram illustrates the flow of blood in the heart during diastole (relaxation and expansion) and systole (contraction). (Illustration by Hans & Cassady.)

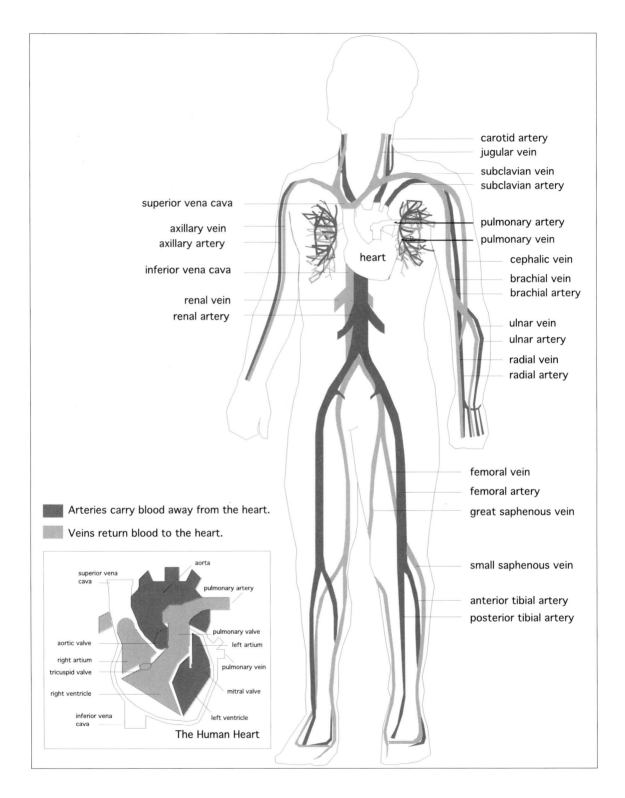

carotid artery
jugular vein

subclavian vein
subclavian artery

superior vena cava

axillary vein
axillary artery

pulmonary artery
pulmonary vein

heart

cephalic vein

inferior vena cava

brachial vein
brachial artery

renal vein
renal artery

ulnar vein
ulnar artery

radial vein
radial artery

Arteries carry blood away from the heart.

Veins return blood to the heart.

femoral vein

femoral artery

great saphenous vein

small saphenous vein

anterior tibial artery
posterior tibial artery

superior vena cava

aorta

pulmonary artery

pulmonary valve

left artium

aortic valve

right artium

pulmonary vein

tricuspid valve

right ventricle

mitral valve

inferior vena cava

left ventricle

The Human Heart

The main blood vessels differ in their structure. Although the walls of both arteries and veins are composed of three coats, they vary in thickness. Arteries have thicker inner and middle coats, which makes them more elastic. They can expand and contract easily when blood pumped from the heart surges through them. Veins, on the other hand, have thinner walls. This allows skeletal muscles surrounding them to contract and press against their flexible walls, squeezing the blood along as it returns to the heart. One-way valves in the walls of veins prevent backflow, keeping the blood flowing in one direction. The valves are most numerous in the legs, where blood must flow against the force of gravity on its way back to the heart. Unlike arteries or veins, the walls of capillaries are only one cell thick. In most capillaries, these singular cells are not joined together tightly. Because of this, oxygen, nutrients, and wastes are able to pass easily between the blood and the surrounding interstitial fluid, which fills the spaces between cells.

THE PULMONARY AND SYSTEMIC CIRCULATIONS. There are two main circulation circuits or routes in the body: the pulmonary circulation and the systemic circulation. Vessels involved in the pulmonary circulation transport blood between the heart and the lungs. Vessels in the systemic circulation transport blood to all other body parts.

The main artery of the systemic circulation is the aorta. In adults, the aorta is about the same size as a standard garden hose. It emerges upward out of the left ventricle for about an inch, then curves left over the heart (a portion called the aortic arch) before plunging downward to divide into branches that carry blood to the major parts of the body.

Branches of the aorta include the carotid arteries (which carry blood to the head), coronary arteries (which supply blood to the muscles of the heart), brachial arteries (which carry blood down the arms), and femoral arteries (which carry blood down the thighs).

The vena cava is the largest vein of the systemic circulation. It has two branches: the superior vena cava accepts blood drained from the head and arms; the inferior vena cava accepts blood drained from the lower body. Both sections (collectively called the venae cavae) empty into the right atrium.

Veins that drain into the venae cavae include the jugular veins (which drain the head), brachial and cephalic veins (which drain the arms), femoral veins (which drain the thighs), and iliac veins (which drain the pelvic or hip region).

The vessels involved in the pulmonary circulation carry blood to the lungs for gas exchange (carbon dioxide is unloaded and oxygen is picked

OPPOSITE: An illustration of the major arteries and veins in the human body. (Reproduced by permission of Gale.)

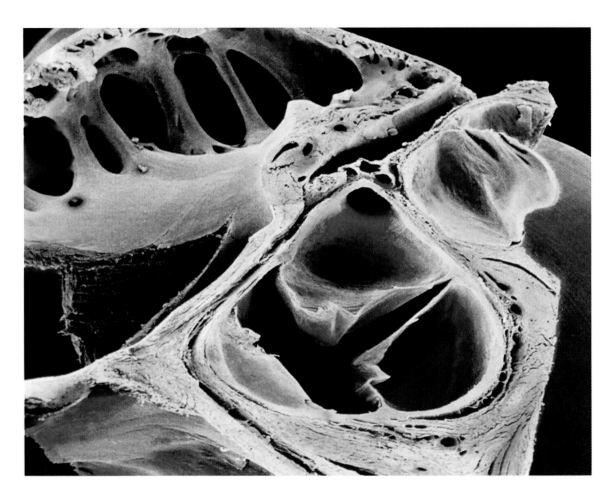

An electron micrograph scan of a human aortic valve. The aorta is the main artery of the systemic circulation. (Photograph by P. Motta. Reproduced by permission of Photo Researchers, Inc.)

up), then return it to the heart. The main vessels are the pulmonary arteries and the pulmonary veins. The two pulmonary arteries branch off from the pulmonary trunk, which originates from the right ventricle. The right pulmonary artery goes to the right lung, the left pulmonary artery to the left lung. After gas exchange occurs in the lungs, the oxygenated (carrying oxygen) blood is transported back to the left atrium of the heart by four pulmonary veins.

Blood

Blood is the fluid pumped by the heart through the blood vessels to all parts of the body. It is connective tissue. As its name suggests, connective tissue connects body parts, providing support, storage, and protection. Found everywhere in the body, connective tissue is the most abundant type of the four types of tissues (the other three are epithelial, muscle, and nervous). Of all the tissues in the body, blood is unique—it is the only one that is *fluid*.

Blood has many functions in the body. It carries everything that must be transported from one place to another within the body: oxygen and nutrients to the cells, hormones (chemical messengers) to the tissues, and waste products to organs responsible for removing them from the body. It helps protect the body by clotting and by acting as a defense against foreign microorganisms. It also keeps the body at a constant temperature by taking heat away from cells.

Stickier and heavier than water, blood ranges in color from scarlet to dull red, depending on the amount of oxygen it is carrying (the brighter the color, the greater the amount of oxygen). Inside the body, blood has a temperature of about 100.4°F (38°C). It makes up approximately 8 percent of a person's body weight. A man of average weight has about 6 quarts (5.6 liters) of blood in his body; a woman of average weight has about 4.8 quarts (4.5 liters). Men tend to have more blood than women due to the presence of testosterone, the male sex hormone that also stimulates blood formation.

Blood is composed of both solid and liquid elements. Red blood cells, white blood cells, and platelets are the solid components that are suspended in plasma, a watery, straw-colored fluid. The living blood cells make up about 45 percent of the blood; the nonliving plasma makes up the remaining 55 percent.

PLASMA. Plasma is approximately 92 percent water. Over 100 different substances are dissolved in this fluid, including nutrients, respiratory gases, hormones, plasma proteins, salts, and various wastes. Of these dissolved substances, plasma proteins are the most abundant. These proteins, most of which are produced by the liver, serve a variety of functions. Fibrinogen is an important protein that aids in blood clotting. Albumins help to keep water in the bloodstream. Proteins called gamma globulins act as antibodies, which are substances produced by the body to help protect it against foreign substances.

The salts present in plasma include sodium, potassium, calcium, magnesium, chloride, and bicarbonate. They are involved in many important body functions, including muscle contraction, the transmission of nerve impulses, and the regulation of the body's pH (acid-base) balance.

RED BLOOD CELLS. Red blood cells, or erythrocytes, are the most prevalent of the three types of blood cells. They number about five million per cubic millimeter of blood (a cubic millimeter is an extremely small drop that is barely visible). Their main function is to transport oxygen from the lungs to all cells in the body. Red blood cells are tiny, flattened, disk-shaped structures

Charles Drew. (Reproduced by permission of AP/Wide World Photos.)

CHARLES DREW AND PLASMA STORAGE

The four main blood types—A, B, O, and AB—were discovered by medical researchers in the early twentieth century. This discovery greatly im-proved the effectiveness of blood transfusions. At the time, however, whole blood could only be kept for seven days before it perished. The prob-lem of having the appropriate blood type readily available during emergencies still existed.

In the late 1930s, American surgeon Charles Drew (1904–1950) began to explore the possi-bility of using plasma as a substitute for whole blood in transfusions. Because plasma lacks red blood cells, it can be given to any patient, re-gardless of that patient's blood type. This prop-erty makes plasma ideal for use in emergencies.

By 1940, Drew had devised a method to process and preserve blood plasma through dehydration so that it could be shipped over great distances and stored for long periods of time. When it was needed, the dried, powderlike plasma was then reconstituted or reformed through the addition of water.

The use of plasma for transfusions proved es-pecially useful during World War II (1939–45), when there was a desperate shortage of blood to treat the wounded. Because of his research, Drew is credited with saving countless numbers of lives.

with depressed centers: under a microscope they look like small doughnuts. Their size allows them to squeeze through the microscopic capillaries.

In adults, red blood cells are formed in the red bone marrow of the ribs, vertebrae, sternum, and pelvis (marrow is the spongylike material that fills the cavities inside most bones). The primary el-ement of red blood cells is a protein pigment called hemoglobin. Hemoglobin molecules ac-count for one-third the weight of each red blood cell. At the center of each hemoglobin molecule is a single atom of iron, which gives red blood cells their color. In the lungs, the iron atoms combine with oxygen to create compounds called oxyhemoglobins. The main function of red blood cells is to transport this form of oxygen to the cells throughout the body. After the oxygen is transferred, hemoglobin combines with the carbon dioxide given off by the cells, and the red

BLOOD TYPES AND THEIR PERCENTAGE

Blood type	Percentage of people in U.S.
O+	37.4%
A+	35.7%
B+	8.5%
O–	6.6%
A–	6.3%
AB+	3.4%
B–	1.5%
AB–	0.6%

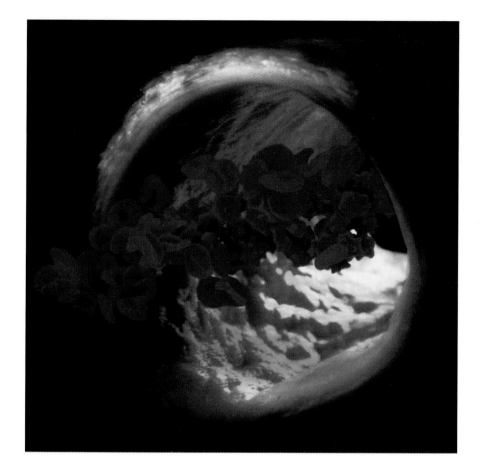

Red blood cells flowing through blood vessels. Also known as erythrocytes, red blood cells are the most prevalent of the three types of blood cells. (Reproduced by permission of Giovaux Communication/Phototake NYC.)

blood cells carry it back to the lungs, where some of the carbon dioxide is exhaled.

Because red blood cells are constantly squeezing through tiny capillaries, their membranes receive much wear and tear. For this reason, each red blood cell lives only about four months. New red blood cells are constantly being produced in the bone marrow to replace old ones.

BLOOD TYPES. On their membranes, red blood cells carry proteins called antigens, or substances that the body recognizes as foreign. These inherited antigens determine to what blood group a person belongs: A, B, AB, or O. A person whose red blood cells carry the A antigen is type A. A person with the B antigen is type B. A person with both A and B antigens is type AB. A person with no antigens is type O.

Knowing a person's blood type is important for blood transfusions. A person with type A blood cannot receive type B blood because they carry antibodies to B antigens. B types carry antibodies to A antigens. AB types do not carry any antibodies to antigens, but O types carry antibodies to both A and B antigens. If a person is given the wrong type of blood, the blood cells clump together and can block small blood vessels. This reaction, called agglutination, can be fatal.

KNOWING A PERSON'S BLOOD TYPE IS IMPORTANT FOR BLOOD TRANSFUSIONS.

Another type of antigen carried on red blood cells is called the Rh antigen (so named because it was originally identified in *Rh*esus monkeys). Most Americans are Rh positive (Rh+), meaning they carry the Rh antigen. Rh negative (Rh–) people do not. Unlike the ABO blood group system, antibodies to the Rh antigen are not automatically found in the blood. The only problem that may arise with the Rh antigen and blood transfusions is when an Rh– individual is given Rh+ blood. In response, that person's body develops antibodies to the Rh+ antigen. Any further transfusions with Rh+ blood would then result in the previously formed antibodies attacking the donor blood.

WHITE BLOOD CELLS. White blood cells, or leukocytes, are far less numerous than red blood cells. Numbering between 4,000 and 11,000 per cubic millimeter of blood, they account for less than 1 percent of total blood volume. Despite their low numbers, white blood cells have a specialized function, serving as an important part of the body's immune system. They help defend the body against damage by bacteria, viruses, parasites, and tumor cells. Like red blood cells, white blood cells are formed in the red bone marrow (some white blood cells are produced in the lymphatic tissue as well). But whereas red blood cells are confined to the blood stream, white blood cells are not. They are able to squeeze through capillary walls on their way to an infected or damaged area of the body.

There are five kinds of white blood cells in the blood: neutrophils, eosinophils, basophils, monocytes, and lymphocytes. Each of the five plays a specific role in the body's defense system, being called into action to fight specific diseases. For example, during chronic (long-term) infections such as tuberculosis (an infectious disease of the lungs), monocytes increase in number. During asthma and allergy attacks, eosinophils increase in number.

Rh ANTIGEN AND PREGNANCY

Rh factor is a special consideration during one type of pregnancy: when an Rh– woman carries an Rh+ baby. During delivery, a tear in the mother's placenta may allow a mother to be exposed to her baby's Rh+ red blood cells. (The placenta is a membrane lining the uterus through which nutrients and oxygen pass from mother to baby.) If this occurs, she then develops antibodies to the Rh+ antigen. During any subsequent pregnancy, if the woman is carrying another Rh+ baby, her anti-Rh antibodies may cross over into the baby's blood and destroy its red blood cells.

To prevent any of this from taking place, doctors will give the Rh– woman RhoGAM, an anti-Rh antibody, within seventy-two hours of her initial delivery. RhoGAM will destroy the Rh+ red blood cells that have entered her circulation before her immune system has had time to develop antibodies.

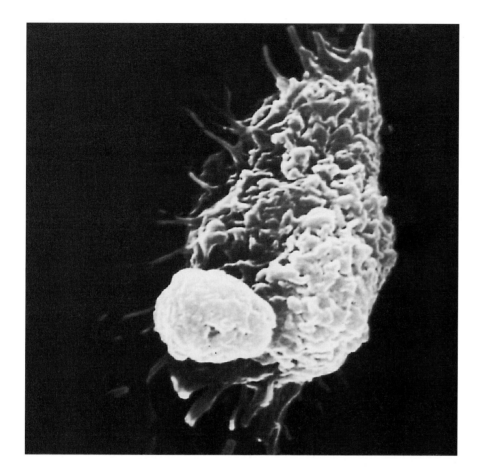

A macrophage (in background) and a lymphocyte (in foreground). Lymphocytes are one of five kinds of white blood cells that help the body's defense system fight disease. (Reproduced by permission of Institut Pasteur/Phototake NYC.)

White blood cells "know" where to go in the body by following certain chemicals. When tissue is infected or damaged, it releases chemicals into the surrounding area that "attract" the proper white blood cells to fight the infection or damage. This process is known as chemotaxis.

PLATELETS. Platelets, or thrombocytes, are not truly cells like red and white blood cells. They are small, disk-shaped fragments of extraordinarily large cells called megakaryocytes that are located in bone marrow. The megakaryocytes rupture, releasing fifty or more fragments that quickly form membranes to become platelets. Numbering about 300,000 per cubic millimeter of blood, platelets help to control bleeding in a complex process called homeostasis, or the stoppage of blood flow.

When an injury to a blood vessel causes bleeding, platelets begin the clotting process by sticking to the ruptured blood vessel. As they do so, they release chemicals that attract other platelets. Soon, a clump of platelets forms a temporary plug. After this, the platelets release serotonin (sir-o-TOE-nin), a chemical that causes the blood vessel to spasm and narrow, decreasing the amount of blood flowing to the site of the injury. While this is occurring, the injured tissue releases a substance that combines with calcium and other clotting factors in blood plasma to create prothrombin activator. This activator converts prothrombin (a substance produced by the liver that is present in plasma), to thrombin (an enzyme). Thrombin then joins with fibrinogen to create long, threadlike molecules called fibrin. Fibrin molecules establish a mesh that traps red blood cells and platelets, forming the basis for the clot.

WORKINGS: HOW THE CARDIOVASCULAR SYSTEM FUNCTIONS

In its continuous work, an average heart contracts more than 100,000 times a day to force blood through the thousands of miles of blood vessels to nourish each of the trillions of cells in the body. With each contraction, the heart forces about 2.5 ounces (74 milliliters) of blood into the bloodstream. At an average adult heart rate of 72 beats per minute, this equals about 1.4 gallons (5.3 liters) of blood every minute, 84 gallons (318 liters) every hour, and 2,016 gallons (7,631 liters) every day. With exercise, this amount may be increased by as much as five times.

Cardiac cycle

Cardiac cycle refers to the series of events that occur in the heart during one complete heartbeat. Each cardiac cycle takes about 0.8 second. During this brief moment, blood enters the heart, passes from chamber to chamber, then is pumped out to all areas of the body. Each cardiac cycle is divided into two phases. The two atria contract while the two ventricles relax. Then, the two ventricles contract while the two atria relax. The contraction phase, especially of the ventricles, is known as systole; the relaxation phase is known as diastole. The cardiac cycle consists of a systole and diastole of both the atria and ventricles.

The process begins as deoxygenated (carrying very little oxygen) blood returns to the right atrium of the heart via the venae cavae. At the

BLOOD DOPING

In order to increase their endurance before competition, some athletes resort to a technique known as *blood doping*. The procedure involves withdrawing some of the athlete's red blood cells. After the blood is removed, the athlete's body responds by quickly producing more red blood cells to replace those withdrawn. Then, a few days before a competitive event, the withdrawn blood is infused back into the body.

The effect is to create a greater number of red blood cells and, in turn, a greater concentration of oxygen in the blood. Blood doping can increase an athlete's aerobic capacity by up to 10 percent.

However, blood doping is not only illegal but risky. It can impair blood flow as well as cause flulike symptoms. Instead of helping an athlete's performance, it can hinder it.

same time, oxygenated blood transported from the lungs by the four pulmonary veins empties into the left atrium. The AV valves open, and as blood flows into the atria it also flows passively into the ventricles. The semilunar valves, however, are closed to prevent blood from flowing out of the ventricles into the arteries. When the ventricles are about 70 percent full, the SA node sends out an impulse that spreads through the atria to the AV node. The atria contract, pumping out the remaining 30 percent of blood into the ventricles.

The AV node slows the impulse briefly, allowing the atria time to complete their contraction. The impulse then travels through the AV bundle, the bundle branches, and the Purkinje fibers to the apex of the heart. As the contraction of the ventricles is initiated at this spot, pressure begins building rapidly in the ventricles and the AV valves close (the "lub" sound heard through a stethoscope) to prevent blood from flowing back into the atria. When the pressure in the ventricles becomes higher than the pressure in the large arteries leaving the heart, the semilunar valves are forced open and blood is pumped out of the ventricles. Deoxygenated blood in the right ventricle is pumped to the lungs via the pulmonary arteries; oxygenated blood in the left ventricle is pumped to the rest of the body via the aorta.

While the ventricles are contracting (systole), the atria are at rest (diastole) and are filling with blood once again. When all the blood is pumped from the ventricles, the semilunar valves close (the "dup" sound heard through a stethoscope) to prevent the backflow of blood into the heart. For a moment, the ventricles are empty, closed chambers. When the pressure in the atria increases above that in the ventricles, the AV valves are forced open and blood begins to flow into the ventricles, starting a new cardiac cycle that will take less than one second to complete.

In short, during the cardiac cycle, the upper half of the heart (the atria) receives blood. The lower half (the ventricles) then pumps out the blood. The right side of the heart (right atrium and right ventricle) receives and pumps out deoxygenated blood; the left side (left atrium and left ventricle) receives and pumps out oxygenated blood.

Blood pressure

When the ventricles contract, they force or propel blood from the heart into the large, elastic arteries that expand as the blood is pushed through them. The pressure the blood exerts against the inner walls of the blood vessels is known as blood pressure. This pressure is necessary to keep the blood flowing to all areas of the body and then back to the heart.

Blood pressure is greatest in the large arteries closest to the heart. Because their walls are elastic, the arteries are able to recoil and keep most of the pressure on the blood as it flows

BLOOD PRESSURE IS GREATEST IN THE LARGE ARTERIES CLOSEST TO THE HEART.

away from the heart. As the blood courses through the system in less elastic vessels—arterioles into capillaries into venules into veins—blood pressure drops. When the blood finally returns to the right atrium via the venae cavae, the pressure behind it is almost zero.

Since the heart contracts and relaxes during a cardiac cycle, blood pressure rises and falls during each beat. It is higher during systole (left ventricle contracting) and lower during diastole (left ventricle relaxing).

Blood pressure is measured in millimeters of mercury (mmHg) with a sphygmomanometer (see box). A blood pressure reading is most often taken on the brachial artery in the arm. The systolic pressure is recorded first, followed by the diastolic pressure. Average young adults have a blood pressure reading of about 120 mmHg for systolic pressure and 80 mmHg for diastolic pressure (written as 120/80 and read as "one-twenty over eighty"). Depending on age, sex, weight, and other factors, normal blood pressure can range from 90 to 135 mmHg for the systolic pressure and 60 to 85 mmHg for the diastolic pressure. Blood pressure normally increases with age.

Regulating the heart rate

Under normal circumstances, the heart controls the rate at which it contracts or beats. But another body system—the nervous system—can and does affect heart rate to help the body adapt to different situations.

The medulla oblongata is a mass of nerve tissue at the top of the spinal cord and at the base of the brain that controls involuntary processes such as breathing and heart rate. Inside the medulla are two cardiac centers, the accelerator center and the inhibitory center. These centers send nerve impulses to the heart to regulate its beating.

The autonomic nervous system is a division of the nervous system that affects internal organs such as the heart, lungs, stomach, and liver. It functions involuntarily, meaning the processes it controls occur without conscious effort on the part of an individual. The autonomic nervous system is divided into two parts, the parasympathetic and sympathetic systems. The parasympathetic system is active primarily in normal, restful situations; the sympathetic system is most active during times of stress or when the body needs energy.

The accelerator center in the medulla sends impulses along sympathetic nerves to the heart to increase heart rate and the force of contraction. The inhibitory center sends impulses along parasympathetic nerves to the heart to decrease heart rate. The centers act in response to changes in blood pressure and the level of oxygen in the blood, often brought about by factors such as exercise, increased body temperature, and emotional stress. Such changes are detected by receptors located in the carotid arteries and the aortic arch.

Receptors in the carotid arteries detect a decrease in blood pressure; those in the aortic arch detect a decrease in the level of oxygen in the blood. Both send out impulses along sensory nerves to the accelerator center, which in turn sends impulses along nerves to the SA node of the heart to increase heart rate. When blood pressure or blood oxygen level has been restored to normal, the inhibitory center sends out impulses along nerves to the SA node to slow heart rate to a normal resting pace.

Exchanges between capillaries and general body tissues

Arteries, arterioles, venules, and veins: the only function of these vessels is to transport blood from or to the heart. The exchange of materials—oxygen, carbon dioxide, nutrients, and wastes—between the blood and interstitial fluid occurs through the capillaries. The movement of these materials is variously brought about by three processes: diffusion, filtration, and osmosis.

Diffusion is the movement of molecules from an area of greater concentration (existing in greater numbers) to an area of lesser concentration (existing in lesser numbers). Diffusion takes place because molecules have free energy, meaning they are always in motion. This is the case especially with molecules in a gas, which move quicker than those in a solid or liquid. Oxygen and carbon dioxide, the gases that pass between the capillaries and the interstitial fluid, move by diffusion. As blood courses through a capillary, the oxygen carried by the hemoglobin in red blood cells exists in a greater amount and thus moves into the surrounding interstitial fluid to be taken up by the cells. Conversely, carbon dioxide exists in a greater amount in the interstitial fluid and so moves into the capillary to be carried away. This exchange of gases between the blood and the interstitial fluid is called internal respiration.

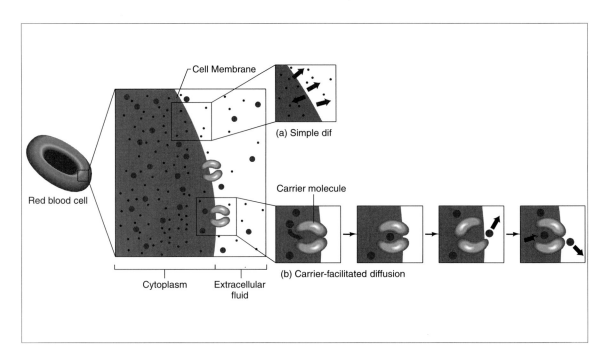

Cell Membrane

(a) Simple dif

Carrier molecule

(b) Carrier-facilitated diffusion

Red blood cell

Cytoplasm

Extracellular fluid

A chart illustrating the process of diffusion. Diffusion is the movement of molecules from an area of greater concentration to an area of lesser concentration. (Illustration by Hans & Cassady.)

Filtration is the movement of water and dissolved materials through a membrane from an area of higher pressure to an area of lower pressure. When blood enters capillaries, it has a pressure reading of about 33 mmHg; the pressure of the interstitial fluid is only about 2 mmHg. Thus, through filtration, plasma and nutrients such as amino acids, glucose, and vitamins are forced through the capillary walls into the surrounding interstitial fluid.

Osmosis is the diffusion of water through a semipermeable membrane (a membrane that allows some materials but not others to flow through it). It is the movement of water from an area where it is abundant to an area where it is scarce or less abundant. Directly related to this is osmotic pressure, which is the tendency of a solution to "pull" water into it. The strength of this pressure is determined by the amount of dissolved material, called solutes, in the solution. The greater the amount of solutes, the lower the amount of water in that solution. A solution containing a high amount of solutes has a high osmotic pressure, and water has a greater tendency to move into the solution.

At the venous end of capillaries, just before they merge to form venules, the osmotic pressure is greater in the capillaries than in the interstitial fluid. This is due to the presence of albumin and other large proteins that have

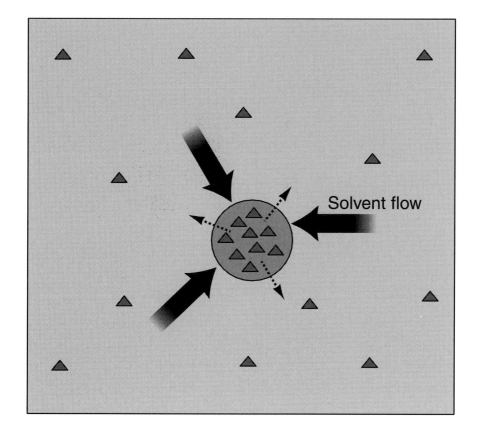

A magnified view of osmosis, the movement of water from an area where it is abundant to an area where it is scarce or less abundant. Osmosis plays a major role in the chemistry of living things. (Illustration by Hans & Cassady.)

remained as solutes in the blood. Interstitial fluid has a low osmotic pressure and is thus "pulled" into the capillaries and carried away.

Capillary exchange in the lungs

After blood has flowed through the tissues of the body, exchanging oxygen and nutrients for carbon dioxide and wastes, it heads back to the heart. The deoxygenated blood empties into the right atrium via the venae cavae, then into the right ventricle. From here it is pumped into the pulmonary trunk, which then divides into the right and left pulmonary arteries. These arteries transport the deoxygenated blood to each lung.

In the lungs, the arteries branch out into successively smaller arteries and successively smaller arterioles. Finally, the smallest arterioles branch into capillaries. These pulmonary capillaries surround the alveoli, the air sacs of the lungs. The exchange of oxygen and carbon dioxide in the lungs, known as external respiration, takes place across the walls of the alveoli and nearby capillaries.

As in internal respiration, the exchange of gases in external respiration occurs according to the process of diffusion. Air in the alveoli has a high concentration of oxygen. The blood in the pulmonary capillaries has a high concentration of carbon dioxide. Following diffusion, oxygen in the alveoli moves into the capillaries while carbon dioxide in the capillaries moves into the alveoli.

Now oxygenated, blood flows from the capillaries into venules, which merge to form larger and larger veins. Finally, the blood exits each lung through two large pulmonary veins and is carried to the left atrium to be pumped back into the systemic circulation once again. The movement of blood from the lungs to the heart is a special occurrence in the body: it is the only time that veins carry oxygenated blood.

Hepatic portal circulation

Another unique circulation route is the hepatic portal circulation, a sub-division of the systemic circulation. Under this circulation pathway, blood from the digestive organs and the spleen flow through the liver before heading to the heart.

Capillaries that drain the stomach, small intestine, colon, pancreas, and spleen flow into two large veins, the superior mesenteric and the splenic. These two veins then unite to form the portal vein, which carries the blood into the liver.

Once in the liver, the portal vein branches to form capillaries called sinusoids. Sinusoids are larger than normal capillaries. Their walls are also more permeable, allowing proteins and blood cells to enter or leave easily. This is important since the blood entering the liver from the digestive organs contains large amounts of nutrients.

As the blood flows slowly through the sinusoids in the liver, some of these nutrients are removed from the blood and either stored in the liver for later use or changed into other materials the body needs. From the sinusoids, blood flows into the right and left hepatic veins, then into the inferior vena cava, and finally into the right atrium.

The complete flow of blood from the digestive organs to the heart is unusual. Normally, arteries flow into capillaries, which flow into veins. In the hepatic portal circulation, no arteries are involved. Here, capillaries merge to form veins, which branch into capillaries that merge again to form veins. This strange route is necessary so that blood may be altered by the liver. Nutrients may be stored or changed and possible poisons (such as alcohol and medicines) may be transformed into less harmful substances before the blood returns to the heart and the rest of circulation.

AILMENTS: WHAT CAN GO WRONG WITH
THE CARDIOVASCULAR SYSTEM

Diseases that affect the heart and the cardiovascular system are among the most serious health problems facing Americans. In fact, cardiovascular or heart disease is the leading cause of death in the United States. The disease does not recognize gender, race, or age: it afflicts all people equally. According to statistics, almost 70 million people in the country suffer from some type of cardiovascular disease. Each year, more than one million of those people die.

The following are just a few of the many diseases and disorders that can impair the cardiovascular system or its parts.

Anemia

The word anemia literally means "lack of blood." It is a condition that results when the number of red blood cells or the amount of hemoglobin is reduced to a low level and the cells of the body do not receive all the oxygen they need to function and produce energy. Weakness, listlessness, drowsiness, headaches, soreness of the mouth, slight fever, and other discomforts are characteristics of anemia. Scientists have identified more than 400 types of anemia. Common forms of the condition may be brought about by rapid blood loss, the destruction or disease of the bone marrow, or an inadequate amount of iron or the vitamin B^{12} in a person's diet.

Atherosclerosis

Atherosclerosis is a type of arteriosclerosis, a general term for hardening of the arteries. Atherosclerosis is a condition in which fatty material and other

---

CARDIOVASCULAR SYSTEM DISORDERS

Anemia (ah-NEE-me-yah): Diseased condition in which there is a deficiency of red blood cells or hemoglobin.

Arteriosclerosis (ar-tir-ee-o-skle-ROW-sis): Diseased condition in which the walls of arteries become thickened and hard, interfering with the circulation of blood.

Atherosclerosis (ath-a-row-skle-ROW-sis): Diseased condition in which fatty material accumulates on the interior walls of arteries, making them narrower.

Hemophilia (hee-muh-FILL-ee-ah): Inherited blood disease in which the blood lacks one or more of the clotting factors, making it difficult to stop bleeding.

Hypertension (hi-per-TEN-shun): High blood pressure.

Leukemia (loo-KEE-mee-ah): Type of cancer that affects the blood-forming tissues and organs, causing them to flood the bloodstream and lymphatic system with immature and abnormal white blood cells.

Sickle cell anemia (SICK-el cell ah-NEE-me-yah): Inherited blood disorder in which red blood cells are sickle-shaped instead of round because of defective hemoglobin molecules.

substances accumulate on and in the walls of large arteries, impairing the flow of blood.

Cholesterol, a fatlike substance produced by the liver, is an essential part of cell membranes and body chemicals. Normally, the body produces all the cholesterol it needs. Eating foods high in saturated fats (found mostly in animal products such as egg yolks, fatty meats, and whole milk dairy products) can cause an increase in blood cholesterol levels. The excess cholesterol not taken up by the cells accumulates on the walls of arteries. There it combines with fatty materials, cellular waste products, calcium, and fibrin to form a waxy buildup known as plaque, which can either partially or totally obstruct blood flow.

CHOLESTEROL IS AN ESSENTIAL PART OF CELL MEMBRANES AND BODY CHEMICALS.

Coronary heart disease (also known as coronary artery disease) arises when atherosclerosis occurs in the coronary (heart) arteries. When the blood flow in these arteries is restricted, the heart muscles do not receive the proper amount of blood and oxygen. Chest pain or pressure, called angina, may occur. If the blood flow is blocked, cardiac muscle cells begin to die and a heart attack may result.

If blood flow is blocked in any cerebral (brain) arteries, brain cells quickly begin to die and a stroke may result. Depending on what area of the brain has been affected, a stroke may cause memory loss, speech impairment, paralysis, coma, or death.

Atherosclerosis is a complex condition, and its exact cause is still unknown. However, scientific studies have shown that smoking, diabetes, a diet high in fats and low in fiber, and lack of exercise can all increase the risk of developing atherosclerosis.

Congenital heart disease

Congenital heart disease (sometimes called congenital heart defect) is any defect in the heart or its main blood vessels that is present at birth. Almost 1 out of every 100 infants are born with some sort of heart abnormality. At present, scientists have recognized thirty-five types of defects. Most of these abnormalities or defects obstruct or alter the flow of blood in the heart or the vessels near it. Defects include openings in the septum between the atria or the ventricles, the emergence of the aorta and pulmonary artery out of the same ventricle, the development of

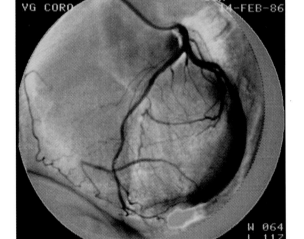

An angiogram of a coronary artery. Coronary artery disease arises when atherosclerosis occurs in the coronary arteries. (Reproduced by permission of CNRI/Phototake NYC.)

Christiaan Barnard (center) at a news conference. (Reproduced by permission of AP/Wide World Photos.)

THE FIRST HUMAN HEART TRANSPLANT

A medical milestone occurred on December 3, 1967, when South African surgeon Christiaan Neethling Barnard performed the first human heart transplant. The procedure, in which a fifty-five-year-old man received the heart of a young accident victim, took place at Groote Schuur Hospital in Cape Town, South Africa.

Barnard, born in 1922, had been focusing his attention on various kinds of open-heart surgery since the late 1950s. Soon after, he had begun to experiment with surgical transplantation. By the late 1960s, he was ready to perform a human heart transplant. All he needed were a proper patient and a donor.

That patient soon turned out to be Louis Washansky, a wholesale grocer who had suffered a series of heart attacks over the previous seven years. Washansky, admitted to the hospital in November 1967, was dying of a failing heart. Doctors estimated he had only weeks to live.

On December 2, twenty-five-year-old Denise Darvall was involved in a severe auto accident. When she was carried into the hospital's emergency room, her brain was dead, but her heart was still beating. Barnard asked her parents if they would donate her heart and they agreed.

The following day, assisted by a team of thirty associates, Barnard placed Darvall's heart into Washansky's chest. Within a few days, Washansky was well enough to sit up in bed. However, to prevent his body from rejecting the new organ, Washansky was given medication that suppressed his immune system. Although the medication worked, it also lowered his body's resistance to infection. Eighteen days after the surgery, Washansky died of pneumonia.

In January 1968, Barnard tried again, this time transplanting the heart of a twenty-four-year-old stroke victim into Philip Blaiberg, a fifty-eight-year-old retired dentist. Blaiberg lived for eighteen months after the surgery.

Today, with the development of more effective immunosuppressant drugs (those that hinder the workings of the immune system), transplant patients survive much longer. Three-quarters of heart-transplant patients currently survive five years after the operation.

---

only one ventricle, or the formation of only one side of the heart. About half of those people with congenital heart disease require surgery to correct the problem.

ALMOST 1 OUT OF EVERY 100 INFANTS ARE BORN WITH SOME SORT OF HEART ABNORMALITY.

Heart murmurs

Murmurs are abnormal, extra heart sounds made by the blood moving through the heart and its valves. Generally, blood flows smoothly and silently through the heart. The only sounds a physician normally hears through a stethoscope are the "lub-dup" sounds created by the closing of the heart valves.

Heart murmurs that are very faint, intermittent, and do not affect a person's health are called "innocent" heart murmurs. They may be caused by the failure of a heart valve to open or close completely. In the healthy hearts of children (or of the elderly), innocent heart murmurs may exist because the heart walls are relatively thin. As blood rushes through, the walls vibrate, creating extra sounds. Innocent heart murmurs in children usually disappear with age.

Murmurs that are caused by severe heart defects, however, are louder and continual. They can bring about chest pain, shortness of breath, dizziness, and, in extreme cases, death. Surgery is often required to correct severely damaged or diseased valves.

Hemophilia

Hemophilia is an inherited blood disease in which the blood lacks one or more of the clotting factors. Because of this, the blood is unable to form a clot, and even a small cut can result in prolonged bleeding and death. Commonly called "bleeder's disease," hemophilia principally affects males. When hemophiliacs (people afflicted with hemophilia) suffer a trauma and begin to bleed, they are given a transfusion of fresh plasma or an injection of the clotting factor they lack.

Hypertension

Hypertension is high blood pressure. It is normal for blood pressure to be elevated for brief periods because of exercise, emotional stress, or a fever.

USING LIGHT TO REDUCE HEART-TRANSPLANT REJECTION

In December 1998, a team of doctors from the U.S. and Europe announced a possible breakthrough technique to reduce the risk of rejection in heart-transplant patients.

Currently, when patients are given new hearts, they are also given drugs, called immunosuppressants, to prevent their immune systems from developing antibodies that would attack the new organs. Unfortunately, these drugs also weaken their immune systems, allowing infections to develop.

Under the new technique, called photophoresis, light is used to destroy cells that prompt the body to reject the transplanted organ. First, blood is pumped from the patient's body. Then the white blood cells in that blood are treated with ultraviolet A light and methoxsalen (a chemical that makes the cells hypersensitive to that type of light). Afterward, the blood is returned to the patient's body.

Of those patients who received the light technique plus immunosuppressant drugs, 81 percent experienced only one episode of rejection. Of those patients receiving only the drugs, the rate was just 52 percent.

The new technique has not yet shown it can increase a patient's long-term chance of survival, but it has helped limit the amount of drugs needed to fight rejection.

Consistent arterial blood pressure measuring 140/90 or higher, however, is hypertension. The condition, the most common one affecting the cardiovascular system, is a serious one. Although it shows no symptoms, hypertension should be treated. If left unchecked, it can lead to atherosclerosis, heart attack, stroke, or kidney damage.

Hypertension most often strikes African Americans, middle-aged and elderly people, obese people, heavy alcohol drinkers, and people suffering from diabetes or kidney disease. Scientists do not know the cause for 90 to 95 percent of hypertension cases. However, studies have shown that reducing salt and fat intake, losing weight, quitting smoking, reducing alcohol consumption, and exercising regularly all combine to reduce blood pressure. Numerous drugs have also been developed to treat hypertension.

Leukemia

Leukemia (pronounced loo-KEE-mee-ah) is a type of cancer that affects the blood-forming tissues and organs, mainly the bone marrow, lymph nodes, and spleen. The disorder causes these blood-forming tissues and organs to flood the bloodstream and lymphatic system with immature and abnormal white blood cells. The overproduction of white blood cells causes a crowding-out of red blood cells and platelets.

Infections develop because these useless white blood cells have no infection-fighting ability. Anemia, easy bruising, and hemorrhaging (bleeding without clotting) also occur because of the lack of red blood cells and platelets. Leukemia is further marked by high fever and continual weakness.

Although ten times as many adults as children are stricken with the disease, leukemia is the number one disease killer of children. There are many types of leukemia, but no one cause of the disease is known. Scientists believe genetic abnormalities, exposure to toxic chemicals, and overexposure to X rays or other radioactive materials may play a part in the development of leukemia.

LEUKEMIA IS THE NUMBER ONE DISEASE KILLER OF CHILDREN.

Chemotherapy—drug therapy to poison and destroy the abnormal cells—is effective against some types of leukemia, especially in children. Blood transfusions and bone marrow transplants have also proven effective in certain cases. With the best treatment, almost 75 percent of children suffering from leukemia survive.

Sickle cell anemia

Sickle cell anemia is an inherited blood disorder in which defective hemoglobin molecules tend to stick to one another in a red blood cell, forming strands of hemoglobin. Red blood cells that contain these strands become rigid, sticky, and crescent or sickle shaped.

These sickle-shaped cells do not last as long as normal red blood cells. They die quickly, leaving a shortage of red blood cells in the body. Anemia then develops. Sickle cells cause further problems by not fitting well through small blood vessels. They become trapped, forming a blockage that prevents normal blood flow. Tissues and organs deprived of oxygenated blood and nutrients begin to deteriorate. Acute pain develops. Over time, damage to the kidneys, lungs, liver, and central nervous and immune systems may be considerable. Severe complications may even lead to strokes and death. Those people who die from sickle cell anemia often do so before the age of thirty.

Sickle cell anemia primarily affects people with African, Mediterranean, Middle Eastern, and Indian ancestry. In the United States, the disease occurs

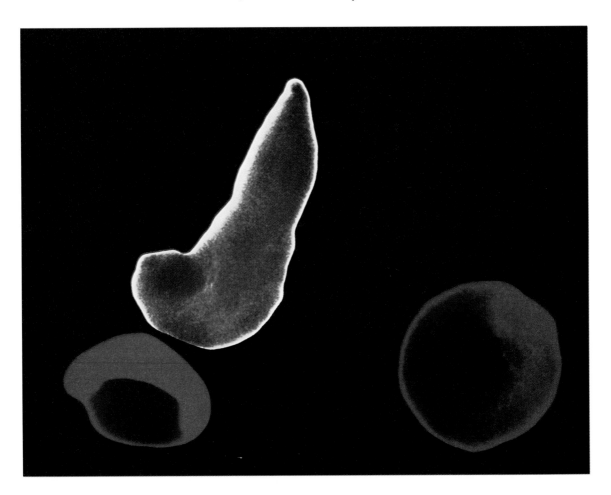

An electron micrograph scan of red blood cells taken from a person with sickle cell anemia. (Photograph by Dr. Gopal Murti. Reproduced by permission of Photo Researchers, Inc.)

in about 1 out of every 500 African American births and 1 out of every 1,000 to 1,400 Hispanic American births.

There is no known cure for the disease. Painkillers, antibiotics (to fight infections), blood transfusions (to boost red blood cell count), and oxygen are treatments given to alleviate symptoms and decrease the chance of complication. Though risky, bone marrow transplants have proven effective for certain children who have been severely affected by sickle cell anemia.

TAKING CARE: KEEPING THE CARDIOVASCULAR SYSTEM HEALTHY

A healthy lifestyle is key to keeping the cardiovascular system healthy. Proper diet, regular exercise, maintaining a healthy weight, not smoking, moderate alcohol drinking, and reducing stress all lead to a healthy heart lifestyle.

A healthy diet can decrease the risk of atherosclerosis from developing, which can lead to heart disease, heart attacks, and strokes. The "Food Guide" Pyramid developed by the U.S. Departments of Agriculture and Health and Human Services provides easy-to-follow guidelines for such a diet. In general, foods that are low in fat (especially saturated fat), low in cholesterol, and high in fiber should be eaten. Fat should make up no more than 30 percent of a person's total daily calorie intake. Breads, cereals, pastas, fruits, and vegetables should form the bulk of a person's diet; meat, fish, nuts, and cheese and other dairy products should make up a lesser portion.

Regular aerobic exercise can lower blood pressure, decrease weight, and keep blood vessels more flexible. The American College of Sports Medicine and the Centers for Disease Control and Prevention recommend that people engage in moderate to intense aerobic activity four or more times per week for at least thirty minutes at a time. Walking, jogging, cycling, swimming, and climbing stairs are just a few examples of aerobic activity that force the large muscles of the body to use oxygen more efficiently.

 WHY DOES THAT HAPPEN?

Q: Why do I feel lightheaded or dizzy when I get up quickly after having lain down?

A: You feel lightheaded because of changes in two related forces: gravity and blood pressure. When you are lying down, gravity is pressing equally along the length of your body. Your heart is able to maintain a constant blood pressure throughout your body by beating at a constant rate.

When you arise suddenly, however, the pressure of gravity is greater upon the upper parts of your body, especially your head. This abrupt change in pressure causes blood in the vessels in your head to flow downward, bringing about a decrease in blood pressure in those vessels. Receptors in the carotid arteries immediately sense this drop in blood pressure and signal the accelerator center in the medulla. The accelerator center then signals the heart to increase the rate of contraction. After a few brief moments, the blood pressure in your brain is restored to normal and the feeling of lightheadedness fades.

Maintaining a healthy weight can reduce blood pressure and lower a person's cholesterol level. Eating a healthy diet and exercising regularly are the principal factors in maintaining a proper body weight.

Smoking is the worst thing a person can do to their heart and lungs. It increases heart rate, constricts major arteries, raises blood pressure, contributes to the development of plaque, and can create irregular heartbeats. A person who smokes can help reverse the negative effects caused by smoking merely by quitting. Within five to ten years, that person will face the same risks of heart disease as a nonsmoker.

SMOKING IS THE WORST THING A PERSON CAN DO TO THEIR HEART AND LUNGS.

People who like to drink alcohol should do so in moderation. The American Heart Association defines moderate alcohol consumption as no more than one ounce of alcohol per day. This roughly equals one cocktail, one 8-ounce glass of wine, or two 12-ounce glasses of beer. Excessive drinking raises blood pressure, can cause abnormal heart rhythms, and can even poison the heart, leading to death. Cocaine, heroin, and all other illegal drugs can seriously damage the heart and should be avoided completely.

Studies have shown that stress can increase heart rate and raise blood pressure. Chronic (long-term) stress can cause plaque to develop in the arteries, increasing the risk of atherosclerosis, heart attacks, and strokes. Exercising, getting enough sleep, practicing relaxation techniques, and thinking positively are a few methods to help reduce stress and keep the cardiovascular system healthy.

FOR MORE INFORMATION

Books

Avraham, Regina, and C. Everett Koop. *The Circulatory System.* New York: Chelsea House, 1989.

Ballard, Carol. *The Heart and Circulatory System.* Austin, TX: Raintree/ Steck-Vaughn, 1997.

Johansson, Philip. *Heart Disease.* Springfield, NJ: Enslow, 1998.

Parramon, Merce. *How Our Blood Circulates.* New York: Chelsea House, 1993.

Seymour, Simon. *The Heart: Our Circulatory System.* New York: Morrow, 1996.

Silverstein, Alvin, Virginia B. Silverstein, and Robert A. Silverstein. *The Circulatory System.* New York: Twenty-First Century Books, 1995.

WWW Sites

American Heart Association National Center
http://www.amhrt.org/

Homepage of the American Heart Association, featuring information on health matters relating to the heart: nutrition, exercise, stroke, diseases and their treatment, and scientific and professional publications.

The Heart: An Online Exploration
http://sln.fi.edu/biosci/biosci.html
Site prepared for the Franklin Institute Science Museum that includes information on topics such as development of the heart, circulation, diet, health, and disease. Also includes graphics and a short video clip of heart-bypass surgery.

The Heart and the Circulatory System
http://www.gene.com/ae/AE/AEC/cc/heart_background.html
Provides an extensive overview of the history of medical approaches to the heart and blood. Also provides information on the types of circulatory systems, a discussion of the anatomy of the heart, a heart glossary, and activities to explore the circulatory system.

NASA K–12 Internet: Shuttle Mir Biology Activity 9
http://quest.arc.nasa.gov/smore/teachers/act9.html
Part of NASA's Quest Project, this site (aimed at grade levels 5–8) provides teachers and students with a "circulatory system relay" activity that brings into focus the workings of the circulatory system. Background information for teachers also provided.

National Heart, Lungs, and Blood Institute Homepage
http://www.nhlbi.nih.gov/nhlbi/nhlbi.htm
Homepage of the NHLBI, part of the federal government's National Institutes of Health. Includes health- and research-related information on the cardiovascular system, the lungs, and blood. Also provides links to other health-related web sites.

2

The Digestive System

The foods we eat—apples, pepperoni pizzas, leafy green salads—taste good to us, but cannot be used by the body as they are. The nutrition the cells of the body need to keeping growing and working must be in a simple form: amino acids, simple sugars, and fatty acids. It is the job of the digestive system to take the complex organic molecules of the foods we ingest—proteins, carbohydrates, and fats—and break them down into their simple building blocks. This process is called digestion. Once digestion has occurred, the simple molecules (nutrients) are absorbed from the digestion system by the cardiovascular and lymphatic systems and transported to cells throughout the body.

DESIGN: PARTS OF THE DIGESTIVE SYSTEM

The digestive system may be broken into two parts: a long, winding, muscular tube accompanied by accessory digestive organs and glands. That open-ended tube, known as the alimentary canal or digestive tract, is composed of various organs. These organs are, in order, the mouth, pharynx, esophagus, stomach, small intestine, and large intestine. The rectum and anus form the end of the large intestine. The accessory digestive organs and glands that help in the digestive process include the tongue, teeth, salivary glands, pancreas, liver, and gall bladder.

The walls of the alimentary canal from the esophagus through the large intestine are made up of four tissue layers. The innermost layer is the mucosa, coated with mucus. This protects the alimentary canal from chemicals and enzymes (proteins that speed up the rate of chemical reactions) that break down food and from germs and parasites that might be in that food. Around the mucosa is the submucosa, which contains blood vessels, nerves, and lymph vessels. Wrapped around the submucosa are two layers of muscles that help move food along the canal. The outermost layer, the serosa, is moist, fibrous tissue that protects the alimentary canal and helps it move against the surrounding organs in the body.

The mouth

Food enters the body through the mouth, or oral cavity. The lips form and protect the opening of the mouth, the cheeks form its sides, the tongue forms its floor, and the hard and soft palates form its roof. The hard palate is at the front; the soft palate is in the rear. Attached to the soft palate is a fleshy, fingerlike projection called the uvula (from the Latin word meaning "little grape"). Two U-shaped rows of teeth line the mouth—one above and one below. Three pair of salivary glands open at various points into the mouth.

THE TONGUE. The muscular tongue is attached to the base of the mouth by a fold of mucous membrane. On the upper surface of the tongue are small projections called papillae, many of which contain taste buds (for a discussion of taste, see chapter 12). Most of the tongue lies within the mouth,

WORDS TO KNOW

Alimentary canal (al-i-MEN-tah-ree ka-NAL): Also known as the digestive tract, the series of muscular structures through which food passes while being converted to nutrients and waste products; includes the oral cavity, pharynx, esophagus, stomach, large intestine, and small intestine.

Amylase (am-i-LACE): Any of various digestive enzymes that convert starches to sugars.

Appendix (ah-PEN-dix): Small, apparently useless organ extending from the cecum.

Bile: Greenish yellow liquid produced by the liver that neutralizes acids and emulsifies fats in the duodenum.

Bolus (BO-lus): Rounded mass of food prepared by the mouth for swallowing.

Cecum (SEE-kum): Blind pouch at the beginning of the large intestine.

Chyle (KILE): Thick, whitish liquid consisting of lymph and tiny fat globules absorbed from the small intestine during digestion.

Chyme (KIME): Soupylike mixture of partially digested food and stomach secretions.

Colon (KOH-lun): Largest region of the large intestine, divided into four sections: ascending, transverse, descending, and sigmoid (colon is sometimes used to describe the entire large intestine).

Colostomy (kuh-LAS-tuh-mee): Surgical procedure where a portion of the large intestine is brought through the abdominal wall and attached to a bag to collect feces.

Defecation (def-e-KAY-shun): Elimination of feces from the large intestine through the anus.

Dentin (DEN-tin): Bonelike material underneath the enamel of teeth, forming the main part.

Duodenum (doo-o-DEE-num or doo-AH-de-num): First section of the small intestine.

Emulsify (e-MULL-si-fie): To break down large fat globules into smaller droplets that stay suspended in water.

Enamel (e-NAM-el): Whitish, hard, glossy outer layer of teeth.

Enzymes (EN-zimes): Proteins that speed up the rate of chemical reactions.

Epiglottis (ep-i-GLAH-tis): Flaplike piece of tissue at the top of the larynx that covers its opening when swallowing is occurring.

Esophagus (e-SOF-ah-gus): Muscular tube connecting the pharynx and stomach.

Feces (FEE-seez): Solid body wastes formed in the large intestine.

but its base extends into the pharynx. Located at the base of the tongue are the lingual tonsils, small masses of lymphatic tissue that serve to prevent infection.

TEETH. Humans have two sets of teeth: deciduous and permanent. The deciduous teeth (also known as baby or milk teeth) start to erupt through the gums in the mouth when a child is about six months old. By the age of two, the full set of twenty teeth has developed. Between the ages of six and twelve, the roots of these teeth are reabsorbed into the body and the teeth begin to fall out. They are quickly replaced by the thirty-two permanent adult teeth. (The third molars, the wisdom teeth, may not erupt because of inadequate space in the jaw. In such cases, they become impacted or embedded in the jawbone and must be removed surgically.)

Flatus (FLAY-tus): Gas generated by bacteria in the large intestine.

Gastric juice (GAS-trick JOOSE): Secretion of the gastric glands of the stomach, containing hydrochloric acid, pepsin, and mucus.

Ileocecal valve (ill-ee-oh-SEE-kal VALV): Sphincter or ring of muscle that controls the flow of chyme from the ileum to the large intestine.

Ileum (ILL-ee-um): Final section of the small intestine.

Jejunum (je-JOO-num): Middle section of the small intestine.

Lacteals (LAK-tee-als): Specialized lymph capillaries in the villi of the small intestine.

Larynx (LAR-ingks): Organ between the pharynx and trachea that contains the vocal cords.

Lipase (LIE-pace): Digestive enzyme that converts lipids (fats) into fatty acids.

Lower esophageal sphincter (LOW-er i-sof-ah-GEE-al SFINGK-ter): Strong ring of muscle at the base of the esophagus that contracts to prevent stomach contents from moving back into the esophagus.

Palate (PAL-uht): Roof of the mouth, divided into hard and soft portions, that separates the mouth from the nasal cavities.

Papillae (pah-PILL-ee): Small projections on the upper surface of the tongue that contain taste buds.

Peristalsis (per-i-STALL-sis): Series of wavelike muscular contractions that move material in one direction through a hollow organ.

Pharynx (FAR-inks): Short, muscular tube extending from the mouth and nasal cavities to the trachea and esophagus.

Plaque (PLACK): Sticky, whitish film on teeth formed by a protein in saliva and sugary substances in the mouth.

Pyloric sphincter (pie-LOR-ick SFINGK-ter): Strong ring of muscle at the junction of the stomach and the small intestine that regulates the flow of material between them.

Rugae (ROO-jee): Folds of the inner mucous membrane of organs, such as the stomach, that allow those organs to expand.

Trypsin (TRIP-sin): Digestive enzyme that converts proteins into amino acids; inactive form is trypsinogen.

Uvula (U-vue-lah): Fleshy projection hanging from the soft palate that raises to close off the nasal passages during swallowing.

Vestigial organ (ves-TIJ-ee-al OR-gan): Organ that is reduced in size and function when compared with that of evolutionary ancestors.

Villi (VILL-eye): Tiny, fingerlike projections on the inner lining of the small intestine that increase the rate of nutrient absorption by greatly increasing the intestine's surface area.

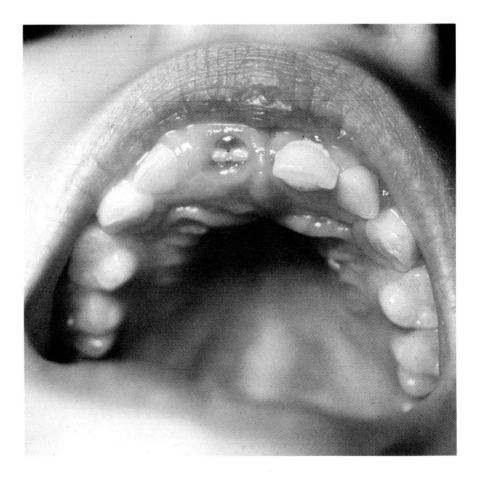

Food enters the body through the mouth. Key structures in the mouth include the lips, the tongue, the hard and soft palates, and the teeth. (Photograph by Keith. Reproduced by permission of Custom Medical Stock Photo.)

Teeth are classified according to shape and function. Incisors, the chisel-shaped front teeth, are used for cutting. Cuspids or canines, the pointed teeth next to the incisors, are used for tearing or piercing. Bicuspids (or premolars) and molars, the back teeth with flattened tops and rounded, raised tips, are used for grinding.

Each tooth consists of two major portions: the crown and the root. The crown is the exposed part of the tooth above the gum line; the root is enclosed in a socket in the jaw. The outermost layer of the crown is the whitish enamel. Made mainly of calcium, enamel is the hardest substance in the body.

OPPOSITE: The human digestive process. The digestive system's job is to take the complex organic molecules of the foods people eat and break them down into their simple building blocks. (Illustration by Hans & Cassady.)

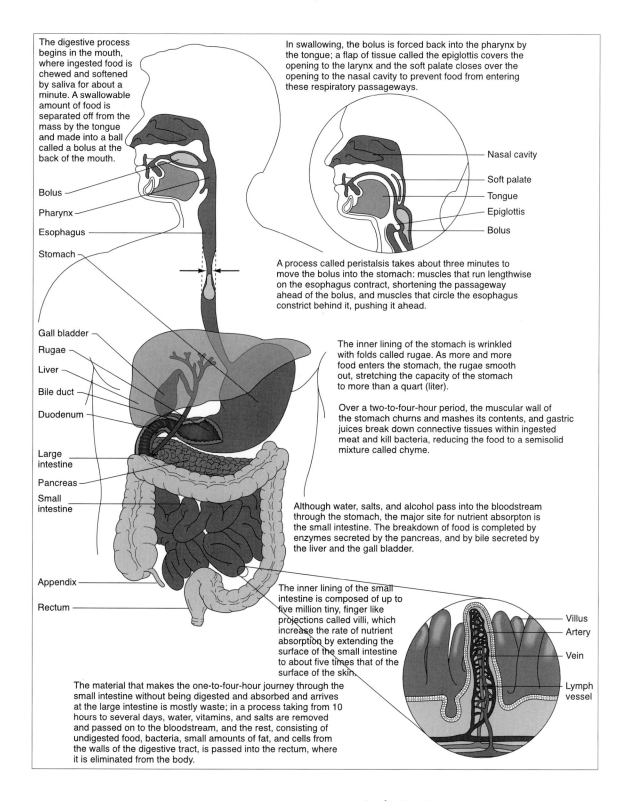

The digestive process begins in the mouth, where ingested food is chewed and softened by saliva for about a minute. A swallowable amount of food is separated off from the mass by the tongue and made into a ball called a bolus at the back of the mouth.

Bolus

Pharynx

Esophagus

Stomach

In swallowing, the bolus is forced back into the pharynx by the tongue; a flap of tissue called the epiglottis covers the opening to the larynx and the soft palate closes over the opening to the nasal cavity to prevent food from entering these respiratory passageways.

Nasal cavity

Soft palate

Tongue

Epiglottis

Bolus

A process called peristalsis takes about three minutes to move the bolus into the stomach: muscles that run lengthwise on the esophagus contract, shortening the passageway ahead of the bolus, and muscles that circle the esophagus constrict behind it, pushing it ahead.

Gall bladder

Rugae

Liver

Bile duct

Duodenum

Large intestine

Pancreas

Small intestine

The inner lining of the stomach is wrinkled with folds called rugae. As more and more food enters the stomach, the rugae smooth out, stretching the capacity of the stomach to more than a quart (liter).

Over a two-to-four-hour period, the muscular wall of the stomach churns and mashes its contents, and gastric juices break down connective tissues within ingested meat and kill bacteria, reducing the food to a semisolid mixture called chyme.

Although water, salts, and alcohol pass into the bloodstream through the stomach, the major site for nutrient absorpton is the small intestine. The breakdown of food is completed by enzymes secreted by the pancreas, and by bile secreted by the liver and the gall bladder.

Appendix

Rectum

The inner lining of the small intestine is composed of up to five million tiny, finger like projections called villi, which increase the rate of nutrient absorption by extending the surface of the small intestine to about five times that of the surface of the skin.

Villus

Artery

Vein

Lymph vessel

The material that makes the one-to-four-hour journey through the small intestine without being digested and absorbed and arrives at the large intestine is mostly waste; in a process taking from 10 hours to several days, water, vitamins, and salts are removed and passed on to the bloodstream, and the rest, consisting of undigested food, bacteria, small amounts of fat, and cells from the walls of the digestive tract, is passed into the rectum, where it is eliminated from the body.

Underneath the enamel is a yellowish, bonelike material called dentin. It forms the bulk of the tooth. Within the dentin is the pulp cavity, which receives blood vessels and nerves through a narrow root canal at the base of the tooth.

THE SALIVARY GLANDS. Three pair of salivary glands produce saliva on a continuous basis to keep the mouth and throat moist. The largest pair, the parotid glands, are located just below and in front of the ears. The next largest pair, the submaxillary or submandibular glands, are located in the lower jaw. The smallest pair, the sublingual glands, are located under the tongue.

Ducts or tiny tubes carry saliva from these glands into the mouth. Ducts from the parotid glands open into the upper portion of the mouth; ducts from the submaxillary and sublingual glands open into the mouth beneath the tongue.

Ivan Pavlov. (Reproduced by permission of the Library of Congress.)

PAVLOV AND HIS SALIVATING DOG

Ivan Petrovich Pavlov (1849–1936) was a Russian physiologist (a person who studies the physical and chemical processes of living organisms) who conducted pioneering research into the digestive activities of mammals. His now-famous experiments with a dog ("Pavlov's dog") to show how the central nervous system affects digestion earned him the Nobel Prize for Medicine or Physiology in 1904.

Interested in the actions of digestion and gland secretion, Pavlov set up an ingenious experiment. In a laboratory, he severed a dog's throat (Pavlov was a skillful surgeon and the animal was unharmed). When the dog ate food, the food dropped out of the animal's throat before reaching its stomach. Through this simulated feeding, Pavlov discovered that the sight, smell, and swallowing of food was enough to cause the secretion of gastric juice. He demonstrated that the stimulation of the vagus nerve (one of the major nerves of the brain) influences the actions of the gastric glands.

In another famous study, Pavlov set out to determine whether he could turn unconditioned (naturally occurring) reflexes or responses of the central nervous system into conditioned (learned) reflexes. He had noticed that laboratory dogs would sometimes salivate merely at the approach of lab assistants who fed them. Pavlov then decided to ring a bell each time a dog was given food. After a while, he rang the bell without feeding the dog. He discovered that the dog salivated at the sound of the bell, even though food was not present. Through this experiment, Pavlov demonstrated that unconditioned reflexes (salivation and gastric activity) could become conditioned reflexes that were triggered by a stimulus (the bell) that previously had no connection with the event (eating).

The salivary glands are controlled by the autonomic nervous system, a division of the nervous system that functions involuntarily (meaning the processes it controls occur without conscious effort on the part of an individual). The glands produce between 1.1 and 1.6 quarts (1 and 1.5 liters) of saliva each day. Although the flow is continuous, the amount varies. Food (or anything else) in the mouth increases the amount produced. Even the sight or smell of food will increase the flow.

Saliva is mostly water (about 99 percent), with waste products, antibodies, and enzymes making up the small remaining portion. At mealtimes, saliva contains large quantities of digestive enzymes that help break down food. Saliva also controls the temperature of food (cooling it down or warming it up), cleans surfaces in the mouth, and kills certain bacteria present in the mouth.

The pharynx

The pharynx, or throat, is a short, muscular tube extending about 5 inches (12.7 centimeters) from the mouth and nasal cavities to the esophagus and trachea (windpipe). It serves two separate systems: the digestive system (by allowing the passage of solid food and liquids) and the respiratory system (by allowing the passage of air).

The esophagus

The esophagus, sometimes referred to as the gullet, is the muscular tube connecting the pharynx and stomach. It is approximately 10 inches (25 centimeters) in length and 1 inch (2.5 centimeters) in diameter. In the thorax (area of the body between the neck and the abdomen), the esophagus lies behind the trachea. At the base of the esophagus, where it connects with the stomach, is a strong ring of muscle called the lower esophageal sphincter. Normally, this circular muscle is contracted, preventing contents in the stomach from moving back into the esophagus.

The stomach

The stomach is located on the left side of the abdominal cavity just under the diaphragm (a membrane of muscle separating the chest cavity from the abdominal cavity). When empty, the stomach is shaped like the letter J and its inner walls are drawn up into long, soft folds called rugae. When the stomach expands, the rugae flatten out and disappear. This allows the average adult stomach to hold as much as 1.6 quarts (1.5 liters) of material.

The dome-shaped portion of the stomach to the left of the lower esophageal sphincter is the fundus. The large central portion of the stomach is the body. The part of the stomach connected to the small intestine (the curve of the J) is the pylorus. The pyloric sphincter is a muscular ring that regulates the flow of material from the stomach into the small intestine by variously opening and contracting. That material, a soupylike mixture of partially digested food and stomach secretions, is called chyme.

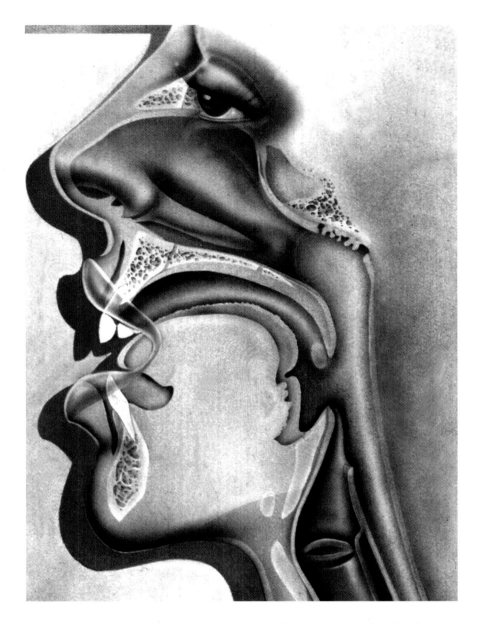

An internal view of the mouth and pharynx, or throat. The throat serves the digestive system by allowing the passage of solid food and liquids. (Reproduced by permission of Photo Researchers, Inc.)

The stomach wall contains three layers of smooth muscle. These layers contract in a regular rhythm—usually three contractions per minute—to mix and churn stomach contents. Mucous membrane lines the stomach. Mucus, the thick, gooey liquid produced by the cells of that membrane, helps protect the stomach from its own secretions. Those secretions—acids and enzymes—

William Beaumont (right) with patient Alexis St. Martin. (Reproduced by permission of Corbis-Bettmann.)

A VIEW OF THE STOMACH

William Beaumont (1785–1853) was an American surgeon who served as an army surgeon during the War of 1812 (1812–15) and at various posts after the war. It was at one of these posts that he saw what perhaps no one before him had seen: the inner workings of the stomach.

In 1882, while serving at Fort Mackinac in northern Michigan, Beaumont was presented with a patient named Alexis St. Martin. The French Canadian trapper, only nineteen at the time, has been accidently shot in the stomach. The bullet had torn a deep chunk out of the left side of St. Martin's lower chest. At first, no one thought he would survive, but amazingly he did. However, his wound never completely healed, leaving a 1 inch-wide (2.5 centimeter-wide) opening. This opening allowed Beaumont to put his finger all the way into St. Martin's stomach.

Beaumont decided to take advantage of opening into St. Martin's side to study human digestion. He started by taking small chunks of food, tying them to a string, then inserting them directly into the young man's stomach. At irregular intervals, he pulled the food out to observe the varying actions of digestion. Later, using a hand-held lens, Beaumont peered into St. Martin's stomach. He observed how the human stomach behaved at various stages of digestion and under differing circumstances.

Beaumont conducted almost 240 experiments on St. Martin. In 1833, he published his findings in *Experiments and Observations on the Gastric Juice and the Physiology of Digestion,* a book that provided invaluable information on the digestive process.

enter the stomach through millions of shallow pits that open onto the surface of the inner stomach. Called gastric pits, these openings lead to gastric glands, which secrete about 1.6 quarts (1.5 liters) of gastric juice each day.

Gastric juice contains hydrochloric acid and pepsin. Pepsin is an enzyme that breaks down proteins; hydrochloric acid kills microorganisms and breaks down cell walls and connective tissue in food. The acid is strong enough to burn a hole in carpet, yet the mucus produced by the mucous membrane prevents it from dissolving the lining of the stomach. Even so, the cells of the mucous membrane wear out quickly: the entire stomach lining is replaced every three days. Mucus also aids in digestion by keeping food moist.

The small intestine

The small intestine is the body's major digestive organ. Looped and coiled within the abdominal cavity, it extends about 20 feet (6 meters) from the stomach to the large intestine. At its junction with the stomach, it measures about 1.5 inches (4 centimeters) in diameter. By the time it meets the large intestine, its diameter has been reduced to 1 inch (2.5 centimeters). Although much longer than the large intestine, the small intestine is called "small" because its overall diameter is smaller.

The small intestine is divided into three regions or sections. The first section, the duodenum, is the initial 10 inches (25 centimeters) closest to the stomach. Chyme from the stomach and secretions from the pancreas and liver empty into this section. The middle section, the jejunum, measures about 8.2 feet (2.5 meters) in length. Digestion and the absorption of nutrients occurs mainly in the jejunum. The final section, the ileum, is also the longest, measuring about 11 feet (3.4 meters) in length. The ileum ends at the ileocecal valve, a sphincter that controls the flow of chyme from the ileum to the large intestine.

The inner lining of the small intestine is covered with tiny, fingerlike projections called villi (giving it an appearance much like the nap of a plush, soft towel). The villi greatly increase the intestinal surface area available for absorbing digested material. Within each villus (singular for villi) are blood capillaries and a lymph capillary called a lacteal. Digested food molecules are absorbed through the walls of the villus into both the capillaries and the lacteal. At the bases of the villi are openings of intestinal glands, which secrete a watery intestinal juice. This juice contains digestive enzymes that convert food materials into simple nutrients the body can readily use. On average, about 2 quarts (1.8 liters) of intestinal juice are secreted into the small intestine each day.

As with the lining of the stomach, a coating of mucus helps protect the lining of the small intestine. Yet again, the digestive enzymes prove too strong for the delicate cells of that lining. They wear out and are replaced about every two days.

The large intestine

Extending from the end of the small intestine to the anus, the large intestine measures about 5 feet (1.5 meters) in length and 3 inches (7.5 centimeters) in diameter. It almost completely frames the small intestine. The large intestine is divided into three major regions: the cecum, colon, and rectum.

Cecum comes from the Latin word *caecum,* meaning "blind." Shaped like a rounded pouch, the cecum lies immediately below the area where the ileum empties into the large intestine. Attached to the cecum is the slender, fingerlike appendix, which measures about 3.5 inches (9 centimeters) in the average adult. Composed of lymphatic tissue, the appendix seems to have no function in present-day humans. For that reason, scientists refer to it as a vestigial organ (an organ that is reduced in size and function when compared with that of evolutionary ancestors).

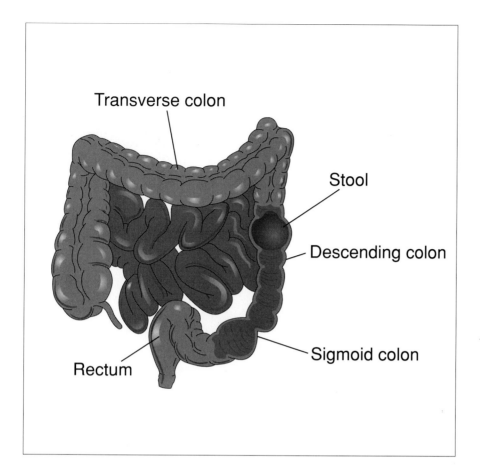

An impacted descending colon. The main part of the large intestine, the colon is divided into four sections: ascending, transverse, descending, and sigmoid. (Illustration by Electronic Illustrators Group.)

Sometimes used to describe the entire large intestine, the colon is actually the organ's main part. It is divided into four sections: ascending, transverse, descending, and sigmoid. The ascending colon travels from the cecum up the right side of the abdominal cavity until it reaches the liver. It then makes a turn, becoming the transverse colon, which travels horizontally across the abdominal cavity. Near the spleen on the left side, it turns down to form the descending colon. At about where it enters the pelvis, it becomes the S-shaped sigmoid colon.

After curving and recurving, the sigmoid colon empties into the rectum, a fairly straight, 6-inch (15-centimeter) tube ending at the anus, the opening to the outside. Two sphincters (rings of muscle) control the opening and closing of the anus.

Roughly 1.6 quarts (1.5 liters) of watery material enters the large intestine each day. No digestion takes place in the large intestine, only the reabsorption or recovery of water. Mucus produced by the cells in the lining of the large intestine help move the waste material along. As more and more water is removed from that material, it becomes compacted into soft masses called feces. Feces are composed of water, cellulose and other indigestible material, and dead and living bacteria. The remnants of worn red blood cells gives feces their brown color. Only about 3 to 7 ounces (85 to 200 grams) of solid fecal material remains after the large intestine has recovered most of the water. That material is then eliminated through the anus, a process called defecation.

ROUGHLY 1.6 QUARTS OF WATERY MATERIAL ENTERS THE LARGE INTESTINE EVERY DAY.

The pancreas

The pancreas is a soft, pink, triangular-shaped gland that measures about 6 inches (15 centimeters) in length. It lies behind the stomach, extending from the curve of the duodenum to the spleen. While a part of the digestive system, the pancreas is also a part of the endocrine system, producing the hormones insulin and glucagon (for a further discussion of this process, see chapter 3).

A posterior view of a human pancreas. The pancreas gland produces pancreatic juice that breaks down all three types of complex food molecules in the small intestine. (Reproduced by permission of Custom Medical Stock Photo.)

Primarily a digestive organ, the pancreas produces pancreatic juice that helps break down all three types of complex food molecules in the small intestine. The enzymes contained in that juice include pancreatic amylase, pancreatic lipase, and trypsinogen. Amylase breaks down starches into simple sugars, such as maltose (malt sugar). Lipase breaks down fats into simpler fatty acids and glycerol (an alcohol). Trypsinogen is the inactive form of the enzyme trypsin, which breaks down proteins into amino acids. Trypsin is so powerful that if produced in the pancreas, it would digest the organ itself. To prevent this, the pancreas produces trypsinogen, which is then changed in the duodenum to its active form.

Pancreatic juice is collected from all parts of the pancreas through microscopic ducts. These ducts merge to form larger ducts, which eventually combine to form the main pancreatic duct. This duct, which runs the length of the pancreas, then transports pancreatic juice to the duodenum of the small intestine.

The liver

The largest glandular organ in the body, the liver weighs between 3 and 4 pounds (1.4 and 1.8 kilograms). It lies on the right side of the abdominal cavity just beneath the diaphragm. In this position, it overlies and almost completely covers the stomach. Deep reddish brown in color, the liver is divided into four unequal lobes: two large right and left lobes and two smaller lobes visible only from the back.

The liver is an extremely important organ. Scientists have discovered that it performs over 200 different functions in the body. Among its many functions are processing nutrients, making plasma proteins and blood-clotting chemicals, detoxifying (transforming into less harmful substances) alcohol and drugs, storing vitamins and iron, and producing cholesterol.

One of the liver's main digestive functions is the production of bile. A watery, greenish yellow liquid, bile consists mostly of water, bile salts, cholesterol, and assorted lipids or fats. Liver cells produce roughly 1 quart (1 liter) of bile each day. Bile leaves the liver through the common hepatic duct. This duct unites with the cystic duct from the gall bladder to form the common bile duct, which delivers bile to the duodenum.

In the small intestine, bile salts emulsify fats, breaking them down from large globules into smaller droplets that stay suspended in the watery fluid in the small intestine. Bile salts are not enzymes and, therefore, do not digest fats. By breaking down the fats in to smaller units, bile salts aid the fat-digesting enzymes present in the small intestine.

The gall bladder

The gall bladder is a small, pouchlike, green organ located on the undersurface of the right lobe of the liver. It measures 3 to 4 inches (7.6 to

10 centimeters) in length. The gall bladder's function is to store bile, of which it can hold about 1.2 to 1.7 ounces (35 to 50 milliliters).

The liver continuously produces bile. When digestion is not occurring, bile backs up the cystic duct and enters the gall bladder. While holding the bile, the gall bladder removes water from it, making it more concentrated. When fatty food enters the duodenum once again, the gall bladder is stimulated to contract and spurt out the stored bile.

WORKINGS: HOW THE DIGESTIVE SYSTEM FUNCTIONS

The digestive system breaks down food into a useful form through mechanical and chemical means. Mechanical digestion is the physical breaking up food into small pieces, such as by chewing. The smaller pieces are then acted upon by digestive enzymes, which change complex chemical molecules into much simpler molecules the body can easily utilize. This process involving enzymes is called chemical digestion.

Digestive activities in the mouth

Food taken into the mouth is broken down by both mechanical and chemical means. Through the process of mastication or chewing, teeth physically break down the tough tissues of meats and fibers of plants into smaller particles. The tongue helps move the food around the mouth, allowing the different sets of teeth variously to cut, tear, or grind the food. The jaw muscles, perhaps some of the strongest muscles in the body, help the teeth break down food in seconds.

Stimulated by the presence of something in the mouth, salivary glands secrete an increased amount of saliva (the sensations of sight, taste, and smell also increase saliva flow). As saliva is mixed with the food, salivary amylase (an enzyme in saliva) begins the chemical digestion of carbohydrates or starches, changing them into the simple sugar maltose.

As the food is broken down into pieces by the teeth and mixed with saliva, the tongue rolls these pieces into a battered, moistened, soft mass or ball called a bolus. Only after food has been compacted into a bolus of proper texture and consistency can swallowing occur.

Swallowing

Swallowing is both a voluntary and involuntary action. Once food has been properly chewed and mixed with saliva to create a bolus, the tongue forces the bolus toward the back of the mouth and into the pharynx. This a voluntary action; the individual has total control over moving the

SWALLOWING IS BOTH A VOLUNTARY AND INVOLUNTARY ACTION.

bolus while it is in the mouth. When the bolus presses against the soft palate, the soft palate and the uvula rise to close off the nasal passages to prevent the bolus from entering them.

Once the bolus enters the pharynx, swallowing becomes an automatic reflex action and cannot be stopped. The larynx, the upper part of the trachea that contains the vocal cords, rises. As it does so, a flaplike piece of tissue at the top of the larynx, the epiglottis, folds down to cover its opening. This prevents the bolus from passing into the trachea.

Sometimes, when a person laughs or talks while eating or drinking, the uvula and the epiglottis may not cover their openings quickly enough. If the uvula does not rise in time, bits of food or liquid may squirt up into the nose. If the epiglottis does not fold down, bits of food or liquid may enter the trachea, causing the person to cough (a protective reflex) until the food or liquid is expelled from the trachea.

Once material reaches the esophagus, the circular muscles in the walls of the esophagus begin alternately to contract and relax in a wavelike manner, pushing the bolus farther and farther down. This series of wavelike muscular motions is known as peristalsis (or peristaltic contractions). Material is pushed down the esophagus regardless what position a person is in: standing up, sitting, lying down, or upside down. Gravity helps move the bolus along, but peristalsis occurs even in the zero gravity of space.

A typical moist bolus takes about 9 seconds to travel through the esophagus. Drier boluses take longer. Liquids often pass through this muscular tube in just seconds, faster than the accompanying peristaltic waves. When the bolus or liquid reaches the lower esophageal sphincter, it presses against the sphincter, causing it to open. The material then passes into the stomach.

Digestive activities in the stomach

Gastric juices begin to flood the stomach even before food arrives. The sight, smell, taste, or even thought of food triggers the central nervous system to send nerve impulses to the gastric glands, which respond by secreting gastric juice. Once food does arrive in the stomach and touches its lining, cells in the lining release gastrin, a hormone. Gastrin, in turn, stimulates the production of even greater amounts of gastric juice.

As food fills the stomach, its wall begin to stretch. This initiates mechanical digestion in the stomach. The muscles in the walls being to contract, compressing and pummeling the food, breaking it apart physically. At the same time, the food is being mixed with gastric juices, and chemical digestion begins. Pepsin, the protein-digesting enzyme in gastric juice, starts to break down complex proteins. Little digestion of carbohydrates or fats takes place in the stomach. Water, alcohol, and drugs such as aspirin, however, are absorbed through the walls of the stomach into the bloodstream.

Once the food has been well mixed and broken down into chyme, peristalsis begins in the lower portion of the stomach. Chyme is moved downward into the pylorus. With each contraction of the stomach walls, the pyloric sphincter opens just a little, allowing a bit of chyme to squirt into the duodenum of the small intestine. When the duodenum is filled and its wall stretched, a nerve impulse is sent to the stomach to slow down its activity. It takes about four hours for the stomach to empty completely after receiving a well-balanced meal. If that meal contains much fat, then the process could take six or more hours.

Digestive activity in the small intestine

When chyme from the stomach enters the small intestine, it contains proteins and carbohydrates that have been only partially digested. Fats have been hardly digested. Over a three- to six-hour period, as chyme moves through the twists and coils of the small intestine, chemical digestion increases. By the time chyme reaches the end of the small intestine, eighty percent of all digestion in the body has taken place.

The presence of chyme in the duodenum stimulates the secretion of intestinal juice. Cells in the lining of the duodenum are also stimulated to produce hormones that, in turn, stimulate the pancreas to produce pancreatic juice and the liver to produce bile (the gall bladder is also stimulated to release its store of concentrated bile). Both enter the duodenum and combine with intestinal juice to digest or break down proteins, carbohydrates, and fats.

Peristalsis occurs in the small intestine, mixing the chyme with the intestinal juices and moving it through the organ. Although water and nutrients are absorbed all along the length of the small intestine, most absorption occurs in the jejunum. In this section, digested carbohydrates, fats, proteins, and most of the vitamins, minerals, and iron are absorbed. These nutrients pass through the walls of the villi into the blood capillaries and lacteals (lymph capillaries). The blood capillaries eventually drain into veins that connect with the portal vein, which transports the nutrient-rich blood to the liver. The lacteals, carrying fat nutrients, eventually drain into larger lymph vessels that connect with the venous system.

By the time material enters the ileum, the last section of the small intestine, all that remains is some water, indigestible food matter (such as plant fibers), and bacteria. This material then enters the large intestine through the ileocecal valve, which closes to prevent material from flowing backward.

Digestive activities in the large intestine

The large intestine does not produce any digestive enzymes; therefore, no digestion takes place. It functions mainly to absorb water and a few minerals from the waste products of digestion. Peristalsis in the large intestine occurs very slowly: material takes between twelve and twenty-four hours to pass through.

Millions of bacteria living in the large intestine feed on the waste products. In doing so, they produce vitamin K and some B vitamins that are absorbed through the wall of the large intestine into the bloodstream and then transported to the liver. The bacteria also produce intestinal gas—methane and hydrogen sulfide—that gives feces their characteristic odor. The amount of that gas, properly known as flatus, may increase if certain foods rich in carbohydrates (such as beans) are eaten.

MILLIONS OF BACTERIA LIVING IN THE LARGE INTESTINE FEED ON WASTE PRODUCTS.

When powerful peristaltic contractions force the feces or compacted waste products from the sigmoid colon into the rectum, the wall of the rectum stretches. This triggers the defecation reflex. Signals from the spinal cord cause the walls of the sigmoid colon and rectum to contract and the anal sphincters to relax. Feces are then eliminated through the anus. The outer sphincter muscle can be controlled voluntarily, allowing an individual to delay defecation when necessary.

DIGESTIVE SYSTEM DISORDERS

Anorexia nervosa (an-ah-REK-see-ah ner-VO-sa): Eating disorder usually occurring in young women that is characterized by an abnormal fear of becoming obese, a persistent aversion to food, and severe weight loss.

Appendicitis (ah-pen-di-SIGH-tis): Inflammation of the appendix.

Biliary atresia (BILL-ee-a-ree ah-TREE-zee-ah): Condition in which ducts to transport bile from the liver to the duodenum fail to develop in a fetus.

Bulimia (boo-LEE-me-ah): Eating disorder characterized by eating binges followed by self-induced vomiting or laxative abuse.

Cirrhosis (si-ROW-sis): Chronic disease of the liver in which normal liver cells are damaged and then replaced by scar tissue.

Crohn's disease (CRONES di-ZEEZ): Disorder that causes inflammation and ulceration of all the layers of the intestinal wall, particularly in the small intestine.

Diverticulosis (di-ver-ti-cue-LOW-sis): Condition in which the inner lining of the large intestine bulges out through its muscular wall; if the bulges become infected, the condition is called diverticulitis.

Gallstones (GAUL-stones): Solid crystal deposits that form in the gall bladder.

Hepatitis (hep-a-TIE-tis): Inflammation of the liver, caused mainly by a virus.

Lactose intolerance (LAK-tose in-TOL-er-ance): Inability of the body to digest significant amounts of lactose, the predominant sugar in milk.

Ulcer (digestive) (UL-sir): Any sore that develops in the lining of the lower esophagus, stomach, or duodenum.

Ulcerative colitis (UL-sir-a-tiv ko-LIE-tis): Disorder that causes inflammation and ulceration of the inner lining of the large intestine and rectum.

AILMENTS: WHAT CAN GO WRONG WITH
THE DIGESTIVE SYSTEM

Many ailments or maladies can afflict the digestive system. Although it is remarkably resistant to abuse, it is still vulnerable and can break down. Some ailments are relatively minor, such as canker sores in the mouth. Others are severe and life-threatening, such as cancers that can target almost every part of the digestive system.

As an individual ages, the activity of the digestive system slows down. Fewer digestive juices are produced and secreted. Peristalsis slows. The sensations of taste and smell wane, and eating becomes less appealing. When less food is ingested, the body receives fewer nutrients. All body systems then weaken and become susceptible to disease.

The following are just a few of the legion of ailments that can beset the many parts of the digestive system.

Appendicitis

Appendicitis is an inflammation of the appendix. It is the most common abdominal emergency found in children and young adults. Because of the appendix's position at the bottom of the cecum, scientists believe one of the main causes of appendicitis is an invasion of bacteria. When infected with bacteria, the appendix may become swollen and filled with pus. It may then eventually rupture. Symptoms of the condition include pain that begins above or around the navel. The pain, which may be severe or only achy, then moves into the right corner of the abdomen. In this position, the pain often becomes more steady and severe. If left untreated, appendicitis is fatal. The treatment for the condition is an immediate appendectomy or surgical removal of the inflamed and ruptured appendix.

Biliary atresia

Biliary atresia is a condition in which ducts to transport bile from the liver to the duodenum fail to develop in a fetus. The condition is the most common fatal liver disease in children. Half of all liver transplants are done for this reason. Scientists have yet to find a convincing cause for this birth defect.

In a child with this condition, bile begins to back up into the liver and eventually into the rest of the body. The child becomes jaundiced (skin turns yellow). The abdomen then begins to swell and the child becomes progressively more ill. If left untreated, liver failure and death will occur within two years.

Surgery is the only treatment for biliary atresia. The surgeon must find a way to create an adequate duct or pathway for the bile to drain from the liver into the intestine. Even if the surgery is successful, persistent disease in the liver will gradually destroy the organ. A liver transplant currently offers the best hope for this condition.

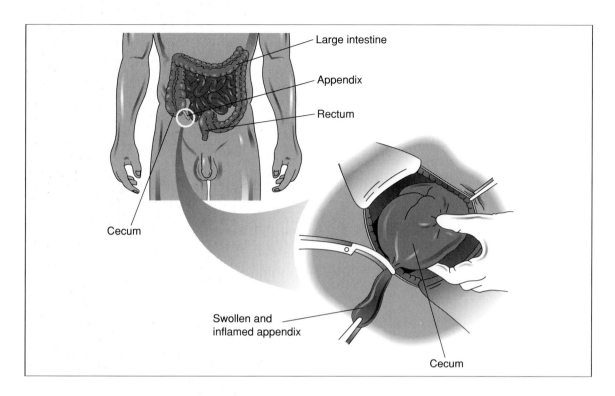

Large intestine

Appendix

Rectum

Cecum

Swollen and
inflamed appendix

Cecum

The treatment for appendicitis is an immediate appendectomy or surgical removal of the inflamed and ruptured appendix. (Illustration by Electronic Illustrators Group.)

Cavities

A dental cavity or tooth decay is the destruction of the enamel or outer surface of a tooth. It is a common health problem, second only to the common cold. It results from the action of bacteria that live in plaque. Plaque is a sticky, whitish film that forms on teeth, composed of a protein in saliva, sugars from foods, and bacteria. The bacteria use the sugars and starches from food particles in the mouth to produce acid that dissolves tooth enamel, creating cavities or holes. If the decay reaches the dentin, the tooth becomes sensitive to temperature and touch. If the decay reaches the pulp cavity, inflammation and pain (toothache) develop.

If left untreated, the decay can eventually destroy the entire tooth. Usually, a dentist is able to treat most cases of tooth decay by removing all decayed parts of the tooth and then filling the cavity with a hard material. If the decay has attacked the pulp, the dentist may perform a root canal treatment, removing the pulp and filling the inside chamber. If a majority of a tooth has to be removed, the dentist covers the tooth with a crown.

Cirrhosis

Cirrhosis is a chronic (long-term) disease in which cells of the liver are damaged and then replaced by scar tissue. The disease obviously affects the liver's ability to perform its many functions. The condition worsens over time and may lead to death. Twice as common in men as in women, cirrhosis is the seventh leading cause of disease-related death in the United States.

Long-term alcoholism is the primary cause of cirrhosis in the United States. Throughout the digestive system, alcohol interferes with the absorption of nutrients. Alcohol provides calories but no nourishment to the body. It also robs the body of vitamins and minerals necessary to maintain proper cell function. Because alcohol is detoxified within the liver, a constant level of alcohol in the organ severely affects it. Cirrhosis may also be brought about by viral infections like hepatitis B and hepatitis C (see page 56).

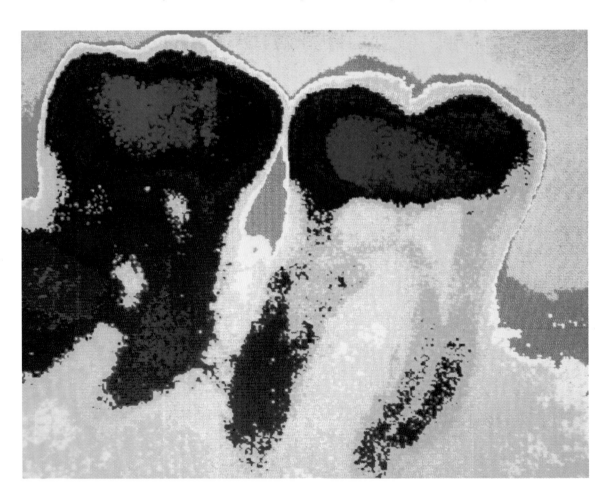

A digitized X ray of molar cavities. (Reproduced by permission of Custom Medical Stock Photo.)

During the early stages of cirrhosis, the liver enlarges. The palms of the hands then turn red. Other symptoms include constipation or diarrhea, dull abdominal pain, fatigue, loss of appetite, nausea, vomiting, weakness, and weight loss. If left untreated, the symptoms increase and worsen, leading to liver failure and death.

The primary treatment for cirrhosis is to reduce the condition causing it. A person suffering from cirrhosis must not consume alcohol. A balanced diet, which helps regenerate healthy liver cells, must be followed. In patients with advanced cirrhosis, a liver transplant may be necessary.

Diverticulosis and diverticulitis

Diverticulosis is a condition in which the inner layer of the large intestine bulges out through the outer, muscular layer. These bulges are called diverticula. When they become infected and inflamed, the resulting condition is known as diverticulitis.

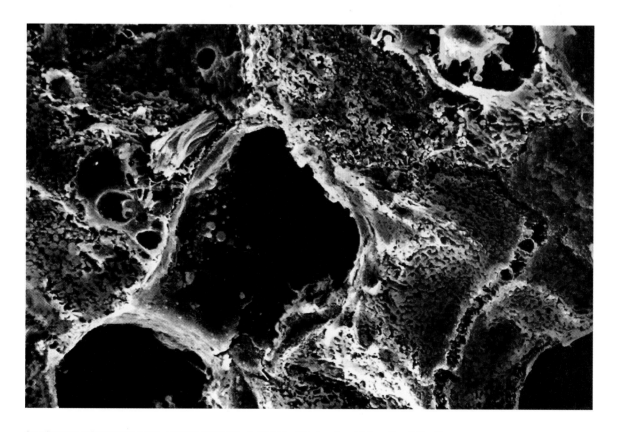

An electron micrograph scan of liver cirrhosis, a chronic disease in which cells of the liver are damaged and then replaced by scar tissue. (Photograph by P. Motta. Reproduced by permission of Photo Researchers, Inc.)

ANOREXIA NERVOSA

Anorexia nervosa is an eating disorder that usually occurs in young women. Anorexia comes from the Greek word *anorektos,* meaning "without appetite." The problem for anorectics (individuals with anorexia) is not that they lack an appetite. The problem is self-image. Anorectics do not eat because they fear gaining weight. They see themselves as "fat" even if they are severely underweight.

Some anorectics refuse to eat at all; others eat only small portions of fruit or vegetables. A few live only on diet drinks. In addition to fasting, anorectics may exercise strenuously to keep their weight low.

The body is severely affected. Skin becomes dry and flaky. Muscles begin to waste away. Bones stop growing and become brittle. The heart weakens. Because the body has almost no fat to keep it warm, downy hair grows on the face, back, and arms. The heart weakens. Muscle cramps, dizziness, tiredness, and even brain damage and kidney and heart failure may occur. An estimated 10 to 20 percent of anorectics die, either from starvation or by committing suicide.

Medical researchers believe anorexia is caused by a combination of biological, psychological, and social factors. Low self-esteem, fear of losing control, and fear of growing up are common characteristics of anorectics. The emphasis on thinness in American culture is believed to contribute to the disorder.

Hospitalization, combined with psychotherapy and family counseling, is often needed to control anorexia. About 70 percent of anorectics who are treated for about six months return to normal body weight.

Diverticula occur most frequently in individuals whose diets are low in fiber. Since the amount of fecal matter produced is low, the large intestine must narrow itself and contract forcefully to move the smaller feces along to the rectum. Over time, this weakens the muscular wall, allowing diverticula to develop.

Diverticulitis occurs when a hardened piece of stool, undigested food or bacteria becomes lodged in the diverticula. Blood supply to the area is disrupted and infection sets in. Symptoms of diverticulitis include pain in the lower left side of the abdomen and fever. Abscesses (walled-off pockets of infection) may develop within the wall of the intestine.

Diverticulitis is quite treatable. Usually, the intestine is "rested" by preventing the individual from eating or drinking anything by mouth. Medications to fight the infection are also given. Once the condition is brought under control, the individual must adhere to a high-fiber diet.

If the condition is severe and surgery is needed to remove a portion of the intestine filled with abscesses, a colostomy is performed. This involves pulling the end of remaining intestine through the abdominal wall and attaching it to a bag on the outside. Because the intestine no longer connects with the rectum, the individual's feces pass out of the intestine into the bag. The colostomy may be temporary (until healing has occurred) or it may be permanent.

Gallstones

Gallstones are solid crystal deposits that form in the gall bladder. They can vary in size from as small as a grain of sand to as large as a golf ball. Eighty percent of all gallstones are composed of cholesterol, a fatlike substance produced by the liver. Gallstones form when the liver produces more cholesterol than intestinal juices can liquefy.

Gallstones are the fifth most common reason adults are hospitalized in the United States. They usually develop in adults between the ages of twenty and fifty. The condition of developing gallstones tends to run in families. In addition, high levels of estrogen (female hormones), insulin (hormone that regulates sugar levels), and cholesterol in the body increase the risk of developing gallstones. A diet high in fat and low in fiber, heavy drinking, and smoking may also play a part.

Gallstones may block the common bile duct, preventing bile from flowing into the duodenum. A gallstone in the cystic duct may cause the gall bladder to become inflamed. Symptoms of a gallbladder attack include pain that begins in the abdomen and moves to the chest and back, chills and sweating, nausea and vomiting, and gas and belching.

Gallstones of a small size may pass out of the body through the urine. So they may more easily pass out, doctors may use high-frequency sound waves to break up the gallstones. To treat painful, severe cases, doctors may surgically remove the gall bladder and gallstones.

BULIMIA

Bulimia is an eating disorder that occurs chiefly in women in their teens and twenties. Bulimia comes from the Greek word *boulimos,* meaning "great hunger." Individuals who are bulimic go on eating binges (often gorging on junk food), then purge their bodies of the food by making themselves vomit or by taking large amounts of laxatives (medicines or foods that stimulate bowel movements).

During an eating binge, bulimics favor high-carbohydrate foods: candy, donuts, cookies, cakes, cereal, bread, soft drinks, and ice cream. At one sitting, bulimics consume more calories than they normally would in an entire day. They usually eat quickly and messily during a binge, stuffing the food in their mouths and gulping it down.

The self-induced vomiting after a binge can cause damage to the stomach and esophagus. Acid in the vomit from the stomach can irritate the throat and erode tooth enamel. Blood vessels in the eyes can burst. The overuse of laxatives can cause muscle cramps, stomach pains, dehydration, and even poisoning. Over time, bulimia causes vitamin deficiencies and an imbalance of critical body fluids. Seizures and kidney failure can ultimately result.

Bulimics know that their eating habits are abnormal. They often suffer from depression, especially after a binge. Bulimics may also suffer from anxiety and low self-esteem. Some medical researchers believe bulimia is related to an imbalance in the brain chemical serotonin, which influences mood. Most research on bulimia, however, focuses on psychological factors. Treatment for bulimia generally involves psychotherapy and, sometimes, the use of antidepressant medications.

Heartburn

Heartburn is a burning sensation in the chest that can extend to the neck, throat, and face. It is caused by a backflow of the stomach's acids through the lower esophageal sphincter into the esophagus, leading to inflammation. More than one third of the population suffers from this disorder, commonly known as acid reflux.

Normally, the lower esophageal sphincter is tightly closed and opens only to allow food to pass from the esophagus into the stomach. However, many different factors may cause the sphincter to open inappropriately or fail to close completely. Fatty or greasy foods, cigarettes, alcohol, chocolate, caffeine, and certain medications can relax the sphincter, increasing reflux. A large meal, obesity, and pregnancy increase pressures with the abdomen, pushing the contents of the stomach into the esophagus.

Heartburn can be prevented by avoiding those foods, drugs, or conditions that cause the disorder. Mild cases of heartburn can be treated with over-the-counter antacids, which decrease the acidity in the stomach. Surgery to correct a defective or damaged sphincter may be necessary in severe cases.

 WHAT IS LACTOSE INTOLERANCE?

Lactose is the primary carbohydrate or sugar in milk. Normally, the enzyme lactase (produced by the cells in the lining of the small intestine) breaks down lactose into simple sugars that can be absorbed into the bloodstream. In individuals who are lactose intolerant, however, the cells have stopped producing lactase. This usually occurs to an individual during adolescence.

When lactose intolerant individuals drink milk or eat small amounts of other dairy products, they can suffer discomfort from nausea, gas, cramps, bloating, and diarrhea. Undigested lactose brings about these symptoms because it provides a source of energy for the bacteria that inhabit the large intestine. The symptoms are a result of the bacteria's activities.

Roughly 30 to 50 million Americans are lactose intolerant. Certain ethnic and racial groups are more widely affected than others. As many as 75 percent of all African Americans and Native Americans and 90 percent of Asian Americans are lactose intolerant.

Hepatitis

Hepatitis is an often fatal disease that causes inflammation of the liver. There are various types of hepatitis, most of which are caused by a virus. The viral forms include hepatitis A, B, C, D, E, and G. The assorted symptoms marking hepatitis include jaundice (yellowing of the skin), nausea, vomiting, fever, weakness, loss of appetite, abdominal and joint pain, and cirrhosis (scarring of the liver).

Alcoholic hepatitis is a noninfectious type of hepatitis. Alcohol, a poison if taken in more than modest amounts, is detoxified in the liver. Too much alcohol causes the liver to become inflamed. The liver cannot function properly and eventually turns to useless fat. If the poisoning continues, cirrhosis develops.

Two viral forms of hepatitis are most common: A and B. Hepatitis A (commonly known as infectious hepatitis) is spread through direct contact with contaminated feces, food, or water. Once infected, an individual usually recovers within two months. Hepatitis B (commonly called serum hepatitis) is much more severe. It is transmitted by sexual activity, blood transfusions, and the use of shared syringes by drug uses. Hepatitis B may destroy the liver through cirrhosis or it may lead to cancer of the liver.

Hepatitis C causes acute (rapidly developing) and chronic (long-term) disease. It is spread mainly through blood transfusions. Medical researchers believe hepatitis C may be caused by several viruses. As with hepatitis B, hepatitis C may lead to cirrhosis of the liver and, eventually, liver cancer. Vaccines have been developed for both hepatitis A and B, but no vaccine has yet been developed to prevent hepatitis C.

Inflammatory bowel disease

Inflammatory bowel disease (IBD) is a disorder that causes inflammation and ulceration (development of ulcers) in the small and large intestine. The two main forms of IBD are ulcerative colitis and Crohn's disease.

Ulcerative colitis, which occurs mainly in people between the ages of fifteen and forty, affects the inner lining of the large intestine and rectum. Inflammation usually begins in the rectum and spreads upward into the entire large intestine. Diarrhea, cramping or abdominal pain, fever, and weight loss

A gall bladder full of gallstones. Solid crystal deposits that form in the gall bladder, gallstones are the fifth most common reason adults are hospitalized in the United States. (Photograph by Martin. Reproduced by permission of Custom Medical Stock Photo.)

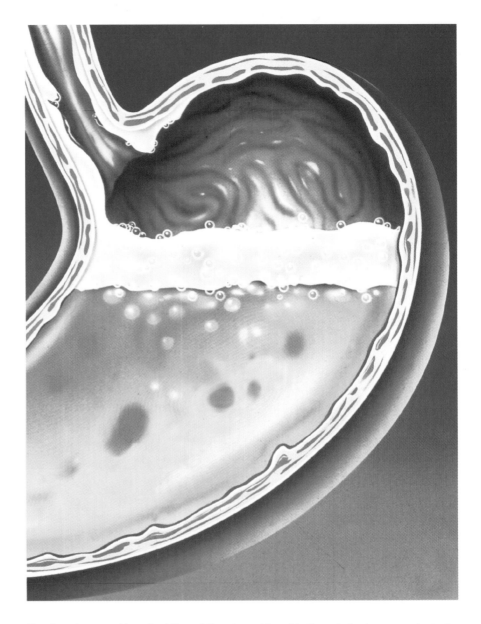

Heartburn is caused by a backflow of the stomach's acids through the lower esophageal sphincter into the esophagus, leading to inflammation. (Illustration by John Bavosi/Science Photo. Reproduced by permission of Custom Medical Stock Photo.)

result. Ulcers (tiny open sores) develop in the intestinal lining, and blood and pus appear in the feces. If the disorder becomes widespread through the large intestine, the risk of cancer increases. The cause of ulcerative colitis is unknown, and the only cure for advanced cases is the surgical removal of the large intestine.

Crohn's disease is a life-long illness that may recur frequently over a person's lifetime. It causes the inflammation of all the layers of the intestinal wall, particularly in the small intestine. In turn, the inflammation brings about ulcerations in the intestinal wall. Crohn's disease can also affect the large intestine, mouth, esophagus, and stomach. The disease is marked by diarrhea, abdominal pain, weight loss, and fever. The cause of Crohn's disease has yet to be found, as well as a cure. Medications to control diarrhea, abdominal pain, and inflammation are the main forms of treatment. Surgery to remove or repair a section of the intestine may be required.

Ulcers (digestive)

A digestive ulcer is any sore that develops in the lining of the stomach or duodenum (sores in the lower esophagus occur less frequently). Because these sores form in areas where gastric juice is present, they are generally referred to as peptic ulcers (pepsin is an enzyme in gastric juice). Peptic ulcers found in the stomach are more specifically called gastric ulcers. Those in the duodenum are called duodenal ulcers. Of the two, duodenal ulcers are the most common type, accounting for about 80 percent of all digestive ulcers. They tend to be smaller than gastric ulcers and heal more quickly. Any ulcer that heals leaves a scar.

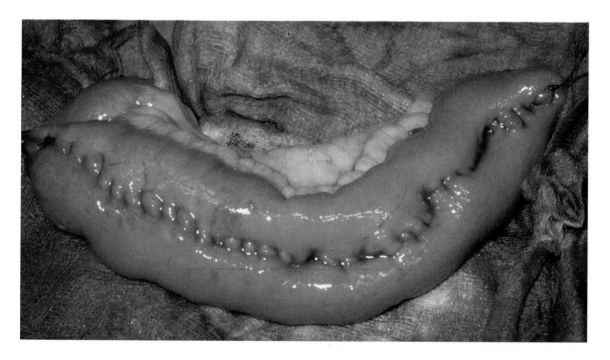

A section of large intestine inflamed by ulcerative colitis. (Reproduced by permission of Photo Researchers, Inc.)

The symptoms for gastric ulcers include feelings of heartburn, nausea, weight loss, and stomach pain. That pain is described as gnawing, dull, aching, or resembling hunger pangs. About one-third of those individuals suffering from gastric ulcers are awakened by pain at night.

The symptoms for duodenal ulcers differ slightly. They include heartburn, stomach pain that is relieved by eating or antacids, and a burning sensation at the back of the throat. Pain is most often felt two to four hours after a meal. Citrus juices, coffee, and aspirin bring on pain more quickly. About 50 percent of individuals suffering from duodenal ulcers are awakened by pain at night.

Before the 1980s, physicians believed ulcers were caused by several factors—including stress and a poor diet—that resulted in excess stomach acid. Medical research has since shown that a certain bacterium that can live undetected in the mucous membrane of the digestive tract is the culprit. This bacterium irritates and weakens the lining, making it more susceptible to

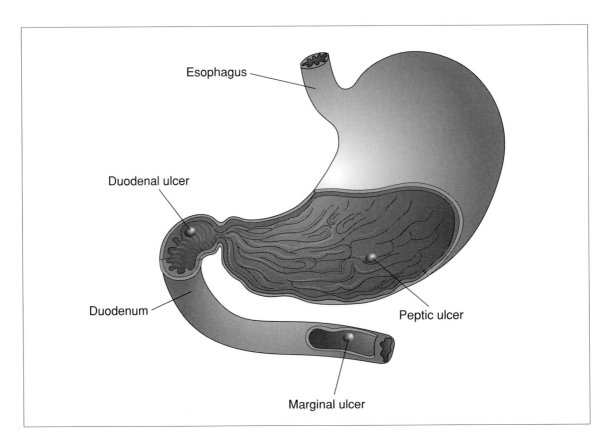

Common sites of ulcers in the human stomach. (Illustration by Electronic Illustrators Group.)

damage by gastric juice. About 95 percent of duodenal ulcers and 70 percent of gastric ulcers are caused by this bacterium.

Treatment for peptic ulcers includes antibiotics to eliminate the bacterium and other drugs to reduce the amount of gastric juice secreted in the stomach. Very few ulcers fail to respond to the medications that are currently used to treat them.

TAKING CARE: KEEPING THE DIGESTIVE SYSTEM HEALTHY

The body is wholly dependent on the digestive system to provide it with the nutrients—fluids, carbohydrates, proteins, lipids, vitamins, and minerals—it needs to continue to function. If the digestive system fails to do this because it is not functioning properly, the entire body suffers.

A healthy lifestyle will keep the digestive system healthy. This includes following a proper diet, exercising regularly, maintaining a healthy weight, not smoking, drinking alcohol only in moderation, and reducing stress.

The "Food Guide" Pyramid developed by the U.S. Departments of Agriculture and Health and Human Services provides easy-to-follow guidelines for a proper diet. In general, foods that are low in fat (especially saturated fat), low in cholesterol, and high in fiber should be eaten. Fiber is especially important in maintaining the workings of the intestines. Fat should make up

WORMS IN THE BODY

Tapeworms are parasites (organisms that live in or on other kinds of organisms) that live in the intestinal tracts of some animals. There are three major species of tapeworms that can infect humans. They are typically acquired from eating raw or undercooked beef, pork, or fish.

Tapeworm eggs are passed along in feces. When improperly treated human sewage is used to fertilize pastures or crops, pigs and cattle can become infected with the eggs. They can also become infected from drinking contaminated water. Freshwater fish become infected when human feces contaminates their water source.

The tapeworm eggs develop into larvae in the infected animals and fish. When humans eat the meat from those animals and fish without properly cooking it, they become infected. The tapeworm travels to the intestine, attaching itself to the inner lining by hooks on its head. If not treated, the tapeworm may stay in the intestine for years, absorbing nutrients through its outer covering. It may grow up to 30 feet (9 meters) in length.

Most individuals infected with a tapeworm have no symptoms. Some, however, may experience pain in the upper abdomen, diarrhea, unexplained weight loss, and weakness. A tapeworm's eggs or worn body parts that appear in an individual's feces are often the only sign of an infection.

Tapeworms are easily treated with medication. Practicing good hygiene and avoiding raw or undercooked meat or fish are important steps in preventing a tapeworm infection.

no more than 30 percent of a person's total daily calorie intake. Breads, cereals, pastas, fruits, and vegetables should form the bulk of a person's diet; meat, fish, nuts, and cheese and other dairy products should make up a lesser portion. Drinking fluids, especially water, helps move material through the digestive system.

Long-term ingestion of cigarette fumes, excessive alcohol, and spicy foods can cause serious damage to the digestive system. Toxins that are taken into the body by way of the mouth are absorbed by the digestive tract and transported to the liver, which can suffer permanent damage. Many medications can injure the lining of the esophagus, stomach, and intestines. Medicines in pill or capsule form should always be taken with plenty of water.

Teeth are an important, yet often overlooked, part of the digestive system. They begin the entire process of digestion. Oral hygiene is, therefore, a primary concern. The best way to prevent tooth decay is to brush the teeth at least twice a day, preferably after every meal and snack. The teeth should also be flossed daily to help prevent gum disease.

Minor irritations of the digestive system are common. Occasional diarrhea, constipation, or excessive gas is to be expected. Often, they are treated with nonprescription drugs. However, if these or any digestive problems persist, they should not be ignored and medical attention should be sought.

FOR MORE INFORMATION

Books

Avraham, Regina. *The Digestive System.* New York: Chelsea House, 1989.

Ballard, Carol. *The Stomach and Digestive System.* Austin, TX: Raintree/ Steck-Vaughn, 1997.

Bryan, Jenny. *Digestion.* Englewood Cliffs, NJ: Silver Burdett Press, 1993.

Epstein, Rachel. *Eating Habits and Disorders.* New York: Chelsea House, 1990.

Parker, Steve. *Digestion.* Brookfield, CT: Copper Beech Books, 1997.

Parramon, Merce. *The Digestive System.* New York: Chelsea House, 1994.

Silverstein, Alvin, Virginia B. Silverstein, and Robert A. Silverstein. *The Digestive System.* New York: Twenty-First Century Books, 1994.

WWW Sites

American Digestive Health Foundation
http://www.gastro.org/adhf.html
Homepage of a national organization that advances digestive health through the financial support of research and education in the cause, prevention, diagnosis, treatment, and cure of digestive diseases.

Digestive System

http://innerbody.com/image/digeov.html

Site includes a large image of the human digestive system with each part/organ linked to a paragraph explanation of its structure and function.

The Digestive System—How It Works

http://www.jeffersonhealth.org/diseases/digestive_disorders/howworks.htm

Site from the Jefferson Health System, a collective of member hospitals and healthcare organizations in the greater Philadelphia region. Information on the digestive system includes a discussion of how it works and the numerous disorders that can afflict it.

MUSC Digestive Disease Center

http://www.ddc.musc.edu

Site of the Medical University of South Carolina focusing on digestive diseases. Includes an overview of the digestive organs, an extensive list of diseases and their symptoms, and links to other sites.

Virtual Anatomy Textbook: The Digestive System

http://www.acm.uiuc.edu/sigbio/project/digestive/index.html

Site provides extensive coverage of the parts of the digestive system, mixing images and text. System parts are grouped into three classes: early digestion, middle digestion, and late digestion.

The Endocrine System

3

The endocrine system is the body's network of glands that produce more than fifty different known hormones or chemical messengers to maintain and regulate basic bodily functions. It is second only to the nervous system as the great controlling system of the body. Whereas nerve impulses from the nervous system immediately prod the body into action, hormones from the endocrine system act more slowly to achieve their widespread and varied effects. The bodily processes regulated by the endocrine system go on for relatively long periods of time. Some go on continuously. These life processes include growth and development, reproduction, immunity (the body's ability to resist disease), and homeostasis (the body's ability to maintain the balance of its internal functions).

DESIGN: PARTS OF THE ENDOCRINE SYSTEM

Glands are any organs that either secrete substances for further use in the body or excrete substances for elimination. Those that excrete substances for elimination are called exocrine glands (*exo* means "outside"). Exocrine glands have ducts or tubes that carry their secretions to the surface of the skin or into body cavities. Sweat glands and the liver are examples of exocrine glands.

Endocrine glands (*endo* means "inside") secrete or release substances that are used in the body. These glands lack ducts, releasing their secretions directly into the surrounding tissues and blood. Those secretions—hormones—then travel in the cardiovascular system to various points throughout the body.

The word hormone comes from a Greek word meaning "to arouse" or "to set in motion." Hormones control or coordinate the activities of other tissues, organs, and organ systems in the body. Most hormones are composed of amino acids, the building blocks of proteins. The smaller class of hormones are steroids, which are built from molecules of cholesterol (fat-like substance produced by the liver).

Each type of hormone affects only specific tissue cells or organs, called target cells or target organs. Each target cell has receptors on its membrane or inside of it to which a particular hormone can attach or bind. Only once this binding has occurred does the hormone bring about a change in the workings of a cell. Some hormones affect nearly every cell in the body; oth-

WORDS TO KNOW

Adrenal cortex (ah-DREE-nul KOR-tex): Outer layer of the adrenal glands, which secretes cortisol and aldosterone.

Adrenal glands (ah-DREE-nul): Glands located on top of each kidney consisting of an outer layer (adrenal cortex) and an inner layer (adrenal medulla).

Adrenal medulla (ah-DREE-nul muh-DUH-luh): Inner layer of the adrenal glands, which secretes epinephrine and norepinephrine.

Adrenocorticotropic hormone (ah-dree-no-kor-ti-koh-TROH-pik): Hormone secreted by the anterior pituitary that stimulates the adrenal cortex to secrete cortisol.

Aldosterone (al-DOS-te-rone): Hormone secreted by the adrenal cortex that controls the salt and water balance in the body.

Androgens (AN-dro-jens): Hormones that control male secondary sex characteristics.

Antidiuretic hormone (an-tee-die-yu-REH-tik HOR-mone): Hormone produced by the hypothalamus and stored in the posterior pituitary that increases the absorption of water by the kidneys.

Calcitonin (kal-si-TOE-nin): Hormone secreted by the thyroid gland that decreases calcium levels in the blood.

Cortisol (KOR-ti-sol): Hormone secreted by the adrenal cortex that promotes the body's efficient use of nutrients during stressful situations.

Epinephrine (ep-i-NEFF-rin): Also called adrenaline, a hormone secreted by the adrenal medulla that

stimulates the body to react to stressful situations.

Estrogens (ES-tro-jenz): Female steroid hormones secreted by the ovaries that bring about the secondary sex characteristics and regulate the female reproductive cycle.

Gland: Any organ that secretes or excretes substances for further use in the body or for elimination.

Glucagon (GLUE-ka-gon): Hormone secreted by the islets of Langerhans that raises the level of sugar in the blood.

Gonad (GO-nad): Sex organ in which reproductive cells develop.

Gonadotropic hormones (gon-ah-do-TROP-ik): Hormones secreted by the anterior pituitary that affect or stimulate the growth or activity of the gonads.

Homeostasis (hoe-me-o-STAY-sis): Ability of the body or a cell to maintain the internal balance of its functions, such as steady temperature, regardless of outside conditions.

Hypothalamus (hi-po-THAL-ah-mus): Region of the brain containing many control centers for body functions and emotions; also regulates the pituitary gland's secretions.

Insulin (IN-suh-lin): Hormone secreted by the islets of Langerhans that regulates the amount of sugar in the blood.

Islets of Langerhans (EYE-lets of LAHNG-er-hanz): Endocrine cells of the pancreas that secrete insulin and glucagon.

Luteinizing hormone (loo-tee-in-EYE-zing): Gonadotropic hormone secreted by the anterior piers affect only a single organ. Some cells have numerous receptors, acting as a target cell for many different hormones.

Unlike the organs or parts of other body systems, the principal endocrine glands are not physically connected together, but are scattered throughout the body. Located in the skull are the hypothalamus, pituitary gland, and pineal gland; in the throat are the thyroid gland and parathyroid glands; in the upper part of the chest is the thymus; in the abdominal region are the

tuitary that stimulates, in women, ovulation and the release of estrogens and progesterone by the ovaries and, in men, the secretion of testosterone by the testes.

Melatonin (mel-a-TOE-nin): Hormone secreted by the pineal gland that helps set the body's twenty-four-hour clock and plays a role in the timing of puberty and sexual development.

Metabolism (muh-TAB-uh-lizm): Sum of all the physiological processes by which an organism maintains life.

Negative feedback: Control system in which a stimulus initiates a response that reduces the stimulus, thereby stopping the response.

Norepinephrine (nor-ep-i-NEFF-rin): Also called noradrenaline, a hormone secreted by the adrenal medulla that raises blood pressure during stressful situations.

Ovaries (O-var-eez): Female gonads in which ova (eggs) are produced and that secrete estrogens and progesterone.

Oxytocin (ahk-si-TOE-sin): Hormone produced by the hypothalamus and stored in the posterior pituitary that stimulates contraction of the uterus during childbirth and secretion of milk during nursing.

Parathyroid glands (pair-ah-THIGH-roid): Four small glands located on the posterior surface of the thyroid gland that regulate calcium levels in the blood.

Pineal gland (PIN-ee-al): Gland located deep in the rear portion of the brain that helps establish the body's day-night cycle.

Pituitary gland (pi-TOO-i-tair-ee): Gland located below the hypothalamus that controls and coordinates the secretions of other endocrine glands.

Progesterone (pro-JESS-te-rone): Female steroid hormone secreted by the ovaries that makes the uterus more ready to receive a fertilized ovum or egg.

Prolactin (pro-LAK-tin): Gonadotropic hormone secreted by the anterior pituitary that stimulates the mammary glands to produce milk.

Testes (TESS-teez): Male gonads that produce sperm cells and secrete testosterone.

Testosterone (tess-TAHS-ter-ohn): Hormone secreted by the testes that spurs the growth of the male reproductive organs and secondary sex characteristics.

Thymosin (thigh-MOE-sin): Hormone secreted by the thymus that changes a certain group of lymphocytes into germ-fighting T cells.

Thymus (THIGH-mus): Glandular organ consisting of lymphoid tissue located behind the top of the breastbone that produces specialized lymphocytes; reaches maximum development in early childhood and is almost absent in adults.

Thyroid gland (THIGH-roid): Gland wrapped around the front and sides of the trachea at the base of the throat just below the larynx that affects growth and metabolism.

Thyroxine (thigh-ROK-seen): Hormone secreted by the thyroid gland that regulates the rate of metabolism and, in children, affects growth.

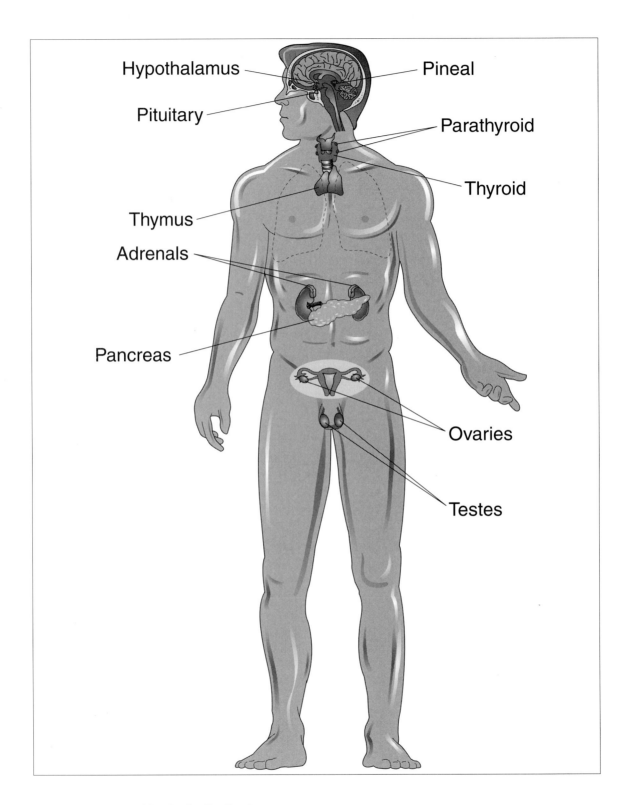

Hypothalamus

Pineal

Pituitary

Parathyroid

Thyroid

Thymus

Adrenals

Pancreas

Ovaries

Testes

pancreas and adrenal glands; in the pelvis of females are the ovaries; and in the scrotum of males are the testes.

Most of the endocrine glands serve only the endocrine system, but a few serve other systems as well. For this reason, they are called mixed glands. The pancreas is also a part of the digestive system because it secretes pancreatic juice into the small intestine (see chapter 2). The ovaries and testes are also part of the reproductive system because they produce gametes or the male and female reproductive cells—sperm cells and ova (see chapter 8). The thymus is also part of the lymphatic system because it helps a certain class of white blood cells to develop in order to fight germs and other foreign invaders (see chapter 5).

The hypothalamus

The hypothalamus is not a gland, but a small region of the brain containing many control centers for body functions and emotions. Composed of gray matter (brain tissue consisting of nerve cells that lack inner protective coverings), it is about the size of an almond and weighs only about 1/300 of the total mass of the brain.

The hypothalamus is often considered a part of the endocrine system for a number of reasons. It sends signals to the adrenal glands to release the hormones epinephrine and norepinephrine. It also produces its own hormones: antidiuretic hormone (ADH), oxytocin, and regulatory hormones. Both ADH and oxytocin are stored in the posterior pituitary gland until the hypothalamus sends nerve signals to the pituitary to release them. Regulatory hormones are divided into two classes: releasing hormones (RH) and inhibiting hormones (IH). Both types control the release of hormones by the pituitary gland. RH stimulate the production of pituitary hormones; IH inhibit or prevent the release of pituitary hormones.

The pituitary gland

Located at the base of the brain behind the nose, the pituitary gland is a small, oval gland approximately the size of a grape. It hangs by a thin piece of tissue from the interior surface of the hypothalamus. The pituitary is divided into two distinct lobes or regions: the anterior pituitary (the front lobe) and the posterior pituitary (the rear lobe). The anterior pituitary produces and secretes six hormones. The posterior pituitary secretes two hormones, but does not produce them. Those hormones are made by the hypothalamus, which uses the posterior pituitary as a storage area for the hormones until they are needed.

OPPOSITE: Components of the endocrine system, including the ovaries (female) and the testes (male). (Illustration by Electronic Illustrators Group.)

Roger Guillemin. (Reproduced by permission of Corbis-Bettmann.)

THE DISCOVERY OF HYPOTHALAMIC HORMONES

For some time, medical researchers have known that the hypothalamus controls the actions of the pituitary gland. Up until the late 1960s, however, they could not explain exactly how. In 1968, French-born American endocrinologist Roger Guillemin (1924–) and others finally answered that unresolved question: hormones.

Prior to this discovery, English anatomist Geoffrey W. Harris had hypothesized that the hypothalamus releases hormones that regulate the pituitary gland. Harris and others, though, could not isolate and identify any hormones coming from the hypothalamus.

In the 1950s, Guillemin began an investigation to find the missing evidence. Working with fellow endocrinologist Andrew V. Schally, Guillemin used a tool developed by physicist Rosalyn Sussman Yalow to isolate and identify the chemical structure of hormones. Soon, Guillemin and Schally ended their scientific cooperation, pursuing their investigations separately.

Finally in 1968, while working with hypothalamic fragments from sheep brains, Guillemin and his coworkers isolated the hypothalamic hormone that causes the pituitary to release thyroid-stimulating hormone (TSH). The following year, both Guillemin and Schally identified the chemical structure of TSH. Guillemin then went on to isolate and determine the chemical structure of other hypothalamic hormones.

For their discoveries, which led to an understanding of the hormone produced by the hypothalamus, Guillemin, Schally, and Yalow shared the 1977 Nobel Prize for physiology or medicine.

Six of the eight hormones released by the pituitary stimulate or "turn on" other endocrine glands. For this reason, they are referred to as tropic hormones (tropic comes from the Greek word *tropos*, meaning "to turn" or "change"). The remaining two hormones control other bodily functions. Because the pituitary's secretions control and regulate the secretions of other endocrine glands, it is often called the "master gland" of the endocrine system.

The pineal gland

The pineal gland or body is a small cone-shaped gland located deep in the rear portion of the brain (pineal comes from the Latin word "pinea," meaning "pine cone"). Scientists are still somewhat mystified as to the endocrine function of this gland, which secretes the hormone melatonin.

The thyroid gland

One of the largest endocrine glands in the body, the thyroid gland is a butterfly-shaped gland that wraps around the front and sides of the trachea (windpipe) at the base of the throat just below the larynx (upper part of the trachea containing the vocal cords). It is divided into two lobes connected by a band of tissue called the isthmus. Because the thyroid contains a large number of blood vessels, it is deep red in color.

The thyroid gland is composed of hollow, spherical structures called thyroid follicles. The follicles release two main hormones, thyroxine and calcitonin. Thyroxine regulates the rate of metabolism and, in children, affects growth. Calcitonin decreases calcium levels in the blood.

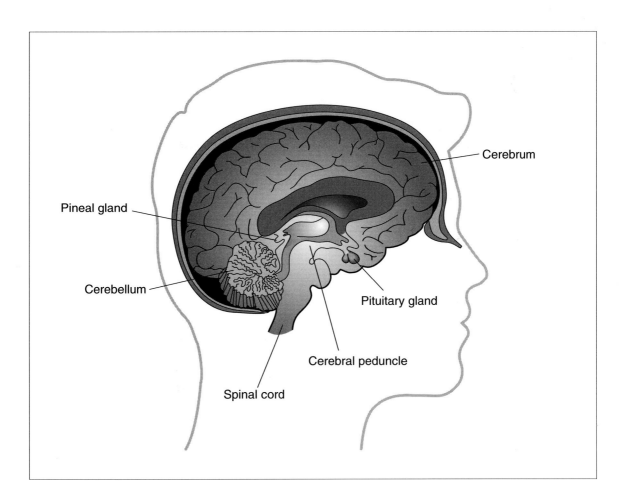

A cutaway view of the brain, including the pituitary gland. Located at the base of the brain behind the nose, this gland is approximately the size of a grape. (Illustration by Electronic Illustrators Group.)

The parathyroid glands

The parathyroid glands are four tiny masses of glandular tissue, each about the size of a pea, located on the posterior or rear surface of the thyroid gland (two on the back of each lobe). The parathyroids secrete parathyroid hormone (PTH) or parathormone, which controls the level of calcium in the blood.

The thymus

The thymus is a soft, flattened, pinkish-gray mass of lymphoid tissue located in the upper chest under the breastbone. In a fetus and newborn infant, the thymus is relatively large (about the size of an infant's fist). Up until about the age of puberty, the thymus continues to grow. After this point

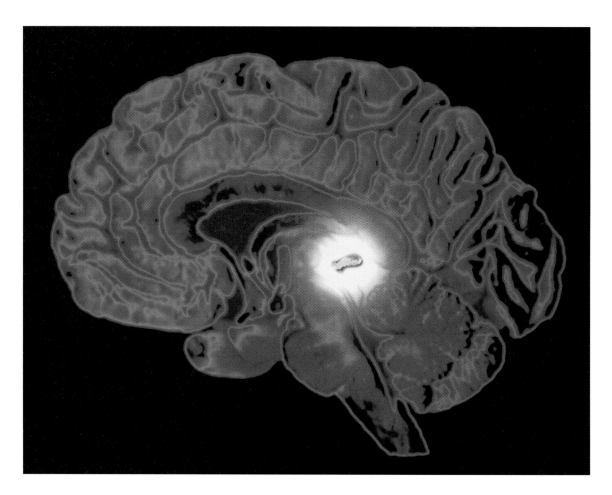

The pineal gland (highlighted) secretes the hormone melatonin. (Reproduced by permission of Custom Medical Stock Photo.)

in life, it shrinks and gradually blends in with the surrounding tissue. Very little thymus tissue is found in adults.

The thymus secretes several hormones that are known collectively as thymosins. Thymosins help change a certain group of white blood cells called lymphocytes into T cells, which are programmed to attack any foreign substance in the body.

The pancreas

The pancreas is a soft, pink, triangular-shaped gland that measures about 6 inches (15 centimeters) in length. It lies behind the stomach, extending from the curve of the duodenum (first part of the small intestine) to the

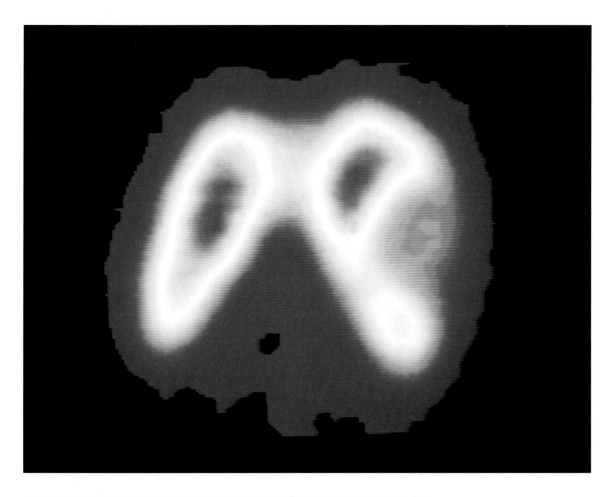

An electron micrograph scan of the parathyroid glands. The parathyroids secrete the hormone PTH, which controls the level of calcium in the blood. (Reproduced by permission of Custom Medical Stock Photo.)

spleen. Primarily a digestive organ, the pancreas secretes pancreatic juice into the duodenum through the pancreatic duct. The digestive enzymes in this juice helps break down carbohydrates, fats, and proteins in the small intestine. While a part of the digestive system, the pancreas is also a part of the endocrine system, producing hormones that maintain blood glucose (sugar) levels.

Scattered like small islands among the cells that produce pancreatic juice are small groups of endocrine cells called the islets of Langerhans (or pancreatic islets). They are named after Paul Langerhans (1847–1888), the German physician and anatomist who discovered them. The pancreas contains between one and two million islets, which account for about 2 percent of the total mass of the pancreas. Each islet contains different cells that produce different hormones, the most important of which are insulin and glucagon. Both regulate the amount of glucose in the blood, but in opposite ways.

Adrenal glands

The adrenals are two glands, each sitting like a cap on top of each kidney. The adrenals are divided into two distinct layers: the adrenal cortex (outer layer) and the adrenal medulla (inner layer).

The adrenal cortex makes up about 80 percent of each adrenal gland. It is grayish yellow in color due to the presence of stored fats, especially cholesterol and various fatty acids. The cortex is extremely important to bodily processes; if it stops functioning, death occurs in just a few days. The cortex secretes about thirty steroid hormones, the most important of which are cortisol (also called hydrocortisone) and aldosterone. Cortisol, released during any stressful situation (physical injury, disease, fear, anger, hunger), regulates the body's metabolism of carbohydrates, proteins, and fats. Aldosterone regulates the body's water and salt balance .

The adrenal medulla is reddish brown in color partly because it contains many blood vessels. It secretes two hormones: epinephrine (also called adrenaline) and norepinephrine (noradrenaline). Both hormones are secreted during dangerous or stressful situations. They prepare the body for emergencies—"flight-or-fight" situations—by increasing heart rate, blood pressure, blood flow to the muscles, and other such processes.

The ovaries

The ovaries are the gonads or sex organs in females. The two almond-sized ovaries are located on each side of the pelvis, one at the end of each fallopian tube. The ovaries are attached to the uterus or womb by an ovarian ligament.

The ovaries secrete two groups of steroid hormones, estrogens and progesterone. Estrogens spur the development of the secondary sex characteristics: enlargement of the breasts, appearance of hair under the arms and in the genital area, and the accumulation of fat in the hips and thighs. Estrogens also act with progesterone to stimulate the growth of the lining of the uterus, preparing it to receive a fertilized egg.

The testes

The testes are the gonads in males. They are two small, egg-shaped structures suspended in the scrotum, a loose sac of skin that hangs outside the pelvic cavity between the upper thighs.

In addition to producing sperm cells, the testes produce male sex hormones called androgens (from the Greek word *andros,* meaning "man"). The

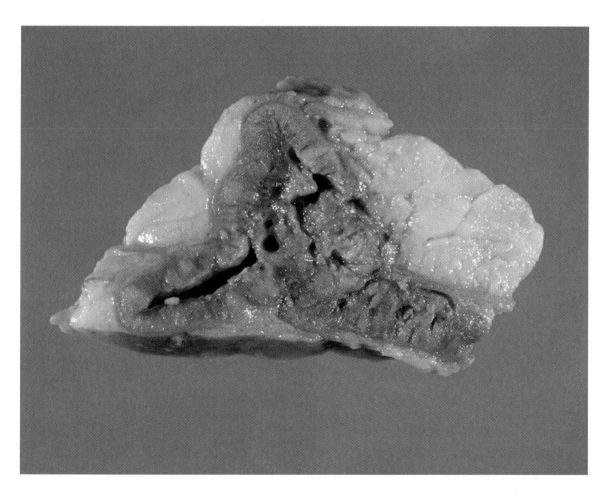

A cross section of a human adrenal gland. The adrenals are divided into two distinct layers: the adrenal cortex and the adrenal medulla. (Reproduced by permission of Custom Medical Stock Photo.)

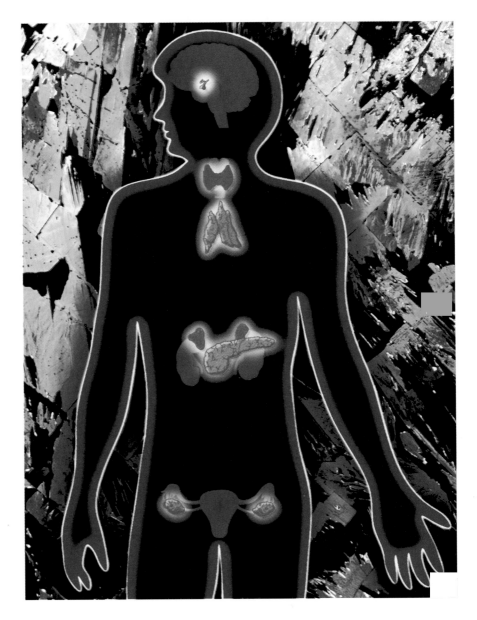

The female hormone system. The ovaries (located on each side of the pelvis) are the sex organs in females. (Photograph by Alfred Pasieka. Reproduced by permission of Photo Researchers, Inc.)

most important of these is testosterone. This hormone spurs the growth of the male reproductive organs and the production of sperm. In addition, testosterone brings about the male secondary sex characteristics: deepening of the voice; appearance of hair under the arms, on the face, and in the genital area; and increased growth of muscles and heavy bones.

ATHLETES AND ANABOLIC STEROIDS

Many professional and amateur athletes around the world take anabolic steroids in the hopes of enhancing their performance. Anabolic steroids are synthetic (man-made) drugs derived from the male hormone testosterone. The full name of the drug is androgenic (promoting masculine characteristics) anabolic (building) steroid (class of drug). Common names for the drug include 'roids, sauce, and juice.

It is estimated that 10 to 20 percent of male high school athletes, up to 30 percent of college and professional athletes, and up to 80 percent of bodybuilders use anabolic steroids to increase skeletal muscle and lean body mass. The drugs are taken either orally or injected.

Anabolic steroids do increase body weight and muscle mass. They also may improve muscular strength and endurance. These are the few benefits.

The drawbacks are many and serious. The major side effects include liver tumors, jaundice (yellowing of the skin), fluid retention, high blood pressure, severe acne, and trembling. In men, steroids can additionally cause shrunken testes, reduced sperm production, sterility, baldness, and the development of breasts. In women, they can also cause the growth of facial hair, menstrual irregularity, smaller breasts, and a deeper voice. In adolescents, the drugs can permanently stop bones from growing, resulting in shortened height for life.

Anabolic steroids not only affect the body but the mind as well. Users suffer from aggression, irritability, delusions, paranoid jealousy, and impaired judgment.

Taking anabolic steroids for nonmedical reasons is illegal under federal law. Hard training is still the most effective and safe way to improve muscle strength and overall athletic performance.

WORKINGS: HOW THE ENDOCRINE SYSTEM FUNCTIONS

The main functions of the endocrine system and its hormone messengers are to maintain homeostasis (a stable internal environment in the body) and to promote permanent structural changes. Maintaining homeostasis is a response to a change in the body, such as low sugar or calcium levels in the blood. Permanent structural changes, occurring over a period of time, are those associated with growth and development.

Hormones bring about their effect on the body's cells mainly by altering the cells' metabolic activity—increasing or decreasing the rate at which they work. The effect is often rapid, such as increased or decreased heart rate. A few hormones, after binding to their target cells, cause those cells to produce proteins, which lead to long-term effects such as growth or sexual maturity.

Hormones travel in the bloodstream or in the interstitial fluid (fluid between cells). Some hormones are long-distance travelers, floating throughout the body in search of their target cells. Others travel shorter distances, having been secreted near theirs.

Negative feedback

Hormones are secreted by endocrine glands in response to a stimulus. That stimulus may be either changing blood levels of certain nutrients or other hormones. When a gland senses a change in the composition of blood or tissue fluid (low blood sugar, for example) and releases its hormones, that action is known as a direct response. When a gland releases its hormones because it has been stimulated by other hormones released by other glands, that action is known as an indirect response.

A feedback system tightly controls the on/off workings of endocrine glands. This system can be compared to a furnace thermostat on a wall in a house. When the temperature in a house falls below the temperature set on the thermostat, the thermostat is triggered and signals the furnace to turn on and begin heating. After the furnace has heated the air in the house to a temperature higher than that set on the thermostat, the thermostat signals the furnace to turn off.

Endocrine glands react to changes in the blood and body in much the same way. When nutrients or chemicals in body fluids are abnormal (either high or low), endocrine glands secrete their hormones. After those levels return to normal (reaching a state of homeostasis), the glands stop secreting their hormones. This control of hormone secretion, where information is fed back to the gland to stop its hormone production, is called negative feedback.

Actions of the hypothalamus

Receiving nerve signals from other parts of the brain, the hypothalamus functions as a monitoring and control station for many body activities. It thus plays an important role in the actions of other endocrine glands, especially the pituitary. Therefore, its role is best considered under the discussions of the actions of those various other glands.

Actions of the pituitary gland

The "master" pituitary gland is small in size, but large in its actions. The eight hormones secreted by its two lobes have a direct effect on the actions of other endocrine glands, controlling growth and fluid balance in the body. The anterior pituitary secretes six hormones: growth hormone, thyroid-stimulating hormone, adrenocorticotropic hormone, and three gonadotropic hormones. The posterior pituitary secretes antidiuretic hormone and oxytocin.

GROWTH HORMONE. Growth hormone (GH) or human growth hormone stimulates overall body growth by spurring target cells to grow in size and divide. GH increases the rate at which those cells take in and utilize proteins (cell structure is made up largely of proteins). GH also causes fats to be broken down and used by the cells for energy. Its greatest effects are on the development of muscles and bones, especially in children. The release of GH is controlled by two regulatory hormones from the hypothalamus: growth hormone releasing hormone (GHRH) and growth hormone inhibiting hormone (GHIH). GHRH stimulates the pituitary to release GH during exercise, when blood sugar levels are low, when amino acid levels in the blood are high, or when the body in under stress. When the body is returned to a state of homeostasis or when blood sugar levels are high, the hypothalamus secretes GHIH, and the pituitary stops releasing GH.

THYROID-STIMULATING HORMONE. Thyroid-stimulating hormone (TSH), as its name implies, influences the growth and activity of the thyroid. TSH prompts the thyroid to release thyroxine, which stimulates the cells in the body to increase their metabolism (energy production) and intake of oxygen. A releasing hormone from the hypothalamus signals the pituitary to secrete TSH. This occurs when the body's metabolic rate decreases.

ADRENOCORTICOTROPIC HORMONE. Adrenocorticotropic hormone (ACTH) stimulates the adrenal cortex to secrete cortisol and other hormones. During any stressful situation such as injury, low blood sugar levels, and exercise, the hypothalamus secretes a releasing hormone that triggers the pituitary to release ACTH.

GONADOTROPIC HORMONES. As their name suggests, the gonadotropic hormones affect the gonads or reproductive organs. Releasing hormones from the hypothalamus regulate the secretion of all three gonadotropic hormones: prolactin, follicle-stimulating hormone (FSH), and luteinizing hormone (LH). In females, prolactin stimulates the development of mammary glands in breasts and their secretion of milk. FSH stimulates the development of

the endocrine system

THE BODY'S NATURAL ALARM CLOCK

It is known that some people can automatically awake in the morning without an alarm clock. German researchers sought an explanation for this phenomenon, and in early 1999 they announced their results. The researchers discovered that the actions of two hormones, adrenocorticotropic hormone (ACTH) and cortisol, were the reason.

In stressful situations, the hypothalamus secretes a releasing hormone that triggers the anterior pituitary to release ACTH. ACTH then travels to the adrenal cortex, stimulating it to release cortisol. In short, cortisol stimulates most body cells to increase their energy production, which heightens the body's ability to react quickly to a stressful or emergency situation.

The researchers found that during the latter stages of sleep, these hormones were released, causing the body to awaken. Most scientists agree that sleep is a state of unconsciousness. From their findings, however, the researchers concluded that even during sleep, the mind maintains some voluntary control. When an individual goes to bed knowing he or she has to get up earlier than normal because of a stressful event (an exam at school or a big presentation at work), the mind "remembers" and so awakens the body in anticipation of that event.

Body By Design **79**

follicles in the ovaries of females. Ovarian follicles are tiny, saclike structures within which ova or eggs develop. FSH also stimulates the secretion of estrogen by the follicle cells. In males, FSH begins the productions of sperm in the testes. LH stimulates ovulation (the release of an egg from an ovary) and the release of estrogens and progesterone from the ovaries in females. In males, LH stimulates the testes to produce testosterone.

ANTIDIURETIC HORMONE. Antidiuretic hormone (ADH) is produced by the hypothalamus and stored in the posterior pituitary. ADH causes the kidneys to reabsorb water from the urine that is being formed. That water is then transported into the bloodstream, maintaining blood pressure. When too much water is lost from the body, such as through sweating, diarrhea, or any type of dehydration, the hypothalamus detects an increased amount of "salt" in the blood. It then triggers the posterior pituitary to release ADH. The kidneys decrease the production of urine and blood pressure increases. Alcohol and certain drugs, however, inhibit the secretion of ADH. Large amounts of urine are consequently excreted from the body and blood pressure decreases. If that fluid is not replaced, an individual may feel dizzy due to low blood pressure.

OXYTOCIN. Oxytocin is also produced by the hypothalamus and stored in the posterior pituitary. The hormone plays an important role in childbirth. When a woman goes into labor, the uterus begins to stretch and nerve impulses are sent to the hypothalamus. The hypothalamus then stimulates the posterior pituitary to release oxytocin, which travels to the uterus. Once there, it triggers strong contractions of the uterine muscles, helping to bring about delivery of the baby. After birth, oxytocin promotes the release of milk from the mammary glands. When a baby suckles a mother's nipple, nerve impulses are sent to the mother's hypothalamus, which then signals the release of oxytocin. The hormone stimulates the contraction of the muscle cells around the mammary ducts, causing the ejection of milk through the nipple.

Actions of the pineal gland

Scientists believe that melatonin, secreted by the pineal gland, establishes the body's sleep and waking patterns. Keeping the body in sync with the cycles of day (light) and night (dark), the pineal gland functions as the body's biological clock. Scientists know that, in general, the secretion of melatonin is spurred by darkness. Known as the sleep "trigger," melatonin is secreted cyclically in response to the fall of darkness at the end of each day. In the morning, when light enters the eyes, that visual information is relayed from the eyes to the hypothalamus. The pineal gland is then stimulated to decrease melatonin production during daylight hours. Scientists also theorize that the hormone plays a role in the timing of puberty and sexual development, preventing it from occurring during childhood before adult body size has been reached.

Actions of the thyroid gland

Thyroxine, the major hormone secreted by the thyroid follicles, is often considered to be the body's major metabolic hormone. When the body's metabolic rate decreases, the anterior pituitary secretes thyroid-stimulating hormone, which triggers the thyroid to secrete thyroxine. Thyroxine then stimulates energy production in cells in the body, increasing the rate at which they consume oxygen and utilize carbohydrates, fats, and proteins. When cells increase their energy production, they generate more heat as a result. This is important when the body is trying to adapt to cold temperatures. In children, thyroxine is essential to the normal development of the muscular, nervous, and skeletal systems. In adults, it is important for continued tissue growth and development. Iodine is an important component of thyroxine. Without the proper amount of iodine in an individual's diet, thyroxine would not be produced, and physical and mental growth and abilities would then diminish.

Calcitonin, the second important hormone secreted by the thyroid, helps maintain normal levels of calcium in the blood. It is secreted directly into the bloodstream when the thyroid detects high levels of calcium in the blood. Calcitonin travels to the bones, stimulating the bone-building cells to absorb calcium from the blood. It also targets the kidneys, stimulating them to

SAD: MORE THAN JUST THE WINTER BLUES

It has been recorded since the time of the ancient Greeks that the varying seasons have had an effect on people's moods and behavior. Generally, the short, dark days of late autumn and winter dampen many people's spirits, and the longer and lighter days of spring and summer have the opposite effect.

While members of the medical community have noted this annual winter depression, they did not fully explore its reasons until the early 1980s. Since then, medical researchers have concluded that the lack of sunlight from November through March is indeed responsible for what is commonly referred to as the "winter blues."

Many people feel mildly "depressed" during the winter, but some suffer from severe symptoms. These include daytime drowsiness, fatigue and low energy level, diminished concentration, irritability, carbohydrate craving and increased appetite, weight gain, and social withdrawal. This mood disorder that affects people only during the autumn and winter seasons is called seasonal affective disorder or SAD.

SAD is a very real problem that affects approximately 10 million people each year in the United States (women suffering from SAD outnumber men four to one). Researchers believe that people with SAD have lost the natural rhythm that signals the body to fall asleep and to awake at the proper times. Melatonin, secreted by the pineal gland when light is low, helps bring the body to rest. Daylight signals the gland to stop producing the hormone to allow the body to come awake.

Researchers do not know why some people are affected more than others. They have discovered, however, that an effective treatment for SAD sufferers is light, particularly morning light. When exposed to a light box that emits bright, artificial sunlight (called phototherapy or light therapy) for thirty minutes a day, almost 80 percent of SAD patients showed marked improvement in their moods.

absorb and excrete the excess calcium. When blood calcium levels return to normal, the thyroid stops secreting calcitonin.

Actions of the parathyroid glands

Like the thyroid's calcitonin, the parathyroid's parathyroid hormone (PTH) also regulates the levels of calcium in the blood. However, its stimulus and effect are just the opposite. Thus, calcitonin and PTH are antagonistic: they work against each other to maintain the normal levels of calcium in the bloodstream.

The parathyroids secrete PTH when blood calcium levels are low. Like calcitonin, PTH targets the bones and the kidneys. In the bones, PTH stimulates the bone-dissolving cells to break down bone, thus releasing calcium (a component of bone) into the bloodstream. In the kidneys, PTH decreases the amount of calcium that is excreted in the urine. Both of these actions raise the levels of calcium in the blood. When those levels have returned to normal, the parathyroids stop secreting PTH.

Actions of the thymus

The thymus and its collective hormones, thymosins, play an important role in helping the body develop immunity (the ability to resist disease). In a fetus and infant, immature or not fully developed lymphocytes (type of white blood cell) are produced in the bone marrow, the spongylike material that fills the cavities inside most bones. A certain group of these lymphocytes then travel to the thymus. There, thymosins changed them into T lymphocytes or T cells (the letter T refers to the thymus). While maturing, dividing, and multiplying in the thymus, T cells are "programmed" to recognize the difference between cells that belong to the body and those that are foreign or abnormal. Once they are fully mature, T cells leave the thymus and enter the bloodstream. They circulate to the spleen, lymph nodes, and other lymphatic tissue where they await the call to defend the body.

Actions of the pancreas

Although the islets of Langerhans make up but a small part of the pancreas, they work tirelessly, acting like an organ within an organ. The main hormones they secrete—glucagon and insulin—are vital to the normal functioning of the body. They regulate blood glucose (sugar) levels in the same way that parathyroid hormone and calcitonin regulate blood calcium levels.

GLUCAGON. Glucagon is secreted by the islets of Langerhans in response to low blood glucose levels. To raise those levels (and the body's energy), glucagon then travels to the liver. The liver performs a multitude of functions in the body. One of those is to store excess glucose that is not immediately required by the body's cells for energy. In order to store that glucose, the liver converts it to glycogen (a starch form of the sugar glucose made up of thousands of glucose units). Glucagon stimulates the liver to change glycogen back into glucose and secrete it into the bloodstream for use by the cells for energy production. When glucose levels rise to normal, the islets of Langerhans stop secreting glucagon.

INSULIN. Insulin has the opposite effect: it lowers blood glucose levels that are too high. When those high levels are detected, the islets of Langerhans secrete insulin, which then travels to almost all cells in the body. Insulin stimulates the cells to take in more glucose and use it to produce energy. Insulin also stimulates the liver to take in more glucose and store it as glycogen for later use by the body. After they break down glucose, the cells use the energy created to build proteins and enhance their energy reserves. Insulin is the only hormone that decreases blood glucose levels and is absolutely necessary in order for the cells to utilize glucose. Without it, the cells cannot take in glucose. After glucose levels return to normal, the islets of Langerhans stop secreting insulin.

Actions of the adrenal glands

The small adrenal glands, capping the kidneys, control numerous activities in the body. The hormones they secrete aid in cell metabolism, adjust the water balance, and increase cardiovascular and respiratory activity.

CORTISOL. In times of physical stress (injury, exercise, anger, fear), the hypothalamus secretes a releasing hormone that causes the anterior pituitary to release adrenocorticotropic hormone (ACTH). ACTH, in turn, targets the adrenal cortex, stimulating it to secrete cortisol. Like insulin, cortisol stimulates most body cells to increase their energy production. Unlike insulin, cortisol causes the cells to increase energy output by using fats and amino acids (proteins) instead of glucose. In stressful situations, this is extremely important because glucose is conserved for use by the brain (glucose is the sole source of energy for neurons or cells in nervous tissue).

Cortisol also has an anti-inflammatory effect, suppressing the activities of white blood cells and other components in the body's defense line. Inflammation is an important first step in tissue repair, but if left unchecked, will lead to excessive tissue destruction. Cortisol limits the inflammation process to what is necessary for immediate tissue repair by blocking the effects of histamine (a chemical released by damaged cells that brings more blood flow to the area).

ALDOSTERONE. Aldosterone, another steroid hormone secreted by the adrenal cortex, targets the kidney cells that regulate the formation of urine. A decrease in blood pressure or volume, a decrease in the sodium (salt) level in blood, and an increase in the potassium level in blood all stimulate the secretion of aldosterone. Once released, aldosterone spurs the kidney cells to reabsorb sodium from the urine and to excrete potassium instead. Sodium is then returned to the bloodstream. When sodium is reabsorbed into the blood, water in the body follows it, thus increasing blood volume and pressure. Aldosterone also reduces the amount of sodium and water lost through the sweat and salivary glands. When normal blood, sodium, and potassium levels are all reached, the adrenal cortex stops releasing aldosterone.

EPINEPHRINE AND NOREPINEPHRINE. When an individual is (or feels) threatened physically or emotionally, the hypothalamus readies the body to "fight" or "take flight" by sending impulses to the adrenal medulla. In response, the medulla secretes norepinephrine (in small amounts) and epinephrine (in larger amounts). Norepinephrine causes blood vessels in the skin and skeletal muscles to constrict, raising blood pressure. Epinephrine causes an increase in heart rate and contraction, stimulates the liver to change glycogen to glucose for use as energy by the cells, and stimulates fatty tissue to break down and release stored fats for use as energy by the cells as well. The actions of both hormones bring about increased levels of oxygen and glucose in the blood and a faster circulation of blood to the body organs, especially the brain, muscles, and heart. Reflexes and body movements quicken and the body is better able to handle a short-term emergency situation.

Actions of the ovaries

The ovaries do not begin to function until puberty, usually between the ages of eleven and fourteen in girls. At this time, the anterior pituitary gland

SCHARRER AND HER SOUTH AMERICAN COCKROACHES

German-born American biologist Berta Scharrer (1906–1995) and her biologist husband Ernst Scharrer pioneered the field of neuroendocrinology, the study of the interaction between the nervous system and the endocrine glands and their secretions. Fighting against accepted scientific beliefs about cells—as well as against prejudice toward women in the sciences—Scharrer established the concept of neurosecretion, or the releasing of substances such as hormones by nerve cells.

Prior to the discoveries of Scharrer and her husband, scientists believed that neurons or nerve cells could not have a dual function. They either secreted hormones, in which case they were endocrine cells belonging to the endocrine system, or they conducted electrical impulses, making them nerve cells belonging to the nervous system.

In the 1930s, after having come to America, Scharrer and her husband set out to prove their theories with no real professional standing and therefore lacking a budget for lab animals. Scharrer reportedly collected cockroaches in the basement of the lab and used them for experiments. Soon she began experimenting on South American cockroaches she had discovered scurrying around in the bottom of a cage of lab monkeys that had arrived from South America. Scharrer found that they made better research subjects because they were slower than the American cockroach. From that point forward, she used the South American cockroaches, which traveled with her wherever she and her husband moved.

By 1950, Scharrer's research and theories on neurosecretion had become accepted as fact by the scientific community. For her pioneering scientific work, Scharrer received many honors. Included among these was the naming of a cockroach species, *scharrerae,* in her honor.

secretes follicle-stimulating hormone, which causes follicles or tiny saclike structures to grow and mature in an ovary. Ova or eggs within these specialized structures also begin to mature. While an egg is developing in an ovarian follicle, the follicle cells surrounding the egg secrete estrogens. Increased levels of estrogens then signal the anterior pituitary gland to secrete luteinizing hormone, which causes the ovary to release a single mature egg—a process called ovulation.

After ovulation has occurred, a structure in the ovary secretes progesterone, which prevents another egg from beginning to develop and causes the lining of the uterus to grow thicker with blood vessels (estrogens also help in this latter action). The mature egg then travels through a fallopian tube to the uterus. If the egg has not fertilized by male sperm, it breaks down. About ten days later, the lining of the uterus begins to break apart and is shed outside the body during the monthly process called menstruation.

If the egg has been fertilized, it attaches to the wall of the uterus and pregnancy occurs. High levels of estrogens and progesterone are then produced to prevent another egg from maturing. In addition, progesterone prevents the muscles of the uterus from contracting so that the developing embryo will not be disturbed. Estrogens and progesterone both prepare the mammary glands to produce milk.

At puberty, the estrogens released by the follicle cells also bring about the female secondary sex characteristics. The breasts enlarge and their duct system to carry milk develops, the uterus enlarges, fat is deposited in the hips and thighs, and hair develops under the arms and in the genital area.

Actions of the testes

Puberty in boys usually occurs between the ages of twelve and sixteen. At this time, the anterior pituitary gland releases luteinizing hormone, which stimulates the testes to produce testosterone. This hormone produces many growth changes in an adolescent boy: growth of all the reproductive organs, growth of facial and body hair, growth of the larynx (resulting in a deeper voice), and growth of the skeletal muscles. Follicle-stimulating hormone, also secreted from the anterior pituitary, initiates the production of sperm in the testes. Testosterone then helps the sperm mature. This process, begun at puberty, continues throughout life.

AILMENTS: WHAT CAN GO WRONG WITH THE ENDOCRINE SYSTEM

As much as 10 percent of the population will experience some endocrine disorder in their lifetime. Most endocrine disorders are caused by an increased

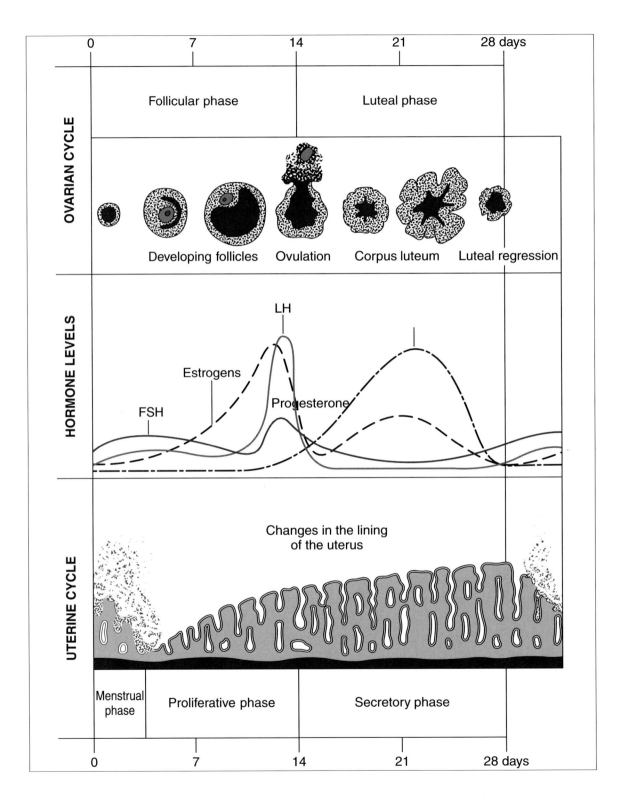

ENDOCRINE SYSTEM DISORDERS

Acromegaly (ak–ro–MEG–ah–lee): Disorder in which the anterior pituitary overproduces growth hormone, resulting in abnormal enlargement of the extremities—nose, jaw, fingers, and toes; in children, the disorder produces gigantism.

Addison's disease (ADD–i–sonz): Disorder in which the adrenal cortex underproduces cortisol and aldosterone, resulting in the disruption of numerous bodily functions.

Cushing's syndrome (KU–shingz SIN–drome): Disorder caused by an overproduction of steroids (mostly cortisol) by the adrenal cortex, resulting in obesity and muscular weakness.

Diabetes mellitus (die–ah–BEE–teez MUL–le–tus): Disorder in which the body's cells cannot absorb glucose, either because the pancreas does not produce enough insulin or the cells do not respond to the effects of insulin that is produced.

Gigantism (jie–GAN–tizm): Disorder in children in which the anterior pituitary overproduces growth hormone, resulting in abnormal enlargement of the extremities (nose, jaw, fingers, and toes) and the long bones, causing unusual height.

Hyperthyroidism (hi–per–THIGH–roy–dizm): Disorder in which an overactive thyroid produces too much thyroxine.

Hypothyroidism (hi–po–THIGH–roy–dizm): Disorder in which an underactive thyroid produces too little thyroxine.

or decreased level of particular hormones. Tumors (abnormal tissue growth) in endocrine glands are one of the major causes of hormone overproduction. Hormone underproduction is often due to defective receptors on cells. The result is that the cells fail to notify an endocrine gland when production of its particular hormone is too low. Injury to or disease of an endocrine gland can also result in low hormone levels.

The following are just a few of the many disorders that can result from an improperly functioning endocrine system.

Acromegaly and gigantism

Acromegaly is a disorder in which the anterior pituitary produces too much growth hormone (GH). This causes an increased growth in bone and soft tissue, especially in the extremities—nose, jaw, fingers, and toes. If the disorder occurs in children who have not yet fully developed, the increased levels of GH also result in the exceptional growth of the long bones. This condition, a variation of acromegaly, is known as gigantism.

Acromegaly is a rare disorder, occurring in approximately 50 out of every 1 million people. Both men and women are affected. Because the symptoms come on gradually, the disorder is often not identified until the patient is middle aged.

OPPOSITE: A chart tracking changing hormone levels during an average ovarian cycle. (Illustration by Hans & Cassady.)

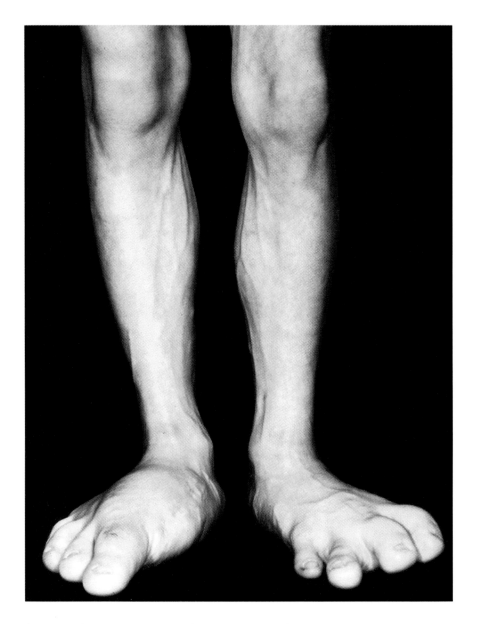

Acromegaly is a rare disorder in which the anterior pituitary produces too much growth hormone. This causes an increased growth in bone and soft tissue. (Reproduced by permission of Custom Medical Stock Photo.)

In 90 percent of the cases, acromegaly is caused by a noncancerous tumor that develops within the pituitary. The tumor causes the anterior pituitary to ignore growth hormone inhibiting hormone (GHIH), a regulating hormone secreted by the hypothalamus that stops the pituitary from producing GH. GH is thus secreted without a stopping mechanism.

The first step in treating acromegaly is the surgical removal of the tumor. Afterward, some patients often require medications that help to reduce the secretion of GH. With treatment, an individual suffering from acromegaly may be able to live a normal life span. Without treatment, an individual will most likely die early because of the disorder's adverse effects on the heart, lungs, and brain.

Addison's disease

Addison's disease is a disorder in which the adrenal cortex produces too little cortisol and aldosterone, resulting in the disruption of numerous bodily functions. About 4 in every 100,000 people suffer from this disorder. It strikes men and women of all ages.

The most common cause of Addison's disease is the destruction or shrinking of the adrenal cortex. In about 70 percent of the cases, this is caused by an autoimmune disorder: a condition in which the body produces antibodies that attack and destroy the body's own tissues instead of foreign invaders such as viruses and bacteria. In the case of Addison's disease, antibodies attack and destroy cells of the adrenal cortex.

Addison's disease tends to be a gradual, slowly developing disease. By the time symptoms are noted, about 90 percent of the adrenal cortex has been destroyed. The most common symptoms include fatigue and loss of energy, decreased appetite, nausea, vomiting, diarrhea, abdominal pain, muscle weakness, dizziness when standing, and dehydration. Unusual areas of darkened skin and dark freckling also appear. Women suffering from the disease may stop having normal menstrual periods. As the disease progresses, the symptoms become more severe: abnormal heart rhythms, uncontrollable nausea and vomiting, a drastic drop in blood pressure, kidney failure, and unconsciousness.

Individuals suffering from Addison's disease are treated with steroid medications that replace cortisol and aldosterone in the body. Taking these medications for the rest of their lives, those individuals can expect to live a normal life span.

Cushing's syndrome

Cushing's syndrome is a disorder caused by an overproduction of steroids—mostly cortisol—by the adrenal cortex, resulting in obesity and muscular weakness. The disorder occurs in about 15 out of every 1 million people per year. It usually strikes adults (men and women) between the ages of twenty and fifty.

Cushing's syndrome can be caused by a tumor either in the pituitary gland or in one of the adrenal glands. The anterior pituitary secretes adrenocorticotropic hormone (ACTH), which stimulates the adrenal cortex to release cortisol. A tumor in the pituitary causes the overproduction of ACTH, which in turn causes the overproduction of cortisol. This is the most common cause. A tumor in the adrenal glands can also lead to the overproduction of cortisol by the adrenal cortex.

The following are some of the symptoms that appear when cortisol is produced in excess: abnormal weight gain (resulting especially in a round or "moon" face), purple and pink stretch marks across the abdomen and sides, high blood pressure, weak bones and muscles, low energy, mood swings and depression, and abnormal hair growth on the face in women.

Treatment for Cushing's syndrome includes the surgical removal of either the pituitary tumor or the adrenal tumor. After surgery, some patients are also given drugs that help decrease cortisol production. If a patient's entire adrenal gland is removed, the patient will have to take steroid medications for the rest of his or her life.

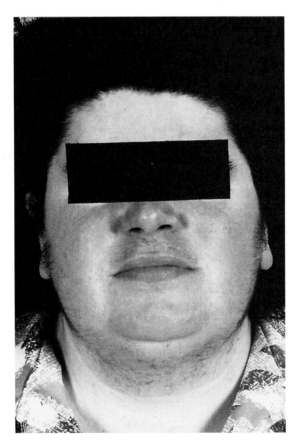

A woman suffering from Cushing's syndrome, a disorder caused by an overproduction of steroids. (Photograph courtesy of John Radcliff Hospital. Reproduced by permission of Photo Researchers, Inc.)

Diabetes mellitus

Diabetes mellitus (commonly referred to simply as diabetes) is a disorder in which the cells of the body cannot absorb glucose. This condition is brought about either because the pancreas no longer produces enough insulin or because the cells do not respond to the effects of the insulin that is produced. Approximately 14 million Americans—about 5 percent of the population-have diabetes, and almost 50 percent of them are unaware they have it. Some 300,000 people in the United States die each year from the disorder.

Common symptoms of diabetes include frequent urination, excessive thirst, tiredness, weight loss, hunger, and slow wound healing. The long-term effects of diabetes include loss of vision decreased blood supply to the hands and feet, and pain. If left untreated, the disorder can lead to kidney failure, heart disease, stroke, coma, and death. There are two types of diabetes mellitus: Type I diabetes and Type II diabetes.

Type I diabetes, sometimes called juvenile diabetes, begins most commonly in childhood or adolescence. In this form of diabetes, the pancreas produces little or no insulin. Scientists believe that Type I diabetes may be brought about by a virus or microorganism that trigger's an autoimmune disorder: antibodies that normally destroy foreign invaders end up destroying the islets of Langerhans, the pancreatic cells that produce insulin.

The disorder can be controlled with daily injections (using a small needle and a syringe) of insulin. A strict diet must also be followed. Too little food (or eating too late to coincide with the action of the injected insulin), alcohol, or increased exercise can all lead to low blood sugar levels. A diabetic (person suffering from diabetes) may then become cranky, confused, tired, sweaty, and shaky. If untreated, the diabetic can lose consciousness and have a seizure. Before the condition becomes too serious, the diabetic should have something sweet to eat or drink like candy, sugar cubes, juice, or some other high-sugar snack to balance his or her sugar levels.

Type II diabetes, sometimes called adult-onset diabetes, is the more common form of diabetes. More than 90 percent of the diabetics in the United States suffer from this form. It occurs most often in people who are overweight and who do not exercise. It is also more common in Native Americans, Hispanic Americans, and African Americans.

In Type II diabetes, the pancreas may produce enough insulin, but the body's cells have become resistant to the effects of insulin. Age, obesity (more than 20 percent above ideal body weight), and a family history of diabetes all play a role in the cause. The symptoms of Type II diabetes can begin so gradually that a person may not know they suffer from the disorder. Sometimes the symptoms can develop over several years in overweight adults over the age of forty.

As is the case for Type I diabetes, there is no cure for Type II diabetes. Treatment focuses on keeping blood glucose levels within the normal range. For many Type II diabetics, weight loss is an important goal in helping to control their diabetes. Moderate exercise and a well-balanced, nutritious diet are key steps. To keep blood glucose levels from surging too high, food intake must be distributed over the course of an entire day. For some Type II diabetics, medications are available to help lower blood glucose levels.

Hyperthyroidism

Hyperthyroidism is a disorder in which an overactive thyroid gland produces too much thyroxine. It generally results from a tumor of the thyroid. It can also be brought about by an autoimmune disorder in which antibodies bind to

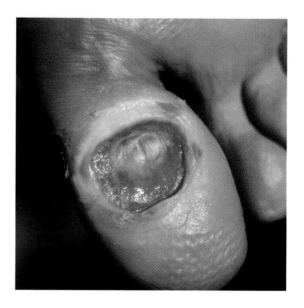

A foot ulcer caused by diabetes. (Photograph by John Smith. Reproduced by permission of Custom Medical Stock Photo.)

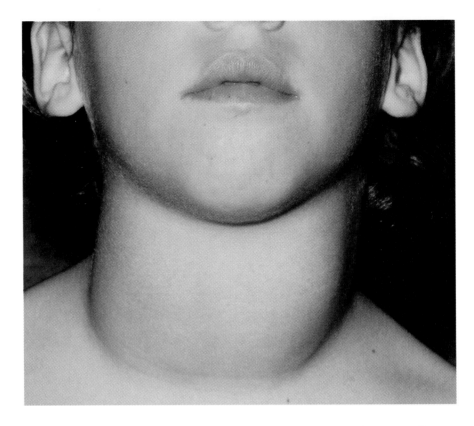

A young boy with a visibly enlarged thyroid—a condition known as a goiter—caused by hyperthyroidism. (Photograph by Lester V. Bergman. Reproduced by permission of Corbis-Bettmann.)

the thyroid cells, forcing them to produce excessive amounts of thyroxine. This latter form of hyperthyroidism is known as Graves' disease.

Regardless of the form, hyperthyroidism has the same symptoms: weight loss with increased appetite, shortness of breath, nervousness and anxiety, rapid heart beat, weak muscles, intolerance of heat, and difficulty relaxing and sleeping. In addition, the eyes may bulge and the thyroid may be visibly enlarged (a condition known as a goiter).

Treatment for hyperthyroidism may include the surgical removal of the thyroid tumor (if one is present) or part of the thyroid. Since the thyroid is the only body part that absorbs iodine, radioactive iodine may be administered to destroy the hormone-producing cells and shrink the enlarged gland. Medications to decrease or block the production of thyroxine may also be given. With proper treatment, most individuals suffering from hyperthyroidism can lead normal lives.

Hypothyroidism

Hypothyroidism is a disorder in which an underactive thyroid gland fails to produce or secrete as much thyroxine as the body needs. Since thyroxine is essential to physical growth and body metabolism, a low supply of this hormone can slow life-sustaining processes and damage organs and tissues in every part of the body.

The disorder is one of the most common chronic (long-term) diseases in the United States. As many as 11 million adults and children may be affected by hypothyroidism. Women are twice as likely as men to suffer from the disorder.

Hypothyroidism is most often the result of Hashimoto's disease. In this disease, the body's defense system fails to recognize that the thyroid gland is part of the body's own tissues and attacks it as if it were a foreign body. Sometimes the gland is destroyed in the process. Infections caused by viruses and bacteria and a diet lacking iodine can also bring about hypothyroidism.

Symptoms, which may not appear until years after the thyroid has stopped functioning, include fatigue, decreased heart rate, weight gain, depression, muscle pain or weakness, dry skin, extreme sensitivity to pain, and puffiness of the face.

If hypothyroidism occurs in early childhood, the condition is known as cretinism. This condition results in dwarfism: the head and trunk, which should be about the same length as the legs, grow about one-and-a-half times larger. Cretins (those suffering from cretinism) have scanty hair and very dry skin. They are often mentally retarded. However, if the condition is discovered early enough and medications to replace thyroxine are given, mental retardation and other symptoms can be prevented.

Synthetic or man-made thyroid hormone medications are also given to adults to treat hypothyroidism. This treatment generally maintains normal thyroid hormone levels, allowing an individual to lead a normal lifestyle.

TAKING CARE: KEEPING THE ENDOCRINE SYSTEM HEALTHY

The endocrine glands and the hormones they secrete are involved in almost all aspects of normal body functioning. Because it is so complex, the system operates on a delicate balance. If it malfunctions, a variety of problems, both great and small, will result.

It is therefore important to monitor the system's workings and seek appropriate treatment if a disorder begins to develop. Preventive measures to protect the endocrine system can be taken. The systems of the body respond well to a healthy diet and regular exercise, and the endocrine system is no exception.

Some endocrine disorders are related to diet. Obesity can lead to Type II diabetes, the most common endocrine disorder in the United States. A lack of iodine in the diet can lead to goiter, or enlargement of the thyroid (with the introduction of iodized table salt, however, goiter is uncommon in the United States). Eating a nutritious, healthy, balanced diet and keeping the body at a healthy weight will diminish the risk of possibly developing certain endocrine disorders.

Stress taxes all body systems. Any condition that threatens the body's homeostasis or steady state is a form of stress. Conditions that cause stress may be physical, emotional, or environmental. One of the main functions of certain endocrine glands is to secrete hormones that help the body respond to stressful situations. However, that function is only meant to be short-term. When stress lasts longer than a few hours, higher energy demands are placed on the body. More hormones are then secreted to meet those demands, but at a price. They tend to weaken the body's defenses, leaving the body open to infection.

Stress over an extended period of time can result in high blood pressure and a lack of cortisol and other steroid hormones released by the adrenal cortex. All this can lead to organ damage and failure. Combining exercise with proper amounts of sleep, relaxation techniques, and positive thinking will help reduce stress and keep hormone levels balanced.

FOR MORE INFORMATION

Books

Landau, Elaine. *Standing Tall: Unusually Tall People.* New York: Franklin Watts, 1997.

Silverstein, Alvin, and Virginia B. Silverstein. *Diabetes: The Sugar Disease.* New York: HarperCollins Children's Books, 1980.

Young, John K. *Hormones: Molecular Messengers.* New York: Franklin Watts, 1994.

WWW Sites

American Diabetes Association
http://www.diabetes.org/
Homepage of the American Diabetes Association, which seeks to prevent and cure diabetes. Site includes the latest news information relating to diabetes.

ECME: Environmental Estrogens (The endocrine system)
http://www.tmc.tulane.edu/ecme/eehome/basics/endosys/ default.html
University site provides extensive information on the endocrine
system. Includes links to other parts of the site focusing on endocrine
glands, hormones, and recent research.

Endocrine Diseases
http://www.endocrineweb.com/Welcome.html
Claims to be the largest web site for thyroid, parathyroid, adrenal, and
pancreas disorders. Presents information on endocrine diseases,
conditions, hormone problems, and treatment options.

The Endocrine Society
http://www.endosociety.org/
Homepage of the Endocrine Society, the world's largest and most
active organization devoted to the research, study, and clinical practice
of endocrinology.

Endocrine System
http://www.innerbody.com/image/endoov.html
Site includes a large image of the human endocrine system with each
part linked to a paragraph explanation of its structure and function.
Also includes an endocrine system overview.

The Endocrine System
http://gened.emc.maricopa.edu/bio/bio181/BIOBK/
BioBookENDOCR.html
Site presents a detailed chapter on the endocrine system—including
hormone action, endocrine organs, and problems—from the On-Line
Biology textbook.

The Endocrine System
http://www3.hmc.edu/~clewis/endocrine/endocrine.htm
Site provides a picture of the location of all the endocrine glands in
the body; also provides information on each.

4

The Integumentary System

The integumentary system, formed by the skin, hair, nails, and associated glands, enwraps the body. It is the most visible organ system and one of the most complex. Diverse in both form and function—from delicate eyelashes to the thick skin of the soles—the integumentary system protects the body from the outside world and its many harmful substances. It utilizes the Sun's rays while at the same time shielding the body from their damaging effects. In addition, the system helps to regulate body temperature, serves as a minor excretory organ, and makes the inner body aware of its outer environment through sensory receptors.

DESIGN: PARTS OF THE INTEGUMENTARY SYSTEM

Integument comes from the Latin word *integumentum,* meaning "cover" or "enclosure." In animals and plants, an integument is any natural outer covering, such as skin, shell, membrane, or husk. The human integumentary system is an external body covering, but also much more. It protects, nourishes, insulates, and cushions. It is absolutely essential to life. Without it, an individual would be attacked immediately by bacteria and die from heat and water loss.

The integumentary system is composed primarily of the skin and accessory structures. Those structures include hair, nails, and certain exocrine glands (glands that have ducts or tubes that carry their secretions to the surface of the skin or into body cavities for elimination).

Skin

Although the skin is not often thought of as an organ, such as the heart or liver, medically it is. An organ is any part of the body formed of two or more tissues that performs a specialized function. As an organ, the skin is the largest and heaviest in the body. In an average adult, the skin covers about 21.5 square feet (2 square meters) and accounts for approximately 7 percent of body weight, or about 11 pounds (5 kilograms) in a 160-pound (73-kilogram) person. It ranges in thickness from 0.04 to 0.08 inches (1 to 2 millimeters), but can measure up to 0.2 inches (6 millimeters) thick on the palms of the hands and the soles of the feet. The skin in these areas is referred to as thick skin (skin elsewhere on the body is called thin skin).

The skin has two principal layers: the epidermis and the dermis. The epidermis is the thin, outer layer, and the dermis is the thicker, inner layer. Beneath the dermis lies the subcutaneous layer or hypodermis, which is composed of adipose or fatty tissue. Although not technically part of the skin, it does anchor the skin to the underlying muscles. It also contains the major blood vessels that supply the dermis and houses many white blood cells, which destroy foreign invaders that have entered the body through breaks in the skin.

WORDS TO KNOW

Apocrine sweat glands (AP-oh-krin): Sweat glands located primarily in the armpit and genital areas.

Arrector pili muscle (ah-REK-tor PI-li): Smooth muscle attached to a hair follicle that, when stimulated, pulls on the follicle, causing the hair shaft to stand upright.

Dermal papillae (DER-mal pah-PILL-ee): Finger-like projections extending upward from the dermis containing blood capillaries, which provide nutrients for the lower layer of the epidermis; also form the characteristic ridges on the skin surface of the hands (fingerprints) and feet.

Dermis (DER-miss): Thick, inner layer of the skin.

Eccrine sweat glands (ECK-rin): Body's most numerous sweat glands, which produce watery sweat to maintain normal body temperature.

Epidermis (ep-i-DER-miss): Thin, outer layer of the skin.

Epithelial tissue (ep-i-THEE-lee-al): Tissue that covers the internal and external surfaces of the body and also forms glandular organs.

Integument (in-TEG-ye-ment): In animals and plants, any natural outer covering, such as skin, shell, membrane, or husk.

Keratin (KER-ah-tin): Tough, fibrous, water-resistant protein that forms the outer layers of hair, calluses, and nails and coats the surface of the skin.

Lunula (LOO-noo-la): White, crescent-shaped area of the nail bed near the nail root.

Melanocyte (MEL-ah-no-site): Cell found in the lower epidermis that produces the protein pigment melanin.

Organ (OR-gan): Any part of the body formed of two or more tissues that performs a specialized function.

Sebaceous gland (suh-BAY-shus): Exocrine gland in the dermis that produces sebum.

Sebum (SEE-bum): Mixture of oily substances and fragmented cells secreted by sebaceous glands.

Squamous cells (SKWA-mus): Cells that are flat and scalelike.

Subcutaneous (sub-kew-TAY-nee-us): Tissues between the dermis and the muscles.

EPIDERMIS. The epidermis is made of stratified squamous epithelial tissue. Epithelial tissue covers the internal and external surfaces of the body and also forms glandular organs. Squamous cells are thin and flat like fish scales. Stratified simply means having two or more layers. In short, the epidermis is composed of many layers of thin, flattened cells that fit closely together and are able to withstand a good deal of abuse or friction.

The epidermis can be divided into four or five layers. Most important of these are the inner and outer layers. The inner or deepest cell layer is the only layer of the epidermis that receives nutrients (from the underlying dermis). The cells of this layer, called basal cells, are constantly dividing and creating new cells daily, which push the older cells toward the surface. Basal cells produce keratin, an extremely durable and water-resistant fibrous protein.

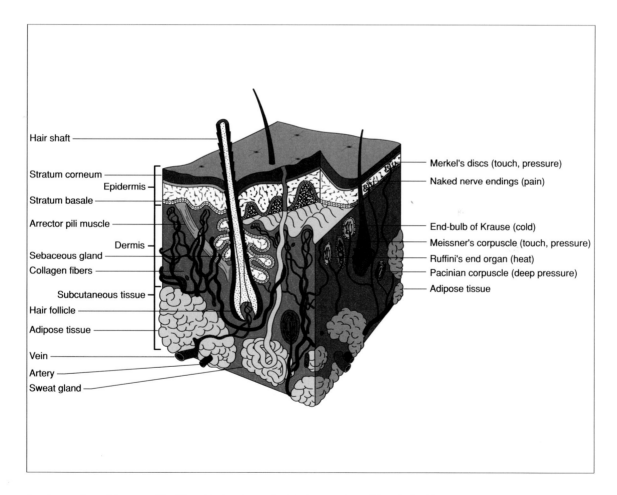

A cutaway view of human skin. The skin has two principle layers: the epidermis (a thin, outer layer) and the dermis (a thicker, inner layer). (Illustration by Hans & Cassady.)

Another type of cell found in the lower epidermis is the melanocyte. Melanocytes produce melanin, a protein pigment that ranges in color from yellow to brown to black. The amount of melanin produced determines skin color, which is a hereditary characteristic. The melanocytes of dark-skinned individuals continuously produce large amounts of melanin. Those of light-skinned individuals produce less. Freckles are the result of melanin clumping in one spot.

The outermost layer of the epidermis consists of about twenty to thirty rows of tightly joined flat dead cells. All that is left in these cells is their keratin, which makes this outer layer waterproof. It takes roughly fourteen days for cells to move from the inner layer of the epidermis to the outer layer. Once part of the outer layer, the dead cells remain for another fourteen days or so before flaking off slowly and steadily.

DERMIS. The dermis, the second layer of skin, lies between the epidermis and the subcutaneous layer. Much thicker than the epidermis, the dermis contains the accessory skin structures. Hair, sweat glands, and sebaceous (oil) glands are all rooted in the dermis. This layer also contains blood vessels and nerve fibers. Nourished by the blood and oxygen provided by these blood vessels, the cells of the dermis are alive.

Connective tissue forms the dermis. Bundles of elastic and collagen (tough fibrous protein) fibers blend into the connective tissue. These fibers provide the dermis strength and flexibility.

The upper layer of the dermis has fingerlike projections that extend into the epidermis. Called dermal papillae, they contain blood capillaries that provide nutrients for the basal cells in the epidermis. On the skin surface of the hands and feet, especially on the tips of the fingers, thumbs, and toes, the dermal papillae form looped and whorled ridges. These print patterns, known as fingerprints or toeprints, increase the gripping ability of the hands and feet. Genetically determined, the patterns are unique to every individual.

Within the dermis are sensory receptors for the senses of touch, pressure, heat, cold, and pain. A specific type of receptor exists for each sensation. For pain, the receptors are free nerve

USING FINGERPRINTS TO IDENTIFY PEOPLE

Fingerprints (the pattern of ridges on an individual's fingertips and thumbs formed by dermal papillae) are unique to each individual and the patterns never change. People have long known about the distinctiveness of fingerprints, but their use in identifying people did not arise until the nineteenth century.

It is generally acknowledged that English scientist Francis Galton (1822–1911) was the first person to devise a system of fingerprint identification. In the 1880s, Galton obtained the first extensive collection of fingerprints for his studies on heredity. He also established a bureau for the registration of civilians by means of fingerprints and measurements.

Galton's ideas were further developed by fellow Englishman Edward R. Henry (1850–1931). In the 1890s, Henry developed a more simplified fingerprint classification system. In 1901, he established England's first fingerprint bureau, called the Fingerprint Branch, within the Scotland Yard police force. Henry's system is still used today in Great Britain and the United States.

endings. For the other sensations, the receptors are encapsulated nerve endings, meaning they have a cellular structure around their endings. The number and type of sensory receptors present in a particular area of skin determines how sensitive that area is to a particular sensation. For example, fingertips have many touch receptors and are quite sensitive. The skin of the upper arm is less sensitive because it has very few touch receptors.

Accessory structures

The accessory structures of the integumentary system include hair, nails, and sweat and sebaceous glands.

HAIR. Roughly 5 million hairs cover the body of an average individual. About 100,000 of those hairs appear on the scalp. Almost every part of the body is covered by hair, except the palms of the hands, the soles of the feet, the sides of the fingers and toes, the lips, and certain parts of the outer genital organs.

ROUGHLY 5 MILLION HAIRS COVER THE BODY OF AN AVERAGE INDIVIDUAL.

Each hair originates from a tiny tubelike structure called a hair follicle that extends deep into the dermis layer. Often, the follicle will project into the subcutaneous layer. Capillaries and nerves attach to the base of the follicle, providing nutrients and sensory information. Inside the base of the follicle, epithelial cells grow and divide, forming the hair bulb or enlarged hair base. Keratin, the primary component in these epithelial cells, coats and stiffens the hair as it grows upward through the follicle. The part of the hair enclosed in the follicle is called the hair root. Once the hair projects from the scalp or skin, it is called a hair shaft.

The older epithelial cells forming the hair root and hair shaft die as they are pushed upward from the nutrient-rich follicle base by newly formed cells. Like the upper layers of the epidermis, the hair shaft is made of dead material, almost entirely protein. The hair shaft is divided into two layers: the cuticle or outer layer consists of a single layer of flat, overlapping cells; the cortex or inner layer is made mostly of keratin.

Hair shafts differ in size, shape, and color. In the eyebrows, they are short and stiff, but on the scalp they are longer and more flexible. Elsewhere on the body they are nearly invisible. Oval-shaped hair shafts produce wavy hair. Flat or ribbonlike hair shafts produce kinky or curly hair. Perfectly round hair shafts produce straight hair. The different types of melanin—yellow, rust, brown, and black—produced by melanocytes at the follicle base combine to create the many varieties of hair color, from the palest blonde to the richest black. With age, the production of melanin decreases, and hair color turns gray.

Attached to each hair follicle is a ribbon of smooth muscle called an arrector pili muscle. When stimulated, the muscle contracts and pulls on the follicle, causing the hair shaft to stand upright.

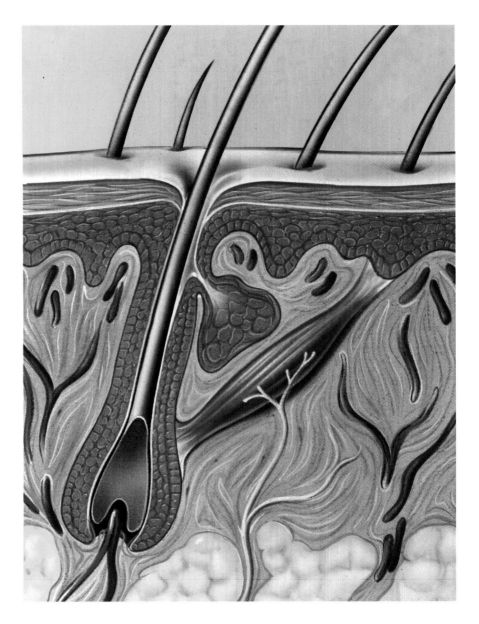

A hair follicle cross-section. (Illustration by SPL/John Bavosi. Reproduced by permission of Custom Medical Stock Photo.)

NAILS. Nails in humans correspond to the hooves of horses and cattle and the claws of birds and reptiles. Found on the ends of fingers and toes, nails are produced by nail follicles just as hair is produced by hair follicles. The nail root is that portion of the nail embedded in the skin, lying very near the bone of the fingertip. Here, cells produce a stronger form of keratin than is found in hair. As new cells are formed, older cells are pushed forward, forming the nail body or the visible attached portion of the nail. The free edge is that portion of the nail that extends over the tip of the finger or toe. Healthy fingernails grow about 0.04 inches (1 millimeter) per week, slightly faster than toenails.

The nail body is made of dead cells, but the nail bed (the tissue underneath the nail body) is alive. The blood vessels running through the nail bed give the otherwise transparent nail body a pink color. Near the nail root, however, these blood vessels are obscured. The resulting white crescent is called the lunula (from the Latin word *luna,* meaning "moon").

SWEAT GLANDS. More than 2.5 million sweat glands are distributed over most surfaces of the human body. They are divided into two types: eccrine sweat glands and apocrine sweat glands.

Eccrine glands, the more numerous of the two types, are found all over the body. They are especially numerous on the forehead, upper lip, palms, and soles. The glands are simply coiled tubes that originate in the dermis. A duct extends from the gland to the skin's surface, where it opens into a pore. Eccrine glands produce sweat or perspiration, a clear secretion that is 99 percent water. Some salts, traces of waste materials such as urea, and vitamin C form the remainder (the salts give sweat its characteristic salty taste).

A polished human nail magnified 105 times its normal size. (Copyright 1988/Keith. Reproduced by permission of Custom Medical Stock Photo.)

Depending on temperature and humidity, an average individual loses 0.6 to 1.7 quarts (0.3 to 0.8 liters) of water every day through sweating. During rigorous physical activity or on a hot day, that amount could rise to 5.3 to 7.4 quarts (5 to 7 liters).

Apocrine glands are found in the armpits, around the nipples, and in the groin. Like eccrine glands, apocrine glands are coiled tubes found in the dermis. However, they are usually larger and their ducts empty into hair follicles. Also, apocrine glands do not function until puberty. At that time, they begin to release an odorless cloudy secretion that contains fatty acids and protein. If the secretion of apocrine glands is allowed to remain on the skin for any length of time, bacteria that lives on the skin breaks down the fatty acids and protein for their growth, creating the unpleasant odor often associated with sweat.

DEPENDING ON TEMPERATURE AND HUMIDITY, AN AVERAGE INDIVIDUAL LOSES 0.6 TO 1.7 QUARTS OF WATER EVERY DAY THROUGH SWEATING.

Apocrine glands are activated by nerve fibers during periods of pain and stress, but their function in humans is not well understood. Scientists theorize they may act as sexual attractants.

SEBACEOUS GLANDS. Sebaceous glands, also known as oil glands, are found in the dermis all over the body, except for the palms and soles. They secrete sebum, a mixture of lipids (fats), proteins, and fragments of dead fat-producing cells. The function of sebum is to prevent the drying of skin and hair. It also contains chemicals that kill bacteria present on the skin surface. While most sebaceous glands secrete sebum through ducts into hair follicles, some secrete sebum directly onto the surface of the skin. Arrector pili muscles, which contract to elevate hairs, also squeeze sebaceous glands, forcing out sebum.

WORKINGS: HOW THE INTEGUMENTARY SYSTEM FUNCTIONS

The integumentary system is essential to the body's homeostasis, or ability to maintain the internal balance of its functions regardless of outside conditions. The system works to protect underlying tissues and organs from infections and injury. It also prevents the loss of body fluids.

Receiving about one-third of the blood pumped from the heart every minute, the skin and its glands help maintain normal body temperature. The system also acts as a mini-excretory system, secreting salts, water, and wastes in the form of sweat. Cells in the skin utilize sunlight to create vitamin D, which is necessary for normal bone growth and function. Finally, the skin contains sensory receptors or specialized nerve endings that allow an individual to "feel" sensations such as touch, pain, pressure, and temperature.

Protection

The outermost epidermal layer of the skin is a barrier between the internal environment of the body and the external world. Keratin, in abundance in this outer layer, waterproofs the body. Without it, handling household chemicals, swimming in a pool, or taking a shower (a necessary everyday activity) would be disastrous to the underlying cells of the body. Not only does keratin keep water out, it also keeps water in. Excessive evaporation or loss of body fluids would result in dehydration and eventual death.

The thickness of the outer layer of the epidermis, combined with the toughness provided by keratin, also prevents microorganisms and viruses from entering the body. In addition, sebum secreted by the sebaceous glands helps prevent microorganisms from living and growing on the skin surface. Since it is slightly acidic, sebum creates a condition in which many microorganisms cannot exist. Sebum serves a further protective function by keeping the skin and hair moist; dry skin would crack, allowing viruses and bacteria to enter.

Karen Wetterhahn. (Reproduced by permission of AP/Wide World Photos.)

WETTERHAHN'S DEADLY RESEARCH

Karen Wetterhahn (1948–1997) was a chemistry professor at Dartmouth College in Hanover, New Hampshire, where she conducted environmental research projects. During an experiment in August 1996, Wetterhahn spilled a tiny drop of di-methyl mercury (a highly toxic chemical) on her hand. Less than a year later, she was dead.

Wetterhahn had been conducting research to determine the effects that heavy metals (metals such as mercury having a high specific gravity) produce on the environment. During her experiment, she was transferring some dimethyl mercury to a tube when she spilled a tiny amount. Although Wetterhahn was wearing latex gloves, the mercury permeated the thin latex and soaked into her skin, passing through its waterproof layers within seconds.

Dimethyl mercury is deadly. Once in the body, it seeps from the bloodstream into brain tissues, causing fatal damage to the central nervous system and the brain. Symptoms of mercury poisoning include loss of motor (movement) control, numbness in the arms and legs, blindness, hearing and speech loss.

Wetterhahn did not feel the effects of the mercury until six months after the accident. Within three months, she was dead. After her death, the U.S. Occupational Safety and Health Administration urged scientists to wear highly resistant laminate gloves (consisting of several bonded layers) under a pair of heavy-duty neoprene gloves when handling compounds such as dimethyl mercury.

If the protective outer layer of the skin is broken because of an injury and microorganisms enter the body, the many blood vessels in the dermis help prevent the microorganisms from reaching internal tissues. As an immune response, the vessels dilate or expand. This increases the amount of blood flowing to the area, which in turn brings in more white blood cells and other protein factors to battle the infection.

Even though the skin forms a protective barrier, it is still slightly permeable or allows certain substances to pass through it. Vitamins A, D, E, and K all pass through the skin and are absorbed in the capillaries in the dermis. Steroid hormones such as estrogen and chemicals such as nicotine also pass through and are absorbed. With this in mind, medical researchers have developed therapeutic patches that are attached to the skin to deliver chemicals or medication (nicotine patches for those individuals trying to quit smoking are an example).

Nails protect the exposed tips of fingers and toes from physical injury. Fingernails also aid the fingers in picking up small objects.

Hair serves a protective function, although it is limited. On the head, hair protects the scalp from damaging ultraviolet (UV) radiation from the Sun, cushions the head from physical blows, and insulates the scalp to a degree. On the eyelids, eyelashes prevent airborne particles and insects from entering the eyes. Hairs in the nostrils and the external ear canals perform a similar function.

WHEN STIMULATED BY COLD OR AN EMOTION SUCH AS FEAR, THE ARRECTOR PILI MUSCLES CONTRACT, PULLING HAIR FOLLICLES UPRIGHT.

When stimulated by cold or an emotion such as fear, the arrector pili muscles contract, pulling hair follicles upright. In animals (and in our evolutionary ancestors, who had much more body hair), this action adds warmth by adding a layer of insulating air to the fur. In present-day humans, who have very little body hair, this action seems to serve no purpose other than to create dimples or "goose bumps" in the skin.

The body is protected against the Sun's harmful UV radiation by melanin, produced by melanocytes in the epidermis. Melanin accumulates within the cells of the epidermis. It then absorbs UV radiation before that radiation can destroy the cells' DNA or deoxyribonucleic acid (large, complex molecules found in the nuclei of cells that carries genetic or hereditary information for an organism's development). Increased exposure to the Sun causes melanocytes to increase their production of melanin. The temporary result is that the skin becomes darker or tanned and is able to withstand further exposure to UV rays.

The protection afforded by melanin, however, is limited. Prolonged or excessive exposure to UV radiation eventually damages the skin. It causes elastic fibers in the dermis to clump, and the skin takes on a leathery appearance. Overexposure can also result in melanoma, a tumor composed of melanocytes.

Body temperature

Normal internal body temperature averages approximately 98.6°F (37°C). The heat-regulating functions of the body are extremely important. If the internal temperature varies more than a few degrees from normal, life-threatening changes take place in the body.

Eccrine glands play an important part in maintaining normal body temperature. When the temperature of the body rises due to physical exercise or environmental conditions, the hypothalamus (region of the brain containing many control centers for body functions and emotions) sends signals to the eccrine glands to secrete sweat. When sweat evaporates on the skin surface, it carries large amounts of body heat with it and the skin surface cools.

Because blood carries heat (a form of energy), blood flow is another regulator of body temperature. Under warm conditions, the hypothalamus signals blood vessels in the dermis to dilate or expand. This increases blood flow (and carries excess heat) to the body's surface. Like a radiator, the skin then gives off heat to the surrounding environment.

During cold conditions, the hypothalamus signals eccrine glands to stop secreting sweat. It also signals blood vessels in the dermis to constrict or close, which reduces blood flow to the skin surface. As a result, heat is kept within the core of the body.

Excretion and vitamin D formation

Excretion is a very minor function of the skin. Sweat does contain salt and urea (a compound produced when the liver breaks down amino acids), but the amounts of these wastes are slight. The kidneys are mainly responsible for removing waste products from the blood.

As explained earlier, too much sunlight is harmful to the body. A limited amount, however, is beneficial. In the lower layers of the epidermis, cells contain a form of cholesterol (fatlike substance produced by the liver that is an essential part of cell membranes and body chemicals). When exposed to UV radiation,

SANDBLASTING YOUR FACE

For years, workers have cleaned old stone and concrete structures by blasting their surfaces with a spray of fine sand. In the late 1990s, dermatologists and beauty salon owners in the United States began using a similar technique to remove the signs of aging on people's faces.

The new treatment, already used in Europe since the early 1990s, is called microdermabrasion. A machine blows tiny sterile sand crystals onto the skin of the face, then suctions them off. The crystals rub off the top layer of the skin, helping remove wrinkles.

The procedure is relatively painless and quick. However, its effects are not permanent, and it only removes fine lines. Deep lines around the mouth, crow's feet around the eyes, and deep lines on the forehead remain, although they are softened.

that cholesterol changes into vitamin D, which the body uses to absorb calcium and phosphorus from food in the small intestine. Those two minerals are then used to build and maintain bones and teeth, among other functions.

Sensory reception

The main function of the sensory receptors in the dermis is to provide the brain with information about the external world and its effect on the skin. Thus, they alert the body to the possible tissue-damaging effects of extreme heat or cold or something that is pressing hard against the skin. They also transmit pleasant sensations, such as a gentle breeze blowing across the face or the soft caress of a loved one.

The skin's sensitive touch receptors help blind readers interpret the raised dot patterns of Braille books. (Reproduced by permission of FPG International.)

The receptors differ in their sensitivity. Touch receptors are the most sensitive, responding to the slightest contact. Found mainly in the fingers, tongue, and lips, they number about 500,000. Pain receptors, however, do not react unless the stimulus is strong enough. Located all over the body, pain receptors number between three and four million. Their high numbers indicate their importance to the body.

Receptors send their information to the brain to be interpreted. The brain then directs the body to respond, whether to remove itself from the situation or remain. Sensation, therefore, is a function of the brain and the nervous system.

AILMENTS: WHAT CAN GO WRONG WITH THE INTEGUMENTARY SYSTEM

Unlike some other body systems, the integumentary system quickly shows when it is afflicted by an aliment or malady. Over one thousand different aliments can affect the skin. The most common skin disorders are those caused by allergies or bacterial or fungal infections. Burns and skin cancers, although less common, are more dangerous. In some cases, they can be lethal.

The following are just a few of the many ailments that can target the integumentary system.

INTEGUMENTARY SYSTEM DISORDERS

Acne (AK-nee): Disorder in which hair follicles of the skin become clogged and infected.

Athlete's foot: Common fungus infection in which the skin between the toes becomes itchy and sore, cracking and peeling away.

Basal cell carcinoma (BAY-sal CELL car-si-NO-ma): Skin cancer that affects the basal cells in the epidermis.

Carcinoma (car-si-NO-ma): Cancerous tumor of the skin, mucous membrane, or similar tissue of the body.

Dermatitis (der-ma-TIE-tis): Any inflammation of the skin.

Malignant melanoma (ma-LIG-nant mel-ah-NO-ma): Cancer of melanocytes; the most serious type of skin cancer.

Psoriasis (so-RYE-ah-sis): Chronic skin disease characterized by reddened lesions covered with dry, silvery scales.

Seborrheic dermatitis (seh-beh-REE-ik der-ma-TIE-tis): Commonly called seborrhea, a disease of the skin characterized by scaly lesions usually on the scalp, hairline, and face.

Squamous cell carcinoma (SKWA-mus CELL car-si-NO-ma): Skin cancer affecting the cells of the second deepest layer of the epidermis.

Vitiligo (vit-i-LIE-go): Skin disorder in which the loss of melanocytes results in patches of smooth, milky white skin.

Warts: Small growths caused by a viral infection of the skin or mucous membrane.

Acne

Acne is a skin disease marked by pimples on the face, chest, and back. The most common skin disease, acne affects an estimated 17 to 28 million people in the United States. Although it can strike people at any age, acne usually begins at puberty and worsens during adolescence.

At puberty, increased levels of androgens (male hormones) cause the sebaceous glands to secrete an excessive amount of sebum into hair follicles. The excess sebum combines with dead, sticky skin cells to form a hard plug that blocks the follicle. Bacteria that normally lives on the skin then invades the blocked follicle. Weakened, the follicle bursts open, releasing the sebum, bacteria, skin cells, and white blood cells into the surrounding tissues. A pimple then forms.

Treatment for acne depends on whether the condition is mild, moderate, or severe. The goal is to reduce sebum production, remove dead skin cells, and kill skin bacteria. In very mild cases, keeping the skin clean by washing with a mild soap is recommended. In other cases, medications applied directly to the skin or taken orally may be prescribed in combination with gentle cleansing.

Athlete's foot

Athlete's foot is a common fungus infection in which the skin between the toes becomes itchy and sore, cracking and peeling away. Properly known as tinea pedis, the infection received its common name because the infection-causing fungi grow well in warm, damp areas such as in and around swimming pools, showers, and locker rooms (areas commonly used by athletes).

The fungi that cause athlete's foot are unusual in that they live exclusively on dead body tissue (hair, the outer layer of skin, and nails). Researchers do not know exactly why some people develop the condition and others do not. It is known that sweaty feet, tight shoes, and the failure to dry feet well after swimming or bathing all contribute to the growth of the fungus.

Symptoms of athlete's foot include itchy, sore skin on the toes, with scaling, cracking, inflammation, and blisters. If the blisters break, raw patches of tissue may be exposed. If the infection spreads, itching and burning may increase.

Athlete's foot usually responds well to treatment. Simple cases are treated with antifungal creams or sprays. In more severe cases, an oral antifungal medication may be prescribed.

Burns

There are few threats more serious to the skin than burns. Burns are injuries to tissues caused by intense heat, electricity, UV radiation (sunburn), or certain chemicals (such as acids). When skin is burned and cells

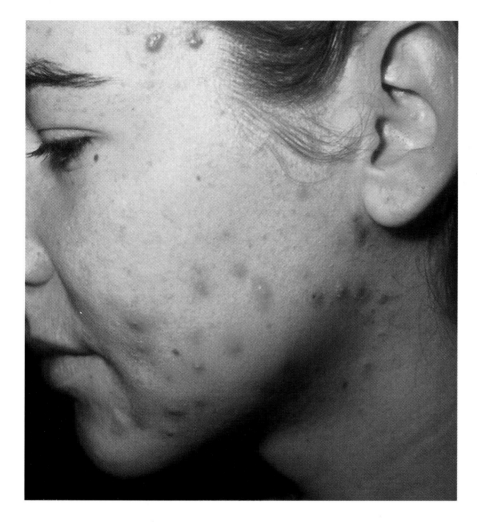

A young woman with acne. (Photograph by Biophoto Associates. Reproduced by permission of Photo Researchers, Inc.)

are destroyed, the body readily loses its precious supply of fluids. Dehydration can follow, leading to a shutdown of the kidneys, a life-threatening condition. Infection of the dead tissue by bacteria and viruses occurs one to two days after skin has been burned. Infection is the leading cause of death in burn victims.

Burns are classified according to their severity or depth: first-, second-, or third-degree burns.

First-degree burns occur when only the epidermis is damaged. The burned area is painful, the outer skin is reddened, and slight swelling may be present. Sunburns are usually first-degree burns. Although they may cause discomfort, these minor burns are usually not serious and heal within a few days.

Second-degree burns occur when the epidermis and the upper region of the dermis are damaged. The burned area is red, painful, and may have a wet, shiny appearance because of exposed tissue. Blisters may form. These moderate burns take longer to heal. If the blisters are not broken and care is taken to prevent infection, the burned skin may regenerate or regrow without permanent scars.

Third-degree burns occur when the entire depth of skin is destroyed. Because nerve endings have been destroyed, the burned area has no sensitivity. The area may be blackened or gray-white in color. Muscle tissue and bone underneath may be damaged. In these serious to critical burns, regeneration of the skin is not possible. Skin grafting—taking a piece of skin from an unburned portion of the burn victim's body and transplanting it to the

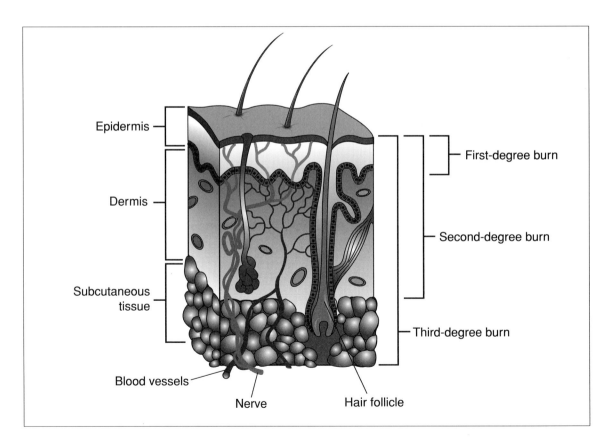

Burns are classified by degree—first, second, or third—according to their severity and skin depth. (Illustration by Electronic Illustrators Group.)

burned area—must be done to cover the exposed tissues. Third-degree burns take weeks to heal and will leave permanent scarring.

Dermatitis

Dermatitis is any inflammation of the skin. There are many types of dermatitis and most are characterized by a pink or red rash that itches. Two common types are contact dermatitis and seborrheic dermatitis.

Contact dermatitis is an allergic reaction to something that irritates the skin. It usually appears within forty-eight hours after touching or brushing against a substance to which the skin is sensitive. The resin in poison ivy, poison oak, and poison sumac is the most common source of contact dermatitis. The skin of some people may also be irritated by certain flowers, herbs, and vegetables. Chemical irritants that can cause contact dermatitis include chlorine, cleaners, detergents and soaps, fabric softeners, perfumes, glues, and topical medications (those applied on the skin). Contact dermatitis can be treated with medicated creams or ointments and oral antihistamines and antibiotics.

Seborrheic dermatitis, known commonly as seborrhea, appears as red, inflamed skin covered by greasy or dry scales that may be white, yellow, or gray. These scaly lesions appear usually on the scalp, hairline, and face. Dandruff is a mild form of seborrheic dermatitis. Medical researchers do not know the exact cause of this skin disease. They believe that a high-fat diet, alcohol, stress, oily skin, infrequent shampooing, and weather extremes (hot or

ARTIFICIAL SKIN

Artificial skin, the synthetic or man-made equivalent of human skin, was first developed in the 1970s. Since then, the lives of many severely burned people have been saved through the use of artificial skin.

In the 1970s, John F. Burke, chief of trauma services at Massachusetts General Hospital in Boston, and Ioannis V. Yannas, chemistry professor at Massachusetts Institute of Technology in Cambridge, teamed up to develop some type of human skin replacement. In their research, the two men found that collagen fibers (protein found in human skin) and a long sugar molecule (called a polymer) could be combined to form a porous material that resembles skin. They then created a kind of artificial skin using polymers from shark cartilage and collagen from cowhide.

Burke and Yannas soon discovered that artificial skin acts like a framework onto which new skin tissue and blood vessels grow. As the new skin grows, the cowhide and shark substances from the artificial skin are broken down and absorbed by the body.

In 1979, Burke and Yannas used their artificial skin on their first patient, a woman who had suffered burns over half her body. After peeling away her burned skin, Burke applied a layer of artificial skin and, where possible, grafted or added on some of her own unburned skin. Three weeks later, the woman's new skin, the same color as her unburned skin, was growing at an amazingly healthy rate.

With continued research and development, synthetic skin may become a more common treatment for burns and other serious skin disorders.

cold) may play some role. The disease may be treated with special shampoos that help soften and remove the scaly lesions. In more severe cases, medicated creams or shampoos containing coal tar may be prescribed.

Psoriasis

Psoriasis is a chronic (long-term) skin disease characterized by inflamed lesions with silvery-white scabs of dead skin. The disease affects roughly four million people in the United States, women slightly more than men. It is most common in fair-skinned people.

Normal skin cells mature and replace dead skin cells every twenty-eight to thirty days. Psoriasis causes skin cells to mature in less than a week. Be-

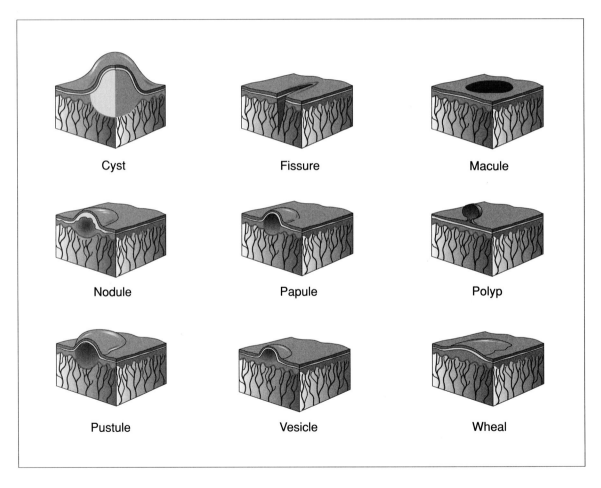

Cyst	Fissure	Macule
Nodule	Papule	Polyp
Pustule	Vesicle	Wheal

Various types of skin lesions. Skin ailments such as dermatitis, psoriasis, and acne are characterized by the size, shape, and texture of lesions present at outbreak. (Illustration by Electronic Illustrators Group.)

cause the body cannot shed old skin as rapidly as new cells are rising to the surface, raised patches of dead skin develop. These patches are seen on the arms, back, chest, elbows, legs, folds between the buttocks, and scalp.

The cause of psoriasis is unknown. In some cases, it may be hereditary or inherited. Attacks of psoriasis can be triggered by injury or infection, stress, hormonal changes, exposure to cold temperature, or steroids and other medications.

The treatment for psoriasis depends on its severity. Steroid creams and ointments are commonly used to treat mild or moderate psoriasis. If the case is more severe, these medications may be used in conjunction with ultraviolet light B (UVB) treatments. Strong medications are reserved for those individuals suffering from extreme cases of psoriasis.

Skin cancer

Skin cancer is the growth of abnormal skin cells capable of invading and destroying other cells. Skin cancer is the single most common type of cancer in humans. The cause of most skin cancers or carcinomas is unknown, but overexposure to ultraviolet radiation in sunlight is a risk factor.

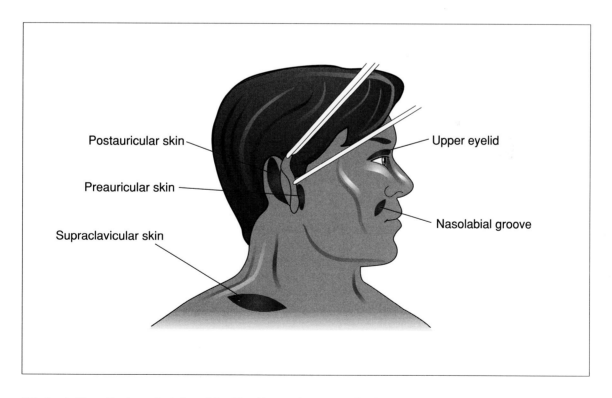

Skin for grafting—the transplantation of healthy skin to a burn or non-healing wound—can be taken from other areas of a patient's body. (Illustration by Electronic Illustrators Group.)

Basal cell carcinoma is the most common form of skin cancer, accounting for about 75 percent of cases. It is also the least malignant or cancerous (tending to grow and spread throughout the body). In this form of skin cancer, basal cells in the epidermis are altered so they no longer produce keratin. They also spread, invading the dermis and subcutaneous layer. Shiny, dome-shaped lesions develop most often on sun-exposed areas of the face. The next most common areas affected are the ears, the backs of the hands, the shoulders, and the arms. When the lesion is removed surgically, 99 percent of patients recover fully.

> **BASAL CELL CARCINOMA IS THE MOST COMMON FORM OF SKIN CANCER, ACCOUNTING FOR ABOUT 75 PERCENT OF CASES.**

Squamous cell carcinoma affects the cells of the second deepest layer of the epidermis. Like basal cell carcinoma, this type of skin cancer also involves skin exposed to the sun: face, ears, hands, and arms. The cancer presents itself as a small, scaling, raised bump on the skin with a crusting center. It grows rapidly and spreads to adjacent lymph nodes if not removed. If the lesion is caught early and removed surgically or through radiation, the patient has a good chance of recovering completely.

Malignant melanoma accounts for about 5 percent of all skin cancers, but it is the most serious type. It is a cancer of the melanocytes, cells in the lower epidermis that produce melanin. In their early stages, melanomas resemble moles. Soon, they appear as an expanding brown to black patch. In addition to invading surrounding tissues, the cancer spreads aggressively to other parts of the body, especially the lungs and liver. Overexposure to the Sun may be a cause of melanomas, but the greatest risk factor seems to be genetic. Early discovery of the melanoma is key to survival. The primary treatment for this skin cancer is the surgical removal of the tumor or diseased area of skin. When the melanoma has spread to other parts of the body, it is generally considered incurable.

Vitiligo

Vitiligo is a skin disorder in which the loss of melanocytes (cells that produce the color pigment melanin) results in patches of smooth, milky white skin. This often inherited disorder affects about 1 to 2 percent of the world's population. Although it is more easily observed in people with darker skin, it affects all races. It can begin at any age, but in 50 percent of the cases it starts before the age of twenty.

Medical researchers do not know the exact cause of the disorder. Some theorize that nerve endings in the skin may release a chemical that destroys melanocytes. Others believe that the melanocytes simply self-destruct. Still others think that vitiligo is a type of autoimmune disease, in which the body targets and destroys its own cells and tissues.

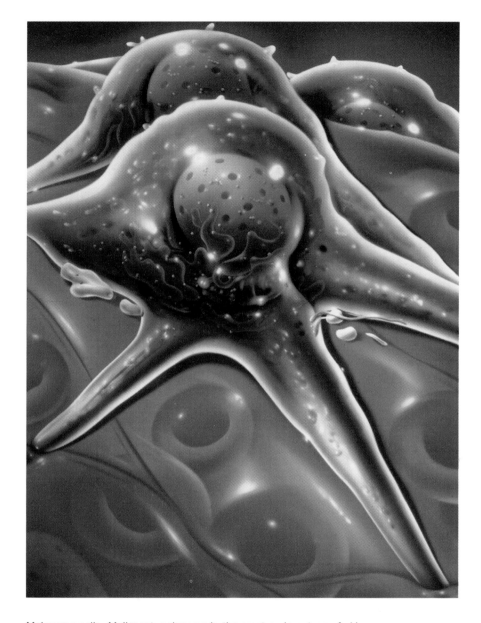

Melanoma cells. Malignant melanoma is the most serious type of skin cancer.
(Reproduced by permission of Photo Researchers, Inc.)

Vitiligo cannot be cured, but it can be managed. Cosmetics can be applied to blend the white areas with the surrounding normal skin. Sunscreens are useful to prevent the burning of affected areas and to prevent normal skin around the patches from becoming darker.

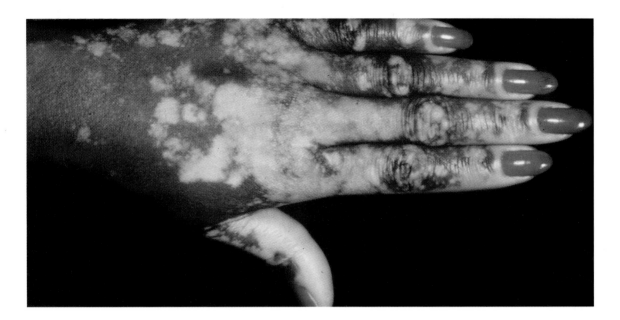

Vitiligo is a skin disorder in which the loss of cells that produce melanin results in patches of smooth, milky white skin. (Reproduced by permission of Custom Medical Stock.)

Warts

Warts are small growths caused by a viral infection of the skin or mucous membrane. The virus infects the surface layer. Warts are contagious. They can easily pass from person to person. They can also pass from one area of the body to another on the same person. Affecting about 7 to 10 percent of the population, warts are particularly common among children, young adults, and women. Common warts include hand warts, foot warts, and flat warts.

Hand warts grow around the nails, on the fingers, and on the backs of the hands. They appear mostly in areas where the skin is broken.

Foot warts (also called plantar warts) usually appear on the ball of the foot, the heel, or the flat part of the toes. Foot warts do not stick up above the surface like hand warts. If left untreated, they can grow in size and spread into clusters of several warts. If located on a pressure point of the foot, these warts can be painful.

Warts are caused by viral infections of the skin. (Reproduced by permission of Custom Medical Stock.)

Flat warts are smaller and smoother than other warts. They grow in great numbers and can erupt anywhere on the body. In children, they appear especially on the face.

Many nonprescription wart remedies are available that will remove simple warts from hands and fingers. Physicians use stronger chemical medications to treat warts that are larger or do not respond to over-the-counter treatments. Freezing warts with liquid nitrogen or burning them with an electric needle are advanced treatment methods.

TAKING CARE: KEEPING THE INTEGUMENTARY SYSTEM HEALTHY

As people age, dramatic changes take place in the integumentary system. The epidermis thins as basal cells divide less and less. The dermis also thins and its elastic fibers decrease in size. As a result, the skin becomes weaker and starts to sag, forming wrinkles. Melanocytes decrease production of melanin, and the skin becomes pale and hair turns white. Sebaceous glands also decrease production of sebum, causing the skin to become dry and scaly. Blood supply to the skin is reduced and body temperature cannot be regulated as well. Finally, the skin takes longer and longer to repair itself.

TATTOOS: BODY ART OR MUTILATION?

Tattoos are relatively permanent marks or designs made on the skin. Tattoo comes from the Tahitian word *tattau,* meaning "to mark." The process of tattooing is accomplished by injecting colored pigment into small deep holes made in the skin. The modern method of tattooing employs an electric needle to inject the pigment.

People have been decorating their bodies with pictures of animals, flowers, supernatural creatures, and various designs for thousands of years. Egyptian mummies dating from 3035 B.C. have been discovered with ornate designs of flowers tattooed on their skin. Many ancient cultures believed that a tattoo of an animal could capture the mystical spirit of that animal and magically link the wearer to the animal depicted.

While many cultures have revered tattoos, many others have considered them vulgar and offensive. For as long as people have applied tattoos to their skin, they have sought ways to remove them.

In modern times, tattoos can be removed medically through one of four ways. If the tattoo is small, it can be surgically cut off and the skin sewn back together. In a method called dermabrasion, the tattoo is "sanded" with a rotary abrasive instrument until the layers of skin peel. Another method that uses abrasion is called salabrasion. In this procedure, which is centuries old, salt water is applied to the tattoo and then it is vigorously rubbed with some sort of sanding device until the tattoo pigments are dispersed. All three of these methods leave some sort of scarring, but the last method, laser surgery, does not. Pulses of light from a laser are directed onto the tattoo, breaking up its pigments. The pigments are then removed over the next few weeks by the body's defense cells.

Although there is no way to avoid aging of the skin, there are ways to decrease the effects of aging. The loss of elasticity in the skin is speeded up by sunlight. The skin should be shielded from the Sun through the use of sunscreens, sunblocks, and protective clothing. Sunburns are never healthy and should always be avoided. This will also help reduce the risk of skin cancer.

As in all other body systems, the following play a part in keeping the integumentary system operating at peak efficiency: proper nutrition, healthy amounts of good-quality drinking water, adequate rest, regular exercise, and stress reduction. Hair loss and graying are both genetically controlled, but stress can add to both conditions. Exercise and relaxation techniques are proven ways to reduce stress.

Proper daily cleansing of the skin is highly recommended. However, harsh detergents and scrubbing will not make the skin cleaner. In fact, they can injure the skin and cause excessive drying. Greater benefits can be gained by cleaning the skin with gentle soaps or lotions, then applying an appropriate moisturizer to all areas of the body.

FOR MORE INFORMATION

Books

Balin, Arthur K., Loretta Pratt Balin, and Marietta Whittlesly. *The Life of the Skin.* New York: Bantam Books, 1997.

Brynie, Faith Hickman. *101 Questions About Your Skin That Got Under Your Skin Until Now.* Brookfield, CT: Millbrook Press, 1999.

Kenet, Barney J., and Patricia Lawler. *Saving Your Skin: Prevention, Early Detection, and Treatment of Melanoma and Other Skin Cancers.* New York: Four Walls Eight Windows, 1998.

Silverstein, Alvin, Robert Silverstein, and Virginia B. Silverstein. *Overcoming Acne: The How and Why of Healthy Skin Care.* New York: Morrow, 1980.

Turkington, Carol A., and Jeffrey S. Dover. *Skin Deep: An A-Z of Skin Disorders, Treatments, and Health.* Updated edition. New York: Facts on File, 1998.

WWW Sites

AcneNet
    http://www.derm-infonet.com/acnenet
    Site developed by Roche Laboratories in association with the American Academy of Dermatology presents a comprehensive online acne information resource, including basic facts, such as how and why acne occurs and various treatments.

American Academy of Dermatology

> http://www.aad.org
>
> Homepage of the American Academy of Dermatology.

Integumentary System

> http://gened.emc.maricopa.edu/bio/bio181/BIOBK/
> BioBookINTEGUSYS.html
>
> Site presents a detailed chapter on the integumentary system—
> including follicles and glands, hair and nails, and skin and sensory
> reception—from the On-Line Biology textbook.

Integumentary System

> http://www.wellweb.com/index/QINTEGUMEN.HTM
>
> Site presents a detailed overview of the main parts of the
> integumentary system.

Integumentary System Color Images

> http://www.udel.edu/Biology/Wags/histopage/colorpage /cin/cin.htm
>
> Site provides links to twenty-six color images of various parts of the
> integumentary system, such as the a nail bed, hair shaft and follicle,
> and sebaceous gland.

Introduction to Skin Cancer

> http://www.maui.net/~southsky/introto.html
>
> Site contains link to the causes of skin cancer, the effects of heredity
> and environment, diagnosis and treatment information, and a glossary
> of terms.

Skin and Connective Tissue Diseases

> http://www.mic.ki.se/Diseases/c17.html
>
> Site compiled by the Karolinska Institutet (Sweden) presents an
> enormous set of links to sites focusing on various skin, nail, and hair
> diseases.

5

The Lymphatic System

The lymphatic system is often considered part of the cardiovascular system (see chapter 1). Excess fluid that leaks out of capillaries to bathe the body's cells is collected by the vessels of the lymphatic system and returned to the blood. By doing so, the lymphatic system maintains the fluid balance in the body. The lymphatic system further assists the cardiovascular system in absorbing nutrients from the small intestine. These necessary actions, however, are only part of the system's vitally important overall function. It is the body's main line of defense against foreign invaders such as bacteria and viruses. The lymphatic system is responsible for body immunity, filtering harmful substances out of tissue fluid (which fills the spaces between the cells) before that fluid is returned to the blood and the rest of the body. For this reason, it is sometimes referred to as the immune system.

DESIGN: PARTS OF THE LYMPHATIC SYSTEM

A network of vessels, tissues, organs, and cells constitute the lymphatic system. Included in this network are lymph vessels, lymph nodes, the spleen, the thymus, and lymphocytes. Running throughout this network is a watery fluid called lymph.

Lymph

Lymph comes from the Latin word *lympha,* meaning "clear water." Slightly yellowish but clear, lymph is any tissue or interstitial fluid that enters the lymph vessels. It is similar to blood plasma, but contains more white blood cells. Lymph also carries other substances, depending on where it is in the body. In the limbs, lymph is rich in protein, especially albumin. In the bone marrow, spleen, and thymus, lymph contains higher concentrations of white blood cells. And in the intestine, lymph contains fats absorbed during digestion.

Lymph vessels

Lymph vessels, also called lymphatics, carry lymph in only one direction—to the heart. Throughout all the tissues of the body, lymph vessels form a complicated, spidery network of fine tubes. The smallest vessels, called lymph capillaries, have closed or dead ends (unlike vessels in the cardiovascular system, which form a closed circuit). The walls of these capillaries are composed of only a single layer of flattened cells. Material in the interstitial fluid passes easily through the gaps between these cells into the capillaries. Lymph capillaries in the villi (tiny fingerlike projections) of the small intestine are called lacteals. These specialized capillaries transport the fat products of digestion, such as fatty acids and vitamin A.

As lymph capillaries carry lymph away from the tissue spaces, they merge to form larger and larger vessels. These larger lymph vessels resemble veins, but their walls are thinner and they have more one-way valves to prevent lymph from flowing backward. Whereas the cardiovascular system has a pump (the heart) to move fluid (blood) through the system, the lymphatic

WORDS TO KNOW

Allergen (AL-er-jen): Substance that causes an allergy.

Antibody (AN-ti-bod-ee): Specialized substance produced by the body that can provide immunity against a specific antigen.

Antibody-mediated immunity (AN-ti-bod-ee MEE-dee-a-ted i-MYOO-ni-tee): Immune response involving B cells and their production of antibodies.

Antigen (AN-ti-jen): Any substance that, when introduced to the body, is recognized as foreign and activates an immune response.

B cell: Also called B lymphocyte, a type of lymphocyte that originates from the bone marrow and that changes into antibody-producing plasma cells.

Cell-mediated immunity (CELL MEE-dee-a-ted i-MYOO-ni-tee): Immune response led by T cells that does not involve the production of antibodies.

Chyle (KILE): Thick, whitish liquid consisting of lymph and tiny fat globules absorbed from the small intestine during digestion.

Edema (i-DEE-mah): Condition in which excessive fluid collects in bodily tissue and causes swelling.

Fever: Abnormally high body temperature brought about as a response to infection or severe physical injury.

Histamine (HISS-ta-mean): Chemical compound released by injured cells that causes local blood vessels to enlarge.

Immunity (i-MYOO-ni-tee): Body's ability to defend itself against pathogens or other foreign material.

Inflammation (in-flah-MAY-shun): Response to injury or infection of body tissues, marked by redness, heat, swelling, and pain.

Interferon (in-ter-FIR-on): Protein compound released by cells infected with a virus to prevent that virus from reproducing in nearby normal cells.

Lacteals (LAK-tee-als): Specialized lymph capillaries in the villi of the small intestine.

Lymph (LIMF): Slightly yellowish but clear fluid found within lymph vessels.

Lymph node: Small mass of lymphatic tissue located along the pathway of a lymph vessel that filters out harmful microorganisms.

system does not. It relies on the contraction of muscles to move lymph throughout the body. The larger lymph vessels have a layer of smooth muscle in their walls that contracts rhythmically to "pump" lymph along. The contraction of skeletal muscles, brought about by simple body movement, and the mechanics of breathing also help to move lymph on its way.

The successively larger lymph vessels eventually unite to return lymph to the venous system through two ducts or passageways: the right lymphatic duct and the thoracic duct. Lymph that has been collected from the right arm and the right side of the head, neck, and thorax (area of the body between the neck and the abdomen) empties into the right lymphatic duct. Lymph from the rest of the body drains into the thoracic duct, the body's main lymph vessel, which runs upward in front of the backbone.

Both ducts then empty the lymph into the subclavian vein, which lies under the clavicle or collarbone. The right lymphatic duct empties into the right subclavian vein; the thoracic duct empties into the left subclavian vein. Flaps in both subclavian veins allow the lymph to flow into the veins, but prevent

Lymphocyte (LIM-foe-site): Type of white blood cell produced in lymph nodes, bone marrow, and the spleen that defends the body against infection by producing antibodies.

Macrophage (MACK-row-fage): Large white blood cell that engulfs and destroys bacteria, viruses, and other foreign substances in the lymph.

Natural killer cell: Also known as an NK cell, a type of lymphocyte that patrols the body and destroys foreign or abnormal cells.

Peyer's patches (PIE-erz): Masses of lymphatic tissue located in the villi of the small intestine.

Phagocyte (FAG-oh-site): Type of white blood cell capable of engulfing and digesting particles or cells harmful to the body.

Phagocytosis (fag-oh-sigh-TOE-sis): Process by which a phagocyte engulfs and destroys particles or cells harmful to the body.

Spleen: Lymphoid organ located in the upper left part of the abdomen that stores blood, destroys old red blood cells, and filters pathogens from the blood.

T cell: Also known as T lymphocyte, a type of lymphocyte that matures in the thymus and that attacks any foreign substance in the body.

Thoracic duct (tho-RAS-ik): Main lymph vessel in the body, which transports lymph from the lower half and upper left part of the body.

Thymus (THIGH-mus): Glandular organ consisting of lymphoid tissue located behind the top of the breastbone that produces specialized lymphocytes; reaches maximum development in early childhood and is almost absent in adults.

Tonsils (TAHN-sills): Three pairs of small, oval masses of lymphatic tissue located on either side of the inner wall of the throat, near the rear openings of the nasal cavity, and near the base of the tongue.

Vaccine (vack-SEEN): Substance made of weakened or killed bacteria or viruses injected (or taken orally) into the body to stimulate the production of antibodies specific to that particular infectious disease.

Villi (VILL-eye): Tiny, fingerlike projections on the inner lining of the small intestine that increase the rate of nutrient absorption by greatly increasing the intestine's surface area.

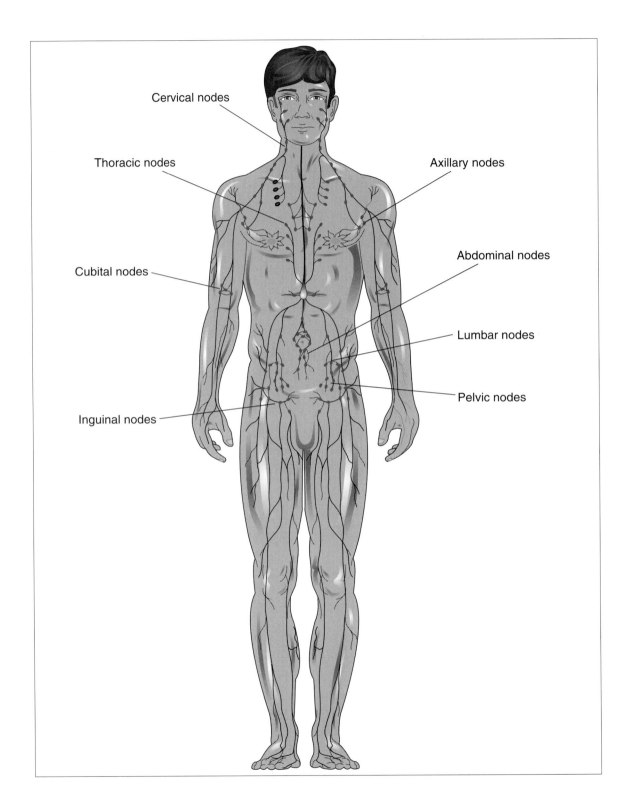

Cervical nodes

Thoracic nodes

Axillary nodes

Cubital nodes

Abdominal nodes

Lumbar nodes

Pelvic nodes

Inguinal nodes

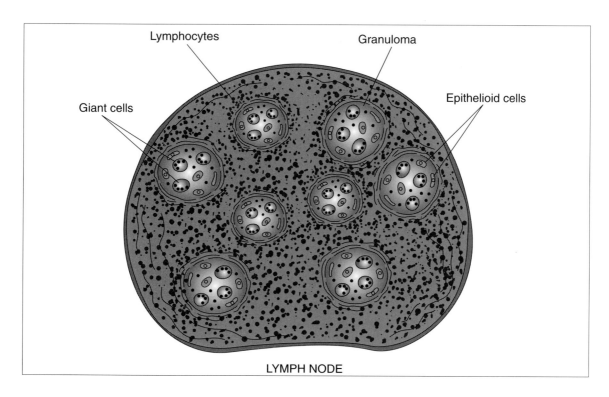

Lymphocytes

Granuloma

Giant cells

Epithelioid cells

LYMPH NODE

Lymph nodes are masses of lymphatic tissue that act as a filtering and cleansing system against disease-causing organisms. (Illustration by Electronic Illustrators Group.)

it from flowing backward into the ducts. The subclavian veins empty into the superior vena cava, which then empties into the right atrium of the heart.

Lymph nodes

Scattered along the pathways of lymph vessels are oval or kidney bean-shaped masses of lymphatic tissue called lymph nodes, which act as filters. These nodes range in size from microscopic to just under 1 inch (2.5 centimeters) in length. The smaller lymph nodes are often called lymph nodules.

Between 500 and 1,500 lymph nodes are located in the body; most of them usually occur in clusters or chains. Principal groupings are based in the neck, armpits, chest, abdomen, pelvis, and groin. The lymph nodes in the neck, armpits, and groin are especially important because they are located where the head, arms, and legs (the extremities) meet the main part of the body (the trunk). Most injuries to the skin, which allow bacteria and other pathogens (disease-causing organisms) to enter the body, are likely to occur

OPPOSITE: The basic components of the lymphatic system. (Illustration by Electronic Illustrators Group.)

along the extremities. The lymph nodes at the junctions of the extremities and trunk destroy the pathogens before they reach the main part of the body and the vital organs.

Each lymph node is enclosed in a fibrous capsule. Lymph enters the node through several small lymph vessels. Inside, bands of connective tissue divide the node into spaces known as sinuses. The specialized tissue in these sinuses harbors macrophages and lymphocytes, both of which are types of white blood cells. Macrophages engulf and destroy bacteria and other foreign substances in the lymph. Lymphocytes identify foreign substances and attempt to destroy them, also. If foreign invaders are abundant and macrophages and lymphocytes have to increase in number to defend the body against them, the lymph node often becomes swollen and tender. Once the lymph has been filtered and cleansed, it leaves the node through one or two other small lymph vessels.

THE BLACK DEATH

In 1347, several Italian merchant ships returned to Messina on the Mediterranean island of Sicily from a trip to the Black Sea. As the ships were docking, many sailors on board were dying of a strange and hideous disease. Within days, many residents of Messina and the surrounding countryside had been infected and were dying. Within four years, the disease had spread across Western Europe and 25 million people—roughly one-third the population of Europe at the time— lay dead in its wake.

The disease was called the "Black Death" because of the black spots it produced on the skin of its victims. It is more properly known as the bubonic plague (a plague is any contagious, widespread disease). In the course of recorded history, a number of major bubonic plagues have swept across Asia and Europe. The worst, however, was the outbreak in the fourteenth century. Because so many people died, there were serious labor shortages throughout Europe. Economic growth on the continent was halted for two centuries.

Historians believe this particular plague started in China sometime in the early 1330s. As one of the world's busiest trading nations at the time, China was a prime destination for the merchant ships of Europe. But those ships brought back to the West something no one bargained for.

Bubonic plague is an infectious disease caused by *Yersinia pestis,* a bacteria transmitted by fleas that have fed on the blood of infected rodents, usually rats. The fleas pass on the bacteria, in turn, when they bite a human. Humans may also become infected if they have a cut or break in the skin and come in direct contact with the body fluids or tissues of infected animals or other humans.

Once inside the human body, *Yersinia pestis* acts quickly. Within two to five days, victims experience fever, headache, nausea, vomiting, and aching joints. The lymph nodes, especially those in the groin, then suddenly become painful and swollen. The inflamed nodes, called *buboes* (from which the disease gets its name), swell with pus to about the size of a chicken's egg. They soon turn black, split open, and ooze pus and blood onto the skin. The infection, rampant in the lymphatic system, quickly spreads throughout the body. Blood appears in the victim's urine and stool, and everything coming out of the body smells horrible. When death finally comes less than a week after the victim contracts the disease, it is painful.

Isolated cases of bubonic plague continue to occur in widespread regions of the world. Since the disease is caused by a bacteria, it can be treated with antibiotics. If treated quickly, the plague can almost always be cured.

Tonsils and Peyer's patches

Both tonsils and Peyer's patches are small masses of lymphatic tissue (some sources consider them specialized lymph nodes). These tissues serve to prevent infection in the body at areas where bacteria is abundant. There are five tonsils: a pair on either side of the inner wall of the throat (palatine tonsils), one near the rear opening of the nasal cavity (pharyngeal tonsil), and a pair near the base of the tongue (lingual tonsils). This "ring" around the throat helps trap and remove any bacteria or other foreign pathogens entering the throat through breathing, eating, or drinking. Peyer's patches, which resemble tonsils, are located in the small intestine. The macrophages of Peyer's patches prevent infection of the intestinal wall by destroying the bacteria always present in the moist environment of the intestine.

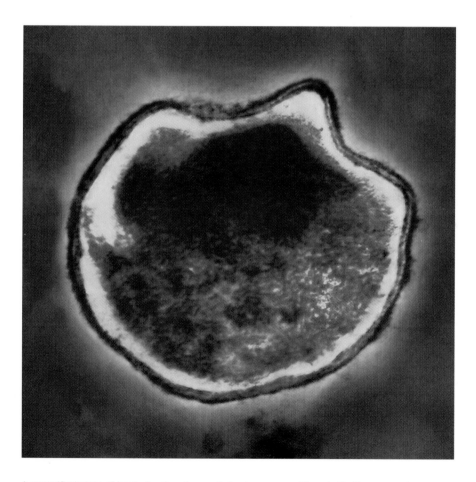

A magnified view of bacteria. Small, specialized masses of lymphatic tissue, such as tonsils and Peyer's patches, help trap and destroy bacteria in the body. (Photograph by Dr. Kari Lounatmaa. Reproduced by permission of Custom Medical Stock Photo.)

The spleen

The spleen is a soft, dark purple, bean-shaped organ located in the upper left side of the abdomen, just behind the bottom of the rib cage. It is the largest mass of lymphoid tissue in the body, measuring about 5 inches (12.7 centimeters) in length.

Though considered to be part of the lymphatic system, the spleen does not filter lymph (only lymph nodes do so). Instead, it filters and cleanses blood of bacteria, viruses, and other pathogens. It also destroys worn or old red blood cells. As blood flows through the spleen, macrophages lining the organ's tissues engulf and destroy both pathogens and worn red blood cells. Any remaining parts of decomposed red blood cells, such as iron, are returned to the body to be used again to form new red blood cells.

Other functions of the spleen include the production of lymphocytes, which the organ releases into the bloodstream, and blood storage. When the body demands additional blood, such as during stress or injury, the spleen contracts, forcing its stored blood into circulation.

The thymus

The thymus is a soft, flattened, pinkish-gray mass of lymphoid tissue located in the upper chest under the breastbone. In a fetus and newborn infant, the thymus is relatively large (about the size of an infant's fist). Up until about the age of puberty, the thymus continues to grow. After this point in life, it shrinks and gradually blends in with the surrounding tissue. Very little thymus tissue is found in adults.

Scientists did not fully understand the function of the thymus until the early 1960s. Only then was its role in developing body immunity discovered.

SCIENTISTS DID NOT FULLY UNDERSTAND THE FUNCTION OF THE THYMUS UNTIL THE EARLY 1960S.

In a fetus and infant, immature or not fully developed lymphocytes are produced in the bone marrow (the spongelike material that fills the cavities inside most bones). A certain group or class of these lymphocytes travel to the thymus where thymic hormones changed them into T lymphocytes or T cells (the letter T refers to the thymus). While maturing and multiplying in the thymus, T cells are "educated" to recognize the difference between cells that belong to the body ("self") and those that are foreign ("nonself"). Each T cell is programmed to respond to a specific chemical identification marker—called an antigen—on the surface of foreign or abnormal cells. Once they are fully mature, T cells then enter the bloodstream and circulate to the spleen, lymph nodes, and other lymphatic tissue.

Lymphocytes

Lymphocytes, the primary cells of the lymphatic system, make up roughly one-fourth of all white blood cells in the body. Like other white blood cells,

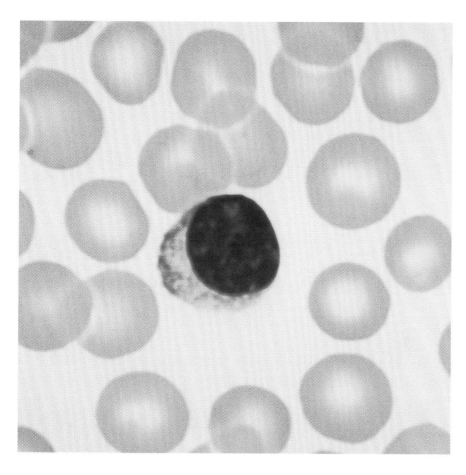

A microscopic view of a lymphocyte cell (center, in purple). Lymphocytes are the primary cells of the lymphatic system. (Photograph by Lester V. Bergman. Reproduced by permission of Corbis-Bettmann.)

they are produced in the red bone marrow. Lymphocytes constantly travel throughout the body, moving through tissues or through the blood or lymph vessels.

There are two major classes of lymphocytes: T cells and B cells. As already stated, the letter T refers to the thymus, where those lymphocytes mature. The letter B refers to the bone marrow, where that group of lymphocytes mature.

About three-quarters of the circulating lymphocytes are T cells. They carry out two main defensive functions: they kill invaders and orchestrate or control the actions of other lymphocytes involved in the immune process or response. In addition, T cells recognize and destroy any abnormal body cells, such as those that have become cancerous.

Like T cells, B cells are also programmed to recognize specific antigens on foreign cells. When stimulated during an immune response (such as when foreign cells enter the body), B cells undergo a change in structure. They then produce antibodies, which are protein compounds. These compounds bind with specific antigens of foreign cells, labeling those cells for destruction.

WORKINGS: HOW THE LYMPHATIC SYSTEM FUNCTIONS

The exchange of materials (oxygen, carbon dioxide, nutrients, and wastes) between the blood and the cells in the body occurs through the capillaries. In the body of an average person, over the course of an average day, roughly 25.4 quarts (24 liters) of plasma fluid are forced out of the capillaries into the interstitial fluid surrounding the cells. After bathing the cells, providing them with nutrients, and picking up their wastes, this fluid is drawn back into the capillaries. However, only 85 percent of the total fluid is drawn back into the bloodstream. The remaining 15 percent, roughly 3.8 quarts (3.6 liters), remains in the interstitial fluid.

If this small amount of fluid were allowed to accumulate over even a brief period of time, massive edema (swelling caused by excessive bodily fluid) would result. If left unchecked, the body would blow up like a balloon, tissues would be destroyed, and death would take place. This condition is prevented by the presence of lymph capillaries, which run alongside blood vessels in most tissue spaces. The lymph capillaries act as "drains," collecting the excess fluid and returning it to the venous blood just before the blood reaches the heart.

Proteins and other large molecules dissolved in the interstitial fluid cannot be absorbed by the blood capillaries. Because the walls of lymph capillaries are much more permeable (allow material to pass through easily), these large substances enter the lymph capillaries and are eventually returned to the blood.

This function of lymph capillaries is particularly important in the small intestine. Whereas carbohydrates and certain other nutrients are small enough to pass directly from the intestine into the bloodstream, fats are not. Lacteals (lymph capillaries in the small intestine) are able to absorb fats and other nutrients that are too large to enter blood capillaries. After digestion, the lymph in lacteals contains as much as 1 to 2 percent fat. Milky-white in appearance, this thick mixture of lymph and tiny fat globules is called chyle. It becomes mixed with the blood after lymph drains into the thoracic duct.

After the vessels of the lymphatic system have collected excess fluid, cellular wastes, proteins, fats, and other substances too large to enter the blood capillaries directly, they return all this material to the bloodstream. Before advancing to the heart and reentering the circulatory system, however, any fluid and matter that enters the lymphatic system must pass through at least one lymph node. It is very likely that foreign substances, such as viruses, bacteria, and even cancer cells, are a part of the lymph that has been collected from all parts of the body. Even the dark, gritty debris of polluted city air finds its way from the lungs of city dwellers into the lymph. Without the filtering abilities of lymph nodes, these foreign substances would overrun the body.

Immunity is the body's ability to defend itself against pathogens or other foreign material. The human body is awash in a sea of infectious agents such

Florence Rena Sabin. (Reproduced by permission of Corbis-Bettmann.)

SABIN AND THE LYMPHATIC SYSTEM

Florence Rena Sabin, a pioneering medical researcher and educator, helped settle a long-standing controversy: how the lymphatic system developed in the human body. In a field dominated by men, Sabin achieved much: she was the first woman faculty member at Johns Hopkins School of Medicine (as well as its first female professor) and the first woman elected to membership in the National Academy of Sciences.

Born in Central City, Colorado, in 1871, Sabin graduated from Smith College in Massachusetts with a bachelor of science degree in 1893. Three years later, she entered Johns Hopkins School

of Medicine. After graduating in 1900, Sabin was accepted as an intern at Johns Hopkins Hospital, a rare occurrence for a woman at the time. But her interest lay in research and teaching, and she was soon awarded a fellowship in the department of anatomy at Johns Hopkins School of Medicine.

In this position, Sabin began her studies of the lymphatic system. At the time, researchers were split over whether the lymphatic system developed separately from the vessels of the cardiovascular system. To find the definitive answer, Sabin studied pig embryos because they developed in a manner similar to humans. (An embryo is an organism in its earliest stages of development.)

After painstaking research, Sabin discovered that lymphatic vessels did, in fact, arise from veins. She found that the outer layer of cells on veins sprouted buds, much like stems growing out of the branches of trees. As these stems grew outward, they connected with each other. This proved that the lymphatic system developed entirely from existing vessels in the body. For her work on lymphatics, Sabin won the 1903 prize of the Naples Table Association, an organization that maintained a research position for women at the Zoological Station in Naples, Italy.

Throughout her career, Sabin continued to study the lymphatic system and the body's immune responses. She paid special attention to the bacterium that causes tuberculosis, an infectious disease marked by lesions on the lungs, bones, and other body tissues.

Sabin died in Denver, Colorado, in 1953.

as bacteria, viruses, fungi, and parasites. It provides an ideal habitat for many of them. If these organisms were to break through the barriers erected by the body, they would ultimately destroy it. To protect itself, the human body relies on two lines of defense: nonspecific and specific.

THE HUMAN BODY IS AWASH IN A SEA OF INFECTIOUS AGENTS SUCH AS BACTERIA, VIRUSES, FUNGI, AND PARASITES.

The nonspecific defense system

The nonspecific defense system prevents the entry and spread of foreign microorganisms throughout the body. It is a general defense that does not discriminate between one threat and another; it responds to protect the body from *all* foreign substances, whatever they are. Present at birth, it includes physical barriers and cellular/chemical defenses.

PHYSICAL BARRIERS. Physical barriers are the body's first line of defense against disease-causing microorganisms. These barriers include the skin and mucous membranes. The skin, the outer tissue covering of the body, forms a strong physical barrier to most microorganisms that swarm on its surface. Microorganisms are unable to penetrate the upper layers of dead skin cells. In addition, the secretions from sweat and sebaceous (oil) glands in the skin contain chemicals that inhibit the growth of bacteria.

The membranes that line all body cavities open to the exterior—digestive, respiratory, urinary, and reproductive tracts—secrete or release sticky mucus that traps microorganisms. To further trap or destroy foreign invaders, the membranes in some of these tracts also contain hairs or secrete a variety of protective chemicals.

For instance, nasal hairs in nasal passages filter and trap large microorganisms before they enter the trachea or windpipe. Those invaders that do get by are often caught in the cilia, the microscopic hairlike structures projecting from the mucous membrane lining the trachea. The cilia wave back and forth in rhythmic movement, and trapped particles are swept along up through the trachea and into the throat. From here, the mucus and particles are either expelled by sneezing or coughing or swallowed into the stomach.

The mucous membrane of the stomach secretes hydrochloric acid and protein-digesting enzymes. Both kill microorganisms. Bacteria is also destroyed by saliva in the mouth and tears in the eyes, which each contain an enzyme that breaks down the walls of bacteria cells.

PHAGOCYTES. If a microorganism is able to break through the body's surface barriers, such as through a scrape or cut, the body uses an enormous number of cells and chemicals to protect itself. Any bacteria or foreign material that enters the body is immediately confronted by phagocytes. These are types of white blood cells that destroy foreign particles by surrounding them and engulfing them—a process called phagocytosis. The largest group of phagocytes are macrophages (literally, "big eaters"). A macrophage, which arises from a white blood cell called a monocyte, can "eat" up to 100 bacteria.

Another group of cells in the nonspecific body defense line are natural killer or NK cells. These type of lymphocytes are a unique group of defensive cells. They constantly patrol the body, floating in blood and lymph, seeking out antigens on foreign or abnormal body cells (such as those infected with viruses or cancer). NK cells can react against any such cells—they are not specific. Unlike macrophages, however, they are not phagocytic. When confronted with a foreign or abnormal cell, an NK cell secretes proteins that dissolve the target cell's membrane and the cell quickly disintegrates.

A MACROPHAGE CAN "EAT" UP TO 100 BACTERIA.

INFLAMMATION. Inflammation is the body's second line of defense. It develops whenever body tissues are damaged by physical injury or infected by bacteria and viruses. Inflammation is localized, meaning it occurs only where the injury or infection has taken place. The four major symptoms marking inflammation are redness, heat, swelling, and pain.

The inflammation process begins when damaged cells release chemicals such as histamine into the surrounding interstitial fluid. Histamine and the other chemicals cause the local blood vessels to expand, which increases blood flow to the area (accounting for the redness and heat). This, in turn, brings more oxygen, nutrients, and white blood cells into the area to fight the infection and begin the healing process. The heat produced by the additional blood increases the rate at which nearby cells "work" and creates unfavorable conditions for bacterial growth. As the blood vessels expand, they also become more permeable, allowing plasma from the bloodstream to seep into the interstitial spaces. This causes edema or swelling, which then activates local pain receptors. Both swelling and pain restrict movement in the area, further aiding healing.

FEVER. The body also uses heat in a more general way to fight infection: fever. A fever is a continued overall body temperature greater than 99°F (37°C). The hypothalamus is a portion of the brain that controls many body functions, including body temperature. In a sense, the hypothalamus is the body's thermostat. When white blood cells and macrophages are exposed to bacteria and other foreign invaders, they secrete chemicals that signal the hypothalamus to raise body temperature. The added heat in the body deters the growth of bacteria and speeds up the repair processes in the damaged cells. However, the temperature range at which fevers are beneficial is limited. High fevers—with temperatures over 104°F (40°C)—can damage many organ systems.

INTERFERONS. In 1957, scientists discovered another nonspecific defense mechanism: small protein compounds called interferons. Once infected with a virus, damaged cells help defend nearby uninfected cells by releasing interferons. These proteins travel to normal cells and bind to their membranes. Once attached, the interferons cause the normal cells to produce substances that prevent the virus from reproducing within those cells.

The specific defense system

The specific defense system is sometimes referred to as the body's third line of defense. Like the nonspecific defense system, it seeks out foreign invaders and acts to disable or destroy them. Unlike its sister system, however, the specific defense system recognizes and acts against particular foreign invaders or abnormal body cells. It is not limited in its actions to the initial site of infection, but functions throughout the entire body. It also has a "memory," mounting a quicker and stronger attack against viruses and bacteria when it encounters them a second time. For all these reasons, the specific defense system is much more effective in defending the body and establishing immunity.

The two separate but overlapping classes of lymphocytes—B cells and T cells—lead the specific immune response. The class called into play depends on the type of foreign or infected cells present in the body. B cells defend against invading bacteria and viruses. Because B cells produce antibodies to attack specific antigens, the immune response launched by B cells is called antibody-mediated immunity. T cells also defend the body against viruses, parasites, fungi, and other invaders. In addition, they attack body cells infected by viruses and bacteria and those that are cancerous. Because T cells attack pathogens directly, their immune response is called cell-mediated immunity.

T CELLS AND IMMUNITY. Cell-mediated immunity is triggered when a macrophage encounters a foreign or infected cell. The macrophage engulfs the cell, breaks it down, then "displays" fragments of that cell's antigens (chemical identification markers) on the outer surface of its membrane. The macrophage then "presents" itself to a T cell that been trained to recognize those specific antigens as nonself or foreign. Once this occurs, the T cell becomes activated and divides into four types: helper T cells, killer (or cytotoxic) T cells, suppressor T cells, and memory T cells. These T cells then travel to the point of infection in the body.

Helper T cells direct or manage the immune response, not only at the site of infection but throughout the body. They stimulate the production of more T cells and antibodies by B cells. They also attract other types of protective white blood cells into the infected area and spur the actions of killer T cells. As their name suggests, killer T cells are responsible for the destruction of foreign or abnormal cells. They kill a target cell by binding with it and injecting a chemical into the target cell, rupturing its membrane.

Once the invading or abnormal cells have been destroyed and the infection has been brought under control, suppressor T cells take over. They release chemicals that slow down and eventually stop the action of other T cells and B cells. This prevents the immune response from remaining active when it is not necessary and possibly harming normal body cells.

Most of the T cells gathered to fight infected or abnormal body cells die after only a few days. Those that remain are called memory T cells. Their job is to "remember" the antigens of each invader or abnormal cell so that if they appear again in the future, the body will be able to respond quickly and efficiently. Memory T cells are long-lived, often surviving in the body for up to twenty years or more.

B CELLS AND IMMUNITY. Antibody-mediated immunity is activated when a B cell encounters its triggering antigen on the surface of a macrophage. B cells can also be activated by chemicals secreted by helper T cells that have already encountered specific antigens. In either case, once a B cell has been activated, it divides numerous times into plasma cells and memory B cells.

Anthony S. Fauci. (Reproduced by permission of AP/Wide World Photos.)

LEADING THE FIGHT AGAINST AIDS

Since 1981, Anthony S. Fauci has play a significant part in AIDS research in the United States. As director of the National Institute of Allergy and Infectious Diseases (NIAID) and the Office of AIDS Research at the National Institutes of Health (NIH), Fauci supervises the ongoing investigation of how the disease works and the development of vaccines and drugs to treat and cure it.

Born in 1940 in Brooklyn, New York, Fauci attended Cornell University Medical School, graduating in 1966. Three years later, he became a clinical associate in the Laboratory of Clinical Investigation of NIAID. He has worked for the NIH ever since.

From the beginning of his medical career, Fauci has focused on the functioning of the body's immune responses and the impact of infectious diseases on them. By 1971, he had found cures for three diseases affecting body immunity.

When AIDS became recognized in the United States in 1981, Fauci was already deputy clinical director of NIAID. He immediately shifted the focus of the Laboratory of Clinical Investigation to the investigation of AIDS. The lab then made the important discovery of how HIV affects helper T cells.

During his tenure at the NIH, Fauci has worked not only against AIDS but against government indifference to the disease. He has won increasingly larger budgets for research. Fauci and his laboratory teams continue to search for an AIDS vaccine and to develop drug therapies to try to help those people already afflicted.

The many plasma cells that descend from a B cell have the ability to produce antibodies (also called gamma globulins). These Y-shaped proteins attach themselves to the foreign antigen. Each antibody produced matches only one antigen, much like a key matches a specific lock. Often the fit is precise; other times it is not. Regardless, once the antibody interlocks with the antigen, it either transforms the cell into a harmless substance or marks the entire antibody-plus-foreign cell package for destruction by phagocytes.

Memory B cells perform the same immunity function as memory T cells: to quicken and strengthen the immune response. Long-lived, they remain in the body to face the same antigens should they appear again. Once that exposure takes place, the memory B cells immediately divide and multiply into antibody-secreting plasma cells.

TYPES OF BODY IMMUNITY. The human body is protected by two types of immunity: genetic and acquired.

Genetic or inherited immunity is present in the body from birth. It does not involve an immune response or the production of antibodies. Because of the structure of human DNA (deoxyribonucleic acid; the genetic material

Edward Jenner. (Reproduced by permission of the Library of Congress.)

HOW THE SMALLPOX VIRUS AROSE

The first effective vaccine was developed against smallpox, a fast-spreading disease characterized by high fever and sores on the skin. Prior to the eighteenth century, the disease was common and often fatal. In 1796, while a smallpox epidemic raged in Europe, English physician Edward Jenner (1749–1823) tested a theory. He had observed that people who had been in contact with cows did not develop smallpox. Instead, they developed cowpox, a similar, milder disease of cows that was not a threat to human life. Jenner believed that individuals who had been infected with cowpox had developed an immunity to the more severe human smallpox.

Taking cowpox fluid from the sores of a milkmaid named Sarah Nelmes, Jenner rubbed it into cuts on the arm of eight-year-old James Phipps. A few days later, the boy came down with a mild case of cowpox, but soon recovered. Six weeks later, Jenner gave young Phipps some fluid from a person who had smallpox and he was not affected. His body had developed an immunity against the disease. Jenner called his procedure vaccination, from the Latin *vaccinus,* meaning "of cows."

In 1980 the World Health Organization declared the eradication of smallpox, the only infectious disease to be completely eliminated.

determining the makeup of all cells), humans are not subject to certain diseases that dogs and other animals are, and vice-versa. For example, humans cannot contract distemper; however, dogs and cats can. Conversely, humans can suffer from measles; dogs and cats cannot. The genetic makeup of human cells (and of animal and plant cells, also) makes it impossible for certain pathogens to infect and reproduce in those cells.

Acquired immunity is just that: resistance to a pathogen that has been acquired or developed. Involving the production of antibodies, that resistance may evolve actively or passively.

Active immunity is formed when B cells encounter antigens and produce antibodies against them. As an individual grows from birth and develops bacterial and viral infections, antibodies are produced in the body to defend it against subsequent attacks. During a lifetime, an individual's active immunity is continually updated and enlarged. Active immunity may also be gained through artificial means: vaccines. A vaccine is a substance made of weakened or killed bacteria or viruses. When injected (or taken orally) into the body, it stimulates the production of antibodies specific to that particular infectious disease. Too weak to take over the body, the harmful microorganisms are destroyed. In the process, the body has developed memory B cells that can react quickly and effectively when threatened by that particular disease in the future. Developing immunity through deliberate exposure to a disease is called immunization.

Passive immunity differs from active immunity in two ways: the antibodies involved come from an outside source and they provide only short-term resistance. Memory B cells are not produced as a result. An example of passive immunity occurs between a pregnant woman and her fetus. During pregnancy, antibodies produced by the mother cross the placenta (the membrane lining the uterus through which nutrients and oxygen pass from mother to fetus) and enter the fetus's circulation. These antibodies remain for several months after birth, protecting the baby from diseases to which the mother is immune (they remain longer if the mother breast-feeds). They are then naturally removed from the baby's circulation and are not replaced. Antibodies may also be given to individuals who are already fighting infection. Antivenins used to treat poisonous snake or spider bites are examples of such antibody preparations that provide immediate but short-term protection.

AILMENTS: WHAT CAN GO WRONG WITH THE LYMPHATIC SYSTEM

By its very nature, the lymphatic system is involved whenever the body is fighting against foreign pathogens or abnormal body cells. The lymph nodes (especially in the neck) often swell with bacteria and lymphocytes when the body is battling common illnesses such as colds and influenza.

However, certain diseases and disorders target the lymphatic system. Some slow down the ability of the system to work; others literally shut it down. The result can be life threatening.

The following are a few of the diseases that can impair the lymphatic system or its parts.

AIDS/HIV

AIDS (acquired immune deficiency syndrome) has been described as the plague of the twentieth century. Since 1981, when it was first recognized in the United States, the disease has claimed almost 14 million lives worldwide. AIDS is currently the leading cause of death among all men between the ages of twenty-five and forty-four. The World Health Organization (a specialized agency of the United Nations) estimates that at the beginning of the twenty-first century, 40 million people worldwide will be infected with HIV, the virus that causes AIDS. Once infected, individuals may not develop symptoms of the disease for as many as ten years or more.

UNITED STATES HIV/AIDS STATISTICS, 1981–1997

Year	Cases diagnosed	Deaths
1981	316	120
1982	1,170	449
1983	3,068	1,478
1984	6,216	3,454
1985	11,740	6,854
1986	18,977	11,942
1987	28,499	16,118
1988	35,343	20,800
1989	42,453	27,423
1990	48,266	31,145
1991	59,318	36,220
1992	78,117	40,674
1993	78,164	44,108
1994	70,431	48,110
1995	65,614	47,858
1996	54,237	34,557
1997	30,986	14,185

HIV (human immunodeficiency virus) impairs the body's ability to produce an immune response. Specifically, the virus infects helper T cells. Once inside a helper T cell, HIV can replicate or reproduce within the cell and kill it in ways that are still not completely understood. When the newly formed viruses break out of the dying helper T cell, they continue the cycle by infecting other helper T cells. In response, the body produces more helper T cells, but this only provides the virus with more hosts in which to grow and spread.

Because helper T cells play a central role in directing the body's immune response, their destruction brings about a drop in cell-mediated immunity. The number of antibodies produced in the body declines, leaving it without defenses against a wide range of invaders. Many different types of infections and cancers can develop, taking advantage of the body's weakened immune response. These infections, normally harmless when the body is functioning properly, are known as opportunistic infections.

HIV is transmitted between humans in blood, semen, and vaginal secretions. The two main ways to contract the virus are by sharing a needle with a drug user who is HIV-positive or by having unprotected sexual relations with a person who is HIV-positive. (A person who is HIV-positive is already infected with the virus.)

HIV/AIDS WORLWIDE ESTIMATES: BEGINNING OF 1999

People living with HIV/AIDS: 33.4 million

New HIV infections in 1998: 5.8 million

Deaths due to HIV/AIDS in 1998: 2.5 million

Total number of deaths due to HIV/AIDS: 13.9 million

It is possible for a pregnant woman who is HIV-positive to transfer the virus to the fetus in her womb. A few individuals have become infected with the virus after receiving a transfusion of contaminated blood.

HIV cannot be transferred through insect bites or stings nor through shaking hands or hugging. No one can contract the virus by sharing telephones or eating utensils, by drinking out of public water fountains, or by swimming in public pools.

There is currently no cure for the disease and no vaccine to prevent its spread. The best defense against AIDS is avoiding sexual contact with infected individuals. Intravenous drug use (injecting drugs into the bloodstream) of any kind should always be avoided. Several antiviral drugs have been developed that slow the progress of the disease in infected individuals. Combinations of these drugs—known informally as cocktails—have proven effective in improving the quality and length of life of AIDS patients, especially those who have been diagnosed in the early stages of the disease.

Medical research findings released in April 1999, however, have shown that the virus can "hide" in memory T cells for up to sixty years. When called upon to fight an infection, such as influenza, the memory T cells could flood an individual's system with HIV.

Allergies

An allergy is an abnormal immune reaction to an otherwise harmless substance. Among the most common of medical disorders, allergies affect an estimated 60 million Americans, or more than one in every five people.

Normally, when a foreign microorganism enters the body, antibodies are produced to bind to the antigens on the foreign particles, and a series of immune reactions take place. When harmless, everyday substances cause the same series of immune reactions, the condition is known as allergy. The offending substance is called an allergen.

Common allergens abound. People may react to airborne particles (plant pollens, animal fur, house dust, cigarette smoke), food (nuts, eggs, fish, milk), drugs (penicillin or other antibiotics), insect bites (bees, wasps, mosquitoes, fleas), or even materials (wool and latex).

Symptoms depend on the specific type of allergic reaction. In the most common type of reaction, antibodies stimulated by the allergen cause certain cells to release histamine into the surrounding interstitial fluid. Histamine causes small blood vessels in the area to expand and become "leaky." Excess fluid and mucus develop, and the common symptoms appear: a runny nose, a scratchy or irritated throat, and red, watery eyes. Allergens that cause a reaction on the skin produce reddened, itchy skin. Those that affect the digestive tract may cause a swelling or tingling in the lips or throat, nausea, cramping, or diarrhea. Most reactions begin within seconds after contact with the allergen and last about half an hour. Some may last from one to several hours after contact.

A large number of prescriptions and over-the-counter drugs can treat the symptoms of allergies. Antihistamines, decongestants, and nasal sprays can all be used to decrease or counteract the effect of histamines. Lotions and creams to reduce skin inflammation caused by allergens are also available.

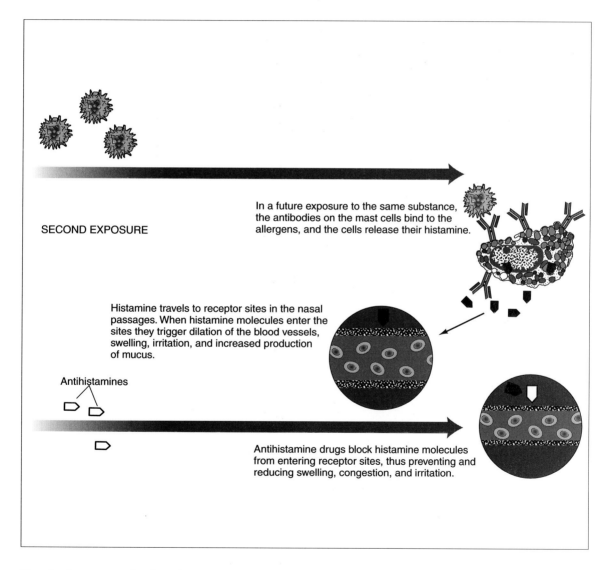

SECOND EXPOSURE

In a future exposure to the same substance, the antibodies on the mast cells bind to the allergens, and the cells release their histamine.

Histamine travels to receptor sites in the nasal passages. When histamine molecules enter the sites they trigger dilation of the blood vessels, swelling, irritation, and increased production of mucus.

Antihistamines

Antihistamine drugs block histamine molecules from entering receptor sites, thus preventing and reducing swelling, congestion, and irritation.

The allergic response. An allergy is an abnormal immune reaction to an otherwise harmless substance. (Illustration by Hans & Cassady.)

Avoiding allergens is the best way to limit allergic reactions. This is especially true for food allergies. Learning to recognize and avoid those items that produce an allergic reaction allows most people with allergies to lead normal lives.

Autoimmune diseases

Autoimmune diseases are those in which the body produces antibodies and T cells that attack and damage the body's own normal cells, causing tissue destruction. It is a puzzling phenomenon. The reaction can either take place in a number of tissues at the same time or in a single organ. The following are just a few of the many types of autoimmune diseases.

Graves' disease, also called hyperthyroidism, occurs when an antibody binds to specific cells in the thyroid gland, forcing them to secrete excess thyroid hormone. Symptoms of the condition include weight loss with increased appetite, shortness of breath, tiredness, weak muscles, anxiety, and visible en-

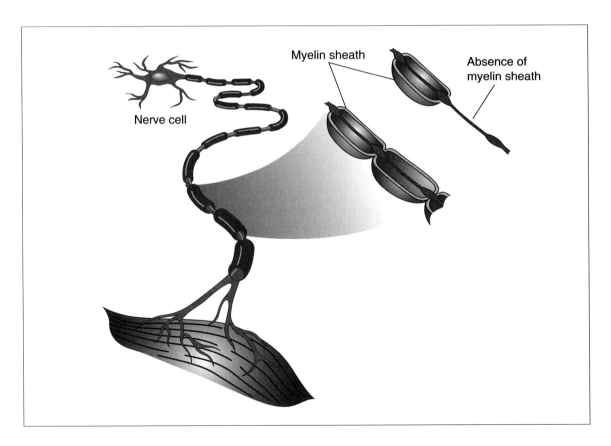

Multiple sclerosis is an immune cell attack on myelin, the insulation covering nerve fibers in the central nervous system. (Illustration by Electronic Illustrators Group.)

largement of the thyroid gland. Treatments include drugs to stop the hormone production, radioactive iodine to destroy the hormone-producing cells and shrink the enlarged gland, and surgery to remove a part or all of the thyroid.

Multiple sclerosis (MS) is a disease in which immune cells attack and destroy the insulation covering nerve fibers (neurons) in the central nervous system (brain and spinal cord). Once the insulation, called myelin, is destroyed, nerve messages are sent more slowly and less efficiently. As a result, the brain and spinal cord no longer communicate properly with the rest of the body. When this occurs, vision, balance, strength, sensation, coordination, and other bodily functions all suffer. More than 250,000 people in the United States are afflicted with MS. Women are twice as likely to get the disease as men. Drugs have been developed that slow the progress of the disease in many patients, but no cure has yet been found.

Systemic lupus erythematosus (also called lupus or SLE) is a disease in which antibodies begin to attack the body's own tissues and organs as if they

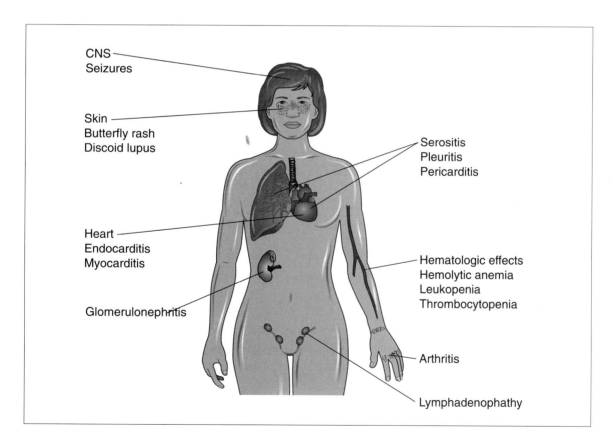

The autoimmune disease systemic lupus erythematosus can affect nearly every system in the body. (Illustration by Electronic Illustrators Group.)

were foreign. The cause of SLE is unknown. It can affect both men and women of all ages, but 90 percent of those afflicted are women. Among the many symptoms of the disease are fevers, weakness, muscle pain, weight loss, skin rashes, joint pain, headaches, vomiting, diarrhea, and inflammation of the lining of the lungs or the lining around the heart. Treatment for SLE depends on how severe the symptoms are. Mild symptoms like inflammation can be treated with aspirin or ibuprofen. Severe symptoms are often treated with stronger drugs, including steroids. Drugs to decrease the body's immune response may also be used for severely ill SLE patients.

Lymphadenitis

Lymphadenitis is the inflammation of lymph nodes. The cause is often an infection of the nodes by bacteria that has entered through a cut or wound in the skin. A virus may also be the cause. The infection may occur in a limited number of nodes in a specific area or in many nodes over a wider area. If the lymph vessels connecting the affected nodes are also inflamed, that condition is known as lymphangitis.

The swollen nodes are often painful to the touch. The skin over the nodes may also be red and warm to the touch. If the accompanying lymph vessels are involved in the infection, they will appear as red streaks from the wound to the lymph nodes. In children, the swollen nodes often appear in the neck because they are close to the ears and throat—locations of frequent bacterial infections in children.

Treatment for lymphadenitis and lymphangitis usually involves medications. Antibiotics, such as penicillin, are often prescribed, and the infection is brought under control in three to four days. If left untreated, the infection may lead to blood poisoning, which is sometimes fatal.

Lymphoma

Lymphoma is a type of cancer in which cells of the lymphatic system (B cells and T cells) become abnormal and begin to grow uncontrollably. Because lymphatic tissue is found throughout the body, lymphomas can occur anywhere. There are many types of lymphomas, but they are generally divided into two main groups: Hodgkin's lymphoma and non-Hodgkin's lymphomas. The exact cause of the cancers in either group is not known.

Hodgkin's lymphoma (or Hodgkin's disease) can occur at any age, although people in early adulthood (ages fifteen to thirty-four) and late adulthood (after age sixty) are most affected. The cancer begins in a lymph node (usually in the neck), causing swelling and possibly pain. After affecting one group of nodes, it progresses on to the next. In advanced cases of the cancer, the spleen, liver, and bone marrow may also be affected. Symptoms

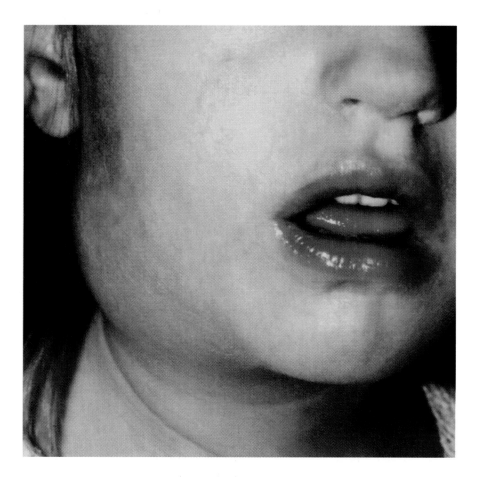

A patient suffering from lymphadenitis, an inflammation of one or more lymph nodes often caused by a bacterial infection. (Reproduced by permission of Custom Medical Stock Photo.)

include fatigue, weight loss, night sweats, and itching. As the cancer spreads throughout the body, the immune response becomes less effective. Common infections caused by bacteria and viruses begin to take over.

Hodgkin's lymphoma is one of the most curable forms of cancer. However, as with any form of cancer, early detection and treatment is highly recommended. Once detected in the body, Hodgkin's is usually treated through chemotherapy (using a combination of drugs to kill the cancer cells and shrink any tumors) or radiation therapy (using X rays or other high-energy rays to kill the cancer cells and shrink any tumors) or a combination of both.

Non-Hodgkin's lymphomas encompass over twenty-nine types of lymphomas. Again, the exact cause of these lymphomas is unknown. In general,

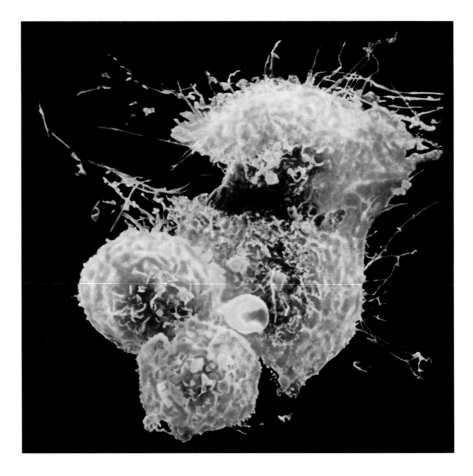

Hodgkin's lymphoma cells. This form of cancer begins in a lymph node—often in the neck—then progresses to other nodes. (Photograph by Andrejs Liepins. Reproduced by permission of Photo Researchers, Inc.)

males suffer from these cancers more than females. People between the ages of sixty and sixty-nine are at the highest risk of contracting these lymphomas. Non-Hodgkin's lymphomas also tend to strike people suffering from AIDS. Symptoms for non-Hodgkin's lymphomas are similar those for Hodgkin's lymphoma. Along with the swelling of lymph nodes, patients may experience loss of appetite, weight loss, nausea, vomiting, pain in the lower back, headaches, fevers, and night sweats. The liver and spleen may enlarge, as well. Immune responses may be weakened.

Treatment for non-Hodgkin's lymphomas also include chemotherapy and radiation therapy (either by themselves or in combination). In severe cases, bone marrow transplants may take place. Since the "cure" rate for non-Hodgkin's lymphomas is not as good as it is for Hodgkin's lymphoma, early detection and treatment is vital.

Tonsillitis

Tonsillitis is an infection and swelling of the tonsils. The condition is caused by bacteria or viruses that have entered the body through the mouth or sinuses. In addition to swollen and red tonsils, symptoms include a mild or severe sore throat, fever, chills, muscle aches, earaches, and tiredness. Although anyone can be afflicted with tonsillitis, the disease is most common in children between the ages of five and ten.

For mild cases of tonsillitis, treatment usually involves bed rest and drinking extra fluids. The body usually brings the infection under control within a few days. If the case is more severe, penicillin or other antibiotics may be prescribed to combat the infection. If an individual suffers repeatedly from

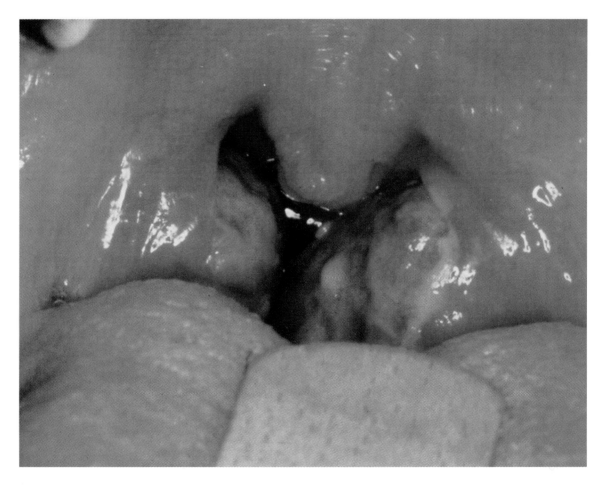

Tonsillitis, an infection and swelling of the tonsils, is caused by bacteria or viruses. (Photograph by NMSB. Reproduced by permission of Custom Medical Stock Photo.)

severe tonsillitis, the tonsils may be removed surgically. That procedure is called a tonsillectomy.

TAKING CARE: KEEPING THE LYMPHATIC SYSTEM HEALTHY

It is important to keep the lymphatic system healthy as it is a vital part of body immunity and overall health. Since the system is closely allied with the cardiovascular system, approaches to keeping that system healthy are recommended for the lymphatic system, also.

> IT IS IMPORTANT TO KEEP THE LYMPHATIC SYSTEM HEALTHY AS IT IS A VITAL PART OF BODY IMMUNITY AND OVERALL HEALTH.

The following all play a part in keeping the lymphatic system operating at peak efficiency: proper nutrition, healthy amounts of good-quality drinking water, adequate rest, regular exercise, and stress reduction.

If left unchecked, infection can quickly weaken the body's immune response, leading to serious health problems. It is best to avoid sources of disease, infection, pollution, and other unsanitary substances. Caring for the body by practicing good hygiene will reduce the threat of infection from ever-present bacteria and viruses in the environment. Injuries such as scrapes, cuts, and wounds should be properly cleansed and cared for to prevent infection or the spread of infection. Serious injuries should be treated immediately by qualified medical personnel.

FOR MORE INFORMATION

Books

Aaseng, Nathan. *Autoimmune Disease.* New York: Franklin Watts, 1995.

Edelson, Edward. *The Immune System.* New York: Chelsea House, 1990.

Friedlander, Mark P., and Terry M. Phillips, Ph.D. *The Immune System: Your Body's Disease-Fighting Army.* Minneapolis, MN: Lerner Publications, 1998.

Kendall, Marion. *Dying to Live: How Our Bodies Fight Disease.* Cambridge, England: Cambridge University Press, 1998.

WWW Sites

Human Body Project: Lymphatic System
http://www.trms.ga.net/~jtucker/students/human/lymphatic
Site provides a brief overview of the lymphatic system: its functions and major organs, its interaction with other body systems, and the various diseases and disorders that can affect it.

Human Lymphatic System Tutorial
    http://www.pblsh.com/Healthworks/lymphart.html
    An article that provides a nontechnical overview of the lymphatic
    system, focusing on its parts and what can go wrong.

Lymphatic System
    http://www.bae.ncsu.edu/bae/courses/bae495g/1998/slides/ lymph/
    index.htm
    Site contains fifty-four slides (links) that provide information or
    answer questions about the lymphatic system and its various parts.

Lymphoma Resources Page
    http://www.alumni.caltech.edu/~mike/lymphoma.html
    An extensive and well-organized site presenting information on
    Hodgkin's disease and non-Hodgkin's lymphoma as they affect both
    adults and children. Also includes a glossary and a list of books
    focusing on lymphomas.

National Center for HIV, STD, & TB Prevention
    http://www.cdc.gov/nchstp/hiv_aids/dhap.htm
    Homepage of the CDC's division of HIV/AIDS prevention. Presents
    recent information on HIV and AIDS.

Non-Hodgkin's Lymphoma Web Page
    http://www.nh-lymphoma.mcmail.com/
    A site developed by a sufferer of non-Hodgkin's lymphoma to provide
    readers with a view of the disease, covering initial symptoms,
    diagnosis, treatment, and possible cures.

Understanding Lymphoma
    http://www.lymphoma.ca/llsdt.htm
    A site run by the Lymphoma Research Foundation of Canada that
    provides an overview of the lymphatic system and the causes,
    diagnosis, and treatment of lymphomas.

Virtual Anatomy Textbook: The Lymphatic System
    http://www.acm.uiuc.edu/sigbio/project/updated-lymphatic/lymph1.html
    Site provides a brief but informative look into the body's defense
    system. Text and illustrations/pictures explain the various parts of
    the lymphatic system.

6

The Muscular System

The muscular system is the body's network of tissues that controls movement both of the body and within it. Walking, running, jumping: all these actions propelling the body through space are possible only because of the contraction (shortening) and relaxation of muscles. These major movements, however, are not the only ones directed by muscular activity. Muscles make it possible to stand, sit, speak, and blink. Even more, were it not for muscles, blood would not rush through blood vessels, air would not fill lungs, and food would not move through the digestive system. In short, muscles are the machines of the body, allowing it to work.

DESIGN: PARTS OF THE MUSCULAR SYSTEM

The muscles of the body are divided into three main types: skeletal, smooth, and cardiac. As their name implies, skeletal muscles are attached to the skeleton and move various parts of the body. They are composed of tissue fibers that are striated or striped. The alternating bands of light and dark result from the pattern of the filaments (threadlike proteins) within each muscle cell. Skeletal muscles are called voluntary muscles because a person controls their use, such as in the flexing of an arm or the raising of a foot.

There are just over 650 skeletal muscles in the whole human body. Some authorities state there are as many as 850 muscles in the body. No exact figure is available because scientists disagree about which ones are separate muscles and which ones are part of larger muscles. There is also some variability in muscular structure between individuals.

Smooth muscles are found in the stomach and intestinal walls, in artery and vein walls, and in various hollow organs. They are called involuntary muscles because a person generally cannot consciously control them. They are regulated by the autonomic nervous system (a division of the nervous

OPPOSITE: Some of the estimated over 800 muscles in the human body. No exact figure is available because scientists disagree about which ones are separate muscles and which ones are part of larger muscles. (Illustration by Kopp Illustration, Inc.)

system that affects internal organs such as the heart, lungs, stomach, and liver). Unlike skeletal muscles, smooth muscles have no striations or stripes.

In a vessel or organ, smooth muscles are arranged in sheets or layers. Often, there are two layers, one running circularly (around) and the other longitudinally (up and down). As the two layers alternately contract and relax, the shape of the vessel or organ changes and fluid or food is propelled along. Smooth muscles contract slowly and can remain contracted for a long period of time without tiring.

Cardiac muscle, called the myocardium, is found in only one place in the body: the heart. It is a unique type of muscle. Like skeletal muscle, it is

WORDS TO KNOW

Acetylcholine (ah-see-til-KOE-leen): Neurotransmitter chemical released at the neuromuscular junction by motor neurons that translates messages from the brain to muscle fibers.

Adenosine triphosphate (ah-DEN-o-seen try-FOS-fate): High-energy molecule found in every cell in the body.

Aerobic metabolism (air-ROH-bic muh-TAB-uh-lizm): Chemical reactions that require oxygen in order to create adenosine triphosphate.

Antagonist (an-TAG-o-nist): Muscle that acts in opposition to a prime mover.

Cramp: Prolonged muscle spasm.

Fascicle (FA-si-kul): Bundle of myofibrils wrapped together by connective tissue.

Lactic acid (LAK-tik ASS-id): Chemical waste product created when muscle fibers break down glucose without the proper amount of oxygen.

Muscle tone: Sustained partial contraction of certain muscle fibers in all muscles.

Myofibrils (my-o-FIE-brilz): cylindrical structures lying within skeletal muscle fibers that are com-

posed of repeating structural units called sarcomeres.

Myofilament (my-o-FILL-ah-ment): Protein filament composing the myofibrils; can be either thick (composed of myosin) or thin (composed of actin).

Neuromuscular junction (nu-row-MUSS-ku-lar JUNK-shun): Region where a motor neuron comes into close contact with a muscle fiber.

Prime mover (or agonist): Muscle whose contractions are chiefly responsible for producing a particular movement.

Rigor mortis (RIG-er MOR-tis): Rigid state of the body after death due to irreversible muscle contractions.

Sarcomere (SAR-koh-meer): Unit of contraction in a skeletal muscle fiber containing a precise arrangement of thick and thin myofilaments.

Spasm: Sudden, involuntary muscle contraction.

Strain: Slight tear in a muscle; also called a pulled muscle.

Synergist (SIN-er-jist): Muscle that cooperates with another to produce a particular movement.

Tendon (TEN-den): Tough, white, cordlike tissue that attaches muscle to bone.

Muscular System

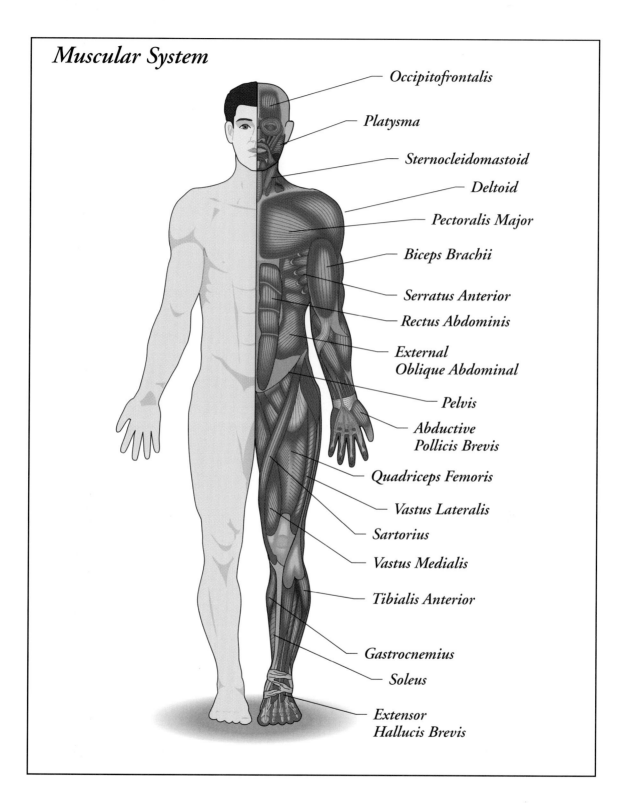

Occipitofrontalis

Platysma

Sternocleidomastoid

Deltoid

Pectoralis Major

Biceps Brachii

Serratus Anterior

Rectus Abdominis

External
Oblique Abdominal

Pelvis

Abductive
Pollicis Brevis

Quadriceps Femoris

Vastus Lateralis

Sartorius

Vastus Medialis

Tibialis Anterior

Gastrocnemius

Soleus

Extensor
Hallucis Brevis

striated. But like smooth muscle, it is involuntary, controlled by the autonomic nervous system. The myocardium is composed of thick bundles of muscle that are twisted and whorled into ringlike arrangements. Forming the walls of the chambers of the heart, the myocardium contracts to pump blood throughout the body (for a further discussion of its actions, see chapter 1).

Of the three types of muscle, skeletal are probably the most familiar. They stabilize joints, help maintain posture, and give the body its general shape. In men, they make up about 40 percent of the body's mass or weight; in women, about 23 percent. Since the term muscular system refers specifically to skeletal muscles, the remainder of this chapter will focus on them.

Structure of muscle cells

Each muscle is made of hundreds to thousands of individual muscle cells. Unlike most other cells in the body, these cells are unusually shaped: they are elongated like a cylinder or a long rod. Because of their shape, muscle cells are normally referred to as muscle fibers. Whereas most cells have a single nucleus (the part of the cell that controls its activities), muscle fibers have as many as 100 or more nuclei. The nuclei are located on the surface of the fiber, just under its thin membrane. Another difference between muscle fibers and other body cells is their size. They can extend the entire length of a muscle. For example, a muscle fiber in a thigh muscle could measure 0.0004 inch (0.001 centimeter) in diameter and 12 to 16 inches (30 to 40 centimeters) in length.

Each muscle fiber is composed of hundreds of smaller filaments or threads called myofibrils (the prefix myo- comes from the Latin word *myos,* meaning "muscle"). Each myofibril contains bundles of threadlike proteins or filaments called myofilaments, which can be either thick or thin. The larger thick myofilaments are made mostly of bundled molecules of the protein myosin. The thin myofilaments are composed of the protein actin.

RIGOR MORTIS

When a person dies, blood stops circulating through the body. The skeletal muscles (along with all other parts of the body) are deprived of oxygen and nutrients, including ATP. Calcium ions leak out of their storage area in the membranes of muscle fibers, causing thick myofilaments to attach to and pull thin myofilaments. While the muscle fibers still have a stored supply of ATP, the heads of thick myofilaments are able to detach from the thin myofilaments. When the supply of ATP runs out, however, the heads cannot detach and the muscle fibers stay in a contracted position.

The rigid state of muscle contraction that results is called rigor mortis. Depending on the person's physical condition at death, the onset of rigor mortis may vary from ten minutes to several hours after death. Facial muscles are usually affected first, followed by other parts of the body. Rigor mortis lasts until the muscle fibers begin to decompose fifteen to twenty-five hours after death.

In each myofibril, the thick and thin myofilaments are combined into thousands of units or segments that repeat over and over. These units are called sarcomeres. Thick myofilaments lie in the center of a sarcomere. Thin myofilaments are attached at either end of a sarcomere and extend toward the center, passing among the thick myofilaments. This regular arrangement of the varying myofilaments within each sarcomere produces the striated or striped appearance of each myofibril and, by extension, of muscle fibers.

As are most living cells, muscle fibers are soft and fragile. Even so, they can exert tremendous power without being ripped apart. The reason is that muscles are composed of different types of tissue (like all other organs in the body). In addition, those tissues are bundled together, providing strength and support. Each myofibril is enclosed in a delicate sheath or covering made of connective tissue (tissue found everywhere in the body that connects body parts, providing support, storage, and protection). Numerous sheathed myofibrils are then bundled together and wrapped with thicker connective tissue to form what is called a fascicle (from the Latin word *fasciculus,* meaning "a bundle"). Many fascicles are then bundled together by an even tougher coat of connective tissue to form the muscle.

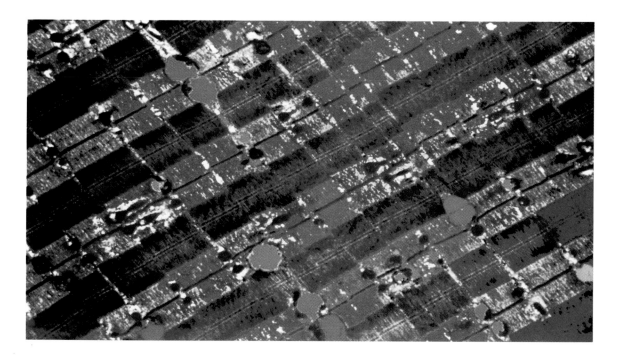

A microscopic view of the proteins myosin and actin. Myosin helps form thick myofilaments, while actin is the main component of thin myofilaments. (Reproduced by permission of Custom Medical Stock Photo.)

Tendons

The layers of connective tissue that bundle the various parts of a muscle usually converge or come together at the end of the muscle to form a tough, white, cord-like tissue called a tendon. Tendons attach muscles to bone. Because they contain fibers of the tough protein collagen, tendons are much stronger than muscle tissue. The collagen fibers are arranged in a tendon in a wavy way so that it can stretch and provide additional length at the muscle-bone junction. As muscles are used, the tendons are able to withstand the constant pulling and tugging.

Muscles are always attached at both of their ends. The end that is attached to a bone that moves when the muscle contracts is called the insertion. The other end, attached to a bone that does not move when the muscle contracts, is called the origin. It is important to note that not all muscles are attached to bones at both ends. The ends of some muscles are attached to other muscles; some are attached to the skin.

Major muscles of the body

Skeletal muscles that support the skull, backbone, and rib cage are called axial skeletal muscles. These include the muscles of the head and neck and those of the trunk. Roughly 60 percent of all skeletal muscles in the body are axial muscles. The skeletal muscles of the limbs (arms and legs) are called distal or appendicular skeletal muscles. These include the muscles of the shoulders and arms and those of the hip and legs.

Muscle names are descriptive. Some muscles are named according to their location in the body. For example, the frontalis muscle overlies the frontal bone of the skull. Other muscles are named for their relative size. Terms such as maximus (largest), minimus (smallest), and longus (long) are often used as part of a muscle's name. Still other muscles are named for their shape. The deltoid muscle is so named because it has the shape of the Greek letter *delta*, which is triangular-shaped. And some muscles are named for their actions. Terms such as flexor (to flex or bend in), extensor (to extend or straighten out), adductor (to draw toward a line that runs down

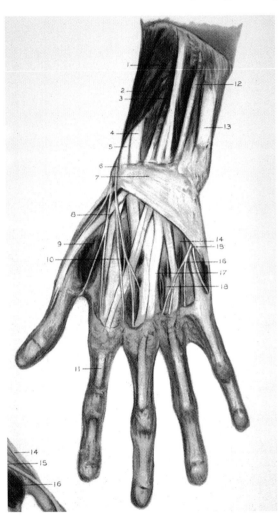

Dissected tendons in a human hand. Tendons attach muscle to bone and are much stronger than muscle tissue. (Reproduced by permission of Custom Medical Stock Photo.)

the middle of the body), and abductor (to draw away from a line that runs down the middle of the body) are often added as part of a muscle's name.

Please note: in the naming of the major muscles of the body on the following pages, pronunciations are provided in parenthesis when necessary.

MUSCLES OF THE HEAD AND NECK. The muscles of the face are unique: they are attached to the skull on one end and to the skin or other muscles on the other end. Muscles that are attached to the skin of the face allow people to express emotions through actions such as smiling, frowning, pouting, and kissing.

As mentioned, the frontalis (frun-TA-lis) covers the frontal bone or forehead. The temporalis (tem-po-RAL-is) is a fan-shaped muscle overlying the temporal bone on each side of the head above the ear. The orbicularis oculi (or-bik-u-LAR-is OK-u-lie) encircles each eye and helps close the eyelid. The orbicularis oris (or-bik-u-LAR-is OR-is) is the circular muscle around the lips. It closes and extends the lips.

The masseter (mas-SE-ter), located over the rear of the lower jaw on each side of the face, opens and closes the jaw, allowing chewing. The buccinator (BUK-si-na-tor), running horizontally across each cheek, flattens the cheek and pulls back the corners of the mouth. The sternocleidomastoid (ster-no-kli-do-MAS-toyd), located on either side of the neck and extending from the

A section of striated muscle tissue. Skeletal muscles are composed of tissue fibers that are striated or striped. (Photograph by M. Abbey. Reproduced by permission of Photo Researchers, Inc.)

clavicle or collarbone to the temporal bone on the side of the head, allows the head to rotate and the neck to flex.

MUSCLES OF THE TRUNK. On the front part of the trunk or torso, the pectoralis major (pek-to-RA-lis MA-jor) are the large, fan-shaped muscles that cover the upper part of the chest. They flex the shoulders and pull the arms into the body. The rectus abdominis (REK-tus ab-DOM-i-nis) are the strap-like muscles of the abdomen, extending from the ribs to the pelvis. Better known as the stomach muscles, they flex the vertebral column or backbone and provide support for the abdomen and its many organs. The muscles making up the side walls of the abdomen are the external oblique (ex-TER-nal o-BLEEK). In addition to helping compress the abdomen, they rotate the trunk and allow it to bend sideways.

On the rear part of the trunk, the trapezius (trah-PEE-zee-us) are the kite-shaped muscles that run from the back of the neck and upper back down to the middle of the back. They raise, lower, and adduct the shoulders. The large, flat muscles that cover the lower back are the latissimus dorsi (lah-TIS-i-mus DOR-see). They adduct and rotate the arms and help extend the shoulders.

MUSCLES OF THE SHOULDERS AND ARMS. The fleshy, triangular-shaped muscles that form the rounded shape of the shoulders are the deltoid (DEL-toyd). They help abduct the arm, or move it away from the middle of the body. The most familiar muscle of the upper arm is the biceps brachii (BI-seps BRAY-key-eye.) Located on the front of the upper arm, the bicep makes a prominent bulge as it flexes the elbow. On the rear portion of the upper arms is the triceps brachii (TRY-seps BRAY-key-eye). Its action is just the opposite of the biceps: it extends or straightens the forearm.

MACHINES WITH MUSCLES

Robots and machines that move and pick up objects like humans may no longer be found only in science fiction novels and movies. Scientists have created various artificial muscles that contract and expand just like human muscles. Unlike human muscles, however, artificial muscles have no limit to their strength.

One such artificial muscle is made out of artificial silk, which is cooked and then boiled to make a rubbery, semiliquid substance. The substance is similar in structure to human muscle, composed of smaller and smaller fibers. These fibers are naturally negatively charged with electricity.

When an acid (which has a positive electrical charge) is applied to this substance, the negative and positive ions attract each other and the substance contracts. When a base material (which has a negative charge) is applied, the ions repel each other and the material expands.

The National Aeronautics and Space Administration (NASA) has plans for artificial muscles. A small NASA rover destined to explore an asteroid in 2002 will be equipped with artificial muscles. Scientists hope tests like this one will eventually lead to the creation of space robots with humanlike flexibility and movement. Beyond that, they hope artificial muscles may someday be used to replace defective muscles in humans.

The muscles of the forearm, which move the bones of the hands, are thin and long. Of these many muscles, the flexor carpi (FLEX-or CAR-pee) bend the wrist and the flexor digitorum (FLEX-or di-ji-TOR-um) bend the fingers. The muscles that have the opposite effect, extending the wrist and fingers, are the extensor carpi and the extensor digitorum.

MUSCLES OF THE HIPS AND LEGS. Muscles of the lower limbs cause movement at the hip, knee, and foot joints. These muscles are among the largest and strongest muscles in the body. Muscles on the thigh (upper portion of the leg) are especially massive and powerful since they hold the body upright against the force of gravity.

The gluteus maximus (GLOO-tee-us MAX-i-mus) are the large muscles that form most of the flesh of the buttocks. These powerful muscles help extend the hip in activities such as climbing stairs and jumping. The adductor (ah-DUC-ter) muscles are a group of muscles that form a mass on the inside of the thighs. As their name indicates, they adduct or press the thighs together.

On the front of the thigh is a group of four muscles known collectively as the quadriceps (KWOD-ri-seps). Together, the quadriceps help powerfully extend or straighten the knee, such as when an individual kicks a soccer ball. On the back of the thigh, a group of three muscles performs the

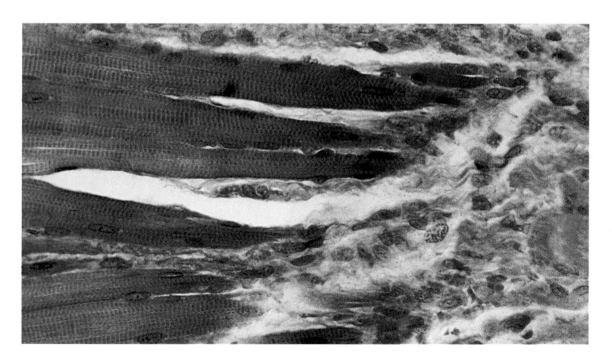

A muscle-tendon junction. As muscles are used, the tendons are able to withstand the constant pulling and tugging. (Reproduced by permission of Photo Researchers, Inc.)

opposite effect. Known as hamstrings (HAM-strings), these muscles flex or bend the knee.

The sartorius (sar-TOR-ee-us) is long, straplike muscle that crosses the front of the thigh diagonally from the outside of the hip to the inside of the knee. Although it is not that powerful, it does lie on upper surface of the thigh and is easily seen. The sartorius helps rotate the leg so an individual can sit in a cross-legged position with the knees wide apart.

On the back part of the lower leg is the calf muscle, properly known as the gastrocnemius (gas-trok-NEE-me-us). This diamond-shaped muscle, formed in two sections, helps extend or lower the foot, such as when an individual walks on his or her toes. The strong tendon that attaches the gastrocnemius to the heel of the foot is the well-known Achilles tendon (ah-KI-leez; in Greek mythology, a hero of the Trojan War who is killed by an arrow shot into his heel). The main muscle on the front part of the lower leg, the tibialis anterior (tib-ee-A-lis), opposes the action of the gastrocnemius. It flexes and inverts or elevates the foot. When runners and other athletes experience tenderness and pain in the front part of the lower leg, a condition commonly known as shin splints, the tibialis anterior has been strained or pulled.

MUSCLE FACTS

Smallest muscle in the body?

Stapedius: the muscle that activates the stirrup, the small bone that sends vibrations from the eardrum to the inner ear. It measures just 0.05 inch (0.13 centimeter) in length.

Largest muscle in the body?

Latissimus dorsi: the large, flat muscle pair that covers the middle and lower back.

Longest muscle in the body?

Sartorius: the straplike muscle that runs diagonally from the waist down across the front of the thigh to the knee.

Strongest muscle in the body?

Gluteus maximus: the muscle pair of the hip that form most of the flesh of the buttocks.

Fastest-reacting muscle in the body?

Orbicularis oculi: the muscle that encircles the eye and closes the eyelid. It contracts in less than 0.01 second.

Number of muscles used to make a smile?

Seventeen.

Number of muscles used to make a frown?

Forty-three.

WORKINGS: HOW THE MUSCULAR SYSTEM FUNCTIONS

Muscles have three important functions: to produce movement, maintain posture, and generate heat. Almost all movements by the human body result from muscle contraction. Muscles lend support to the body and help it maintain posture against the force of gravity. Even when the body is at rest (or asleep), muscle fibers are contracting to maintain muscle tone. Finally, any activity by muscles generates heat as a by-product, which is vital in maintaining normal body temperature.

The link between nerve cells and muscle fibers

In order to contract or shorten, muscle fibers must be stimulated by nerve impulses sent through motor neurons or nerves. These impulses originate in the brain, then run down the spine. From there, they branch out to all parts of the body.

A single motor neuron may stimulate a few muscle fibers or hundreds of them. A motor neuron along with all the fibers it stimulates is called a motor unit. When a motor neuron reaches a muscle fiber, it does not touch the fiber, but fits into a hollow on the surface of the muscle fiber. This region where the end of the motor neuron and the membrane of the muscle fiber come close together is called the neuromuscular junction.

When a nerve impulse reaches the end of the motor neuron at the neuromuscular junction, acetylcholine (a neurotransmitter chemical) is released. Acetylcholine then travels across the small gap between the motor neuron and the muscle fiber and attaches to receptors on the membrane of the muscle fiber. This triggers an electrical charge that quickly travels from one end of the muscle fiber to the other, causing it to contract.

The sliding filament theory

In 1950, while working to explain exactly how muscles contract, two teams of scientists developed the same theory at the same time: the sliding filament theory. Today, medical researchers accept this theory as a good description of what happens to make a muscle contact.

Victor Albrecht von Haller. (Reproduced by permission of the Library of Congress.)

DISCOVERING THE LINK BETWEEN NERVES AND MUSCLES

Swiss biologist Victor Albrecht von Haller (1708–1777) was the first scientist to discover the relationship between nerves and muscles. Prior to his research, scientists knew little about the structure and function of nerves or about their interaction with muscles. A popular theory at the time even held that nerves were hollow tubes through which a spirit or fluid flowed.

Haller rejected this theory, especially since no one had ever been able to locate or identify such a spirit or fluid. Instead, he sought to prove that a muscle contracts when a stimulus is applied to it. Haller labeled this action irritability.

In his research, Haller soon found that irritability increased when a stimulus was applied to a nerve connected to a muscle. He then rightly concluded that in order for a muscle to contract, a stimulus had to come from its connecting nerve.

According to the sliding filament theory, thick myofilaments have branches or arms that extend out from their main body. At the end of the branches are thickened heads (the appearance of a thick myofilament can be likened to a racing shell or a long narrow boat with many oars attached on either side). Normally, when a muscle is relaxed, the thick and thin myofilaments do not interact. When the muscle is stimulated to contract, they do.

The electrical charge triggered by acetylcholine stimulates the release of calcium ions (an ion is an atom or group or atoms that has an electrical charge) stored within the muscle fiber. The ions attach to the thin myofilaments and remove their protective coverings. The arms of the thick myofilaments then reach out, and the heads on the arms attach to open sites on the thin myofilaments. The arms pivot (an action called a power stroke), pulling the thin myofilaments toward the center of the sarcomere. This shortens the sarcomere. As this event occurs simultaneously throughout all sarcomeres in a muscle fiber, the muscle fiber shortens or contracts.

A single nerve impulse produces only one contraction, which lasts between 0.01 and 0.04 second. For a muscle fiber to remain contracted, the brain must send additional nerve impulses. When nerve impulses cease, so do the electrical charges, the release of calcium ions, and the connection between thin myofilaments and thick myofilaments.

When a muscle fiber contracts, it does so completely and always produces the same amount of pull (tension). The muscle fiber is either "on" or "off." This is known as the all-or-nothing principle of muscle contraction. While this principle applies to individual muscle fibers, it does not apply to entire muscles. A muscle would be useless if it could only contract completely or not at all. The amount of tension or pull in a muscle can vary depending on how many muscle fibers in that muscle are stimulated to contract.

MUSCLES IN SPACE

In the zero gravity of space, astronauts face many challenges. Chief among these is the effect of weightlessness on muscles. Even after spending as little as four or five days in space, astronauts have experienced significant muscle and bone changes.

The reason is that more than half the muscles in the human body are designed primarily to fight gravity. In a weightless environment, those muscles are not used. As a result, they quickly weaken and atrophy or waste away. Without the stress of pumping blood through the body against the force of gravity, the muscles of the heart also begin to weaken considerably.

Exercising during space flights is one way astronauts have tried to counter the effects of zero gravity. Unfortunately, they have had to exercise two to three hours a day just to maintain muscle and cardiovascular strength. The National Aeronautics and Space Administration (NASA) and research centers are currently working to develop exercising devices that recreate the forces on Earth so astronauts can spend more time exploring instead of exercising.

Muscle fiber energy

In order to contract, muscles need energy. That energy comes from adenosine triphosphate (ATP), a high-energy molecule found in every cell in the body. ATP is the **only** energy source that muscles can use to power their activity. Thick myofilaments need ATP in order to detach their heads from thin myofilaments. They then use the energy from the ATP to complete their next power stroke.

Yet, muscle fibers store only a limited supply of ATP—about 4 to 6 seconds' worth. For muscles to continue working, ATP must be supplied continuously. The most abundant energy source for ATP is glycogen—a starch form of the simple sugar glucose made up of thousands of glucose units. In the human body, the liver stores glucose by converting it to glycogen. When the body needs energy, the liver is stimulated to change glycogen back into glucose and secrete it into the bloodstream for use by the cells.

In the cells, glucose combines with oxygen to yield or produce carbon dioxide, water, heat, and ATP. This process of energy production that uses oxygen in the reaction is called aerobic ("with air") metabolism. Carbon dioxide, water, and heat are all waste products of this chemical reaction. Carbon dioxide moves from the cells into the blood to be carried to the lungs, where it is exhaled. The water becomes a necessary part of a cell's internal fluid. The heat contributes to normal body temperature. If too much heat is generated, such as during vigorous physical activities, the excess heat is carried away and removed from the body through the process of sweating.

EXERCISE AND MUSCLE FATIGUE. Even though muscle fibers store some oxygen, that oxygen is quickly used up, especially during strenuous exercise. In order to convert glucose into ATP so they can continue working, muscles must receive more oxygen via the blood. That is why respiration or breathing rate increases during physical exertion. In times where work or play activities are exhausting, muscle fibers may literally run out of oxygen. If not enough oxygen is present in muscle fibers, the fibers convert glucose into lactic acid, a chemical waste product.

When lactic acid builds up in muscle fibers, it increases the acidity in the fibers. Key enzymes in the fibers are then deactivated, and the fibers can no longer function properly. As a result, muscles are not as effective, contracting less and less. This condition is known as muscle fatigue.

WHY DOES THAT HAPPEN?

Q: Why do I shiver when I become cold?

A: When muscles need to create ATP, their only energy source, they combine glucose with oxygen. This reaction also creates heat as a by-product. The body uses this heat to maintain normal body temperature.

When the temperature of the body drops below normal, the brain signals the muscles to contract rapidly—what we perceive as shivering. The heat generated by these rapid muscle contractions helps to raise or at least stabilize body temperature.

In a state of fatigue, muscle contractions may be painful. Finally, muscles may simply stop working.

Lactic acid is normally carried away from muscles by the blood. It is then transported to the liver, where it is changed back into glucose. In order to do this, however, the liver needs ATP. To produce ATP in the liver, oxygen is once again needed. This is why breathing rate remains high even after vigorous physical activity is stopped. Only after the liver produces the necessary ATP does breathing gradually return to normal.

Movement and muscle arrangement

Muscles cannot push; they can only pull. In order to create movement, muscles must act in pairs. Muscles are arranged on the skeleton in such a way that the flexing or contracting of one muscle or group of muscles is usually balanced by the lengthening or relaxation of another muscle or group of muscles. In other words, when a muscle performs an action, another can undo or reverse that action.

For example, when the biceps (muscle on the front of the upper arm) contracts, the forearm moves in at the elbow toward the biceps; at the same time, the triceps (muscle on the rear of the upper arms) lengthens. When the forearm is moved out in a straight-arm position, the opposite occurs: the triceps contracts and the biceps lengthens.

A muscle whose contraction is responsible for producing a particular movement is called a prime mover (or an agonist). A muscle that opposes or reverses the movement of a prime mover is called an antagonist. Generally, antagonistic muscles are located on the opposite side of a limb or portion of the body from prime mover or agonist muscles.

In the previous example, the biceps is the prime mover behind the flexing of the elbow. In this movement, the triceps is the antagonist of the biceps. When the forearm is straightened out (and the elbow is extended), the triceps becomes the prime mover and the biceps is the antagonist.

Most muscles do not act by themselves to produce a particular movement. Muscles that help prime movers by producing the same movement or by reducing unnecessary movement are called synergists. When the biceps flexes the elbow, smaller muscles in the upper arm also come into play. If the elbow is flexed with the palm of the hand up, the biceps is the prime mover. However, if the elbow is flexed with the palm down or the thumb up (palm in), the other muscles become the prime movers. These particular synergistic muscles allow for greater mobility or movement of the hand when the elbow is flexed.

MOST MUSCLES DO NOT ACT BY THEMSELVES TO PRODUCE A PARTICULAR MOVEMENT.

Although prime movers are mainly responsible for producing certain body movements, the actions of antagonists and synergists are equally important. Without the combined efforts of all three types of muscles, body movements would not be smooth, coordinated, and precise.

Muscle tone

Even when the body is at rest, certain muscle fibers in all muscles are contracting. This activity is directed by the brain and cannot be controlled consciously. This state of continuous partial muscle contractions is known as muscle tone. These contractions are not strong enough to produce movement, but do tense and firm the muscles. In doing so, they keep the muscles firm, healthy, and ready for action. Muscles with moderate muscle tone are firm and solid, whereas ones with little muscle tone are limp and soft.

Muscle tone is the result of different motor units throughout a muscle being stimulated by the nervous system in an orderly way. First one group of motor units is stimulated, then another. Alternate fibers contract so the muscle as a whole does not become fatigued.

Muscle tone is important because it helps human beings maintain an upright posture. Without muscle tone, an individual would not be able to sit up straight in a chair or hold his or her head up. Muscle tone is also important because it generates heat to help maintain body temperature. Normal muscle tone accounts for about 25 percent of the heat in a body at rest.

MUSCLE TONE IS IMPORTANT BECAUSE IT HELPS HUMAN BEINGS MAINTAIN AN UPRIGHT POSTURE.

AILMENTS: WHAT CAN GO WRONG WITH THE MUSCULAR SYSTEM

With their rich supply of blood, skeletal muscles are fairly resistant to infection. When following a healthy lifestyle, few people will experience a life-threatening muscular ailment. Though rare, serious disorders can target the muscles. A few disorders can affect the muscles indirectly by attacking the nerves that stimulate muscles. Among these ailments are botulism and tetanus.

The following are a few of the disorders that can affect the muscular system, from common injuries caused by misuse to indirectly caused serious disorders.

Botulism

Botulism, or severe food poisoning, is caused by a toxin (poison) produced by a certain bacteria that is sometimes present in foods not properly canned or preserved. Once released by the bacteria in the body, the toxin prevents motor neurons from releasing acetylcholine at neuromuscular junctions. Muscle fibers are then not stimulated to contract and paralysis (partial or complete loss of the ability to move) results. As botulism progresses, the muscles controlling breathing fail and the affected individual suffocates.

Botulism is a serious disease that requires prompt medical attention. Antibiotics are not effective in preventing or treating the disease. Medical researchers have developed an antitoxin (antibody capable of acting against a toxin) for treating botulism. However, since it only works on the toxin when it is not attached to nerve endings, the antitoxin must be given to an infected individual as soon as possible. Motor neuron endings that have already been affected by the toxin cannot be saved. If an individual survives a severe case of botulism, it may weeks to months to years for the body to recover fully, if at all.

THE MOST FREQUENT AND MOST DREADED TYPE OF MUSCULAR DYSTROPHY APPEARS IN BOYS AGED THREE TO SEVEN.

Muscular dystrophy

The most common type of genetic (inherited) muscular disorder is muscular dystrophy. This disease causes skeletal muscles to waste away slowly and progressively. Medical researchers generally recognize nine types of muscular dystrophy. The causes behind some of these types are not well understood. In others, researchers believe that proteins used by muscle fibers to protect their membranes are defective, leading to deterioration of the membranes and the muscle fibers.

The most frequent and most dreaded type of muscular dystrophy appears in boys aged three to seven. (Boys are usually affected because it is a sex-linked condition; girls are carriers of the disease and are usually not affected.) In the United States, this type of the disease occurs in about 1 in 3,500 births and affects approximately 8,000 boys and young men.

The first symptom of this disease type is clumsiness in walking and a tendency to fall due to muscle weakness in the legs and pelvis. The disease then spreads to other areas in the body. Sometimes, muscle tissue is replaced by fatty tissue, giving the false impression that the muscles have become enlarged. By the age of ten, a boy is usually confined to a wheelchair or a bed.

MUSCULAR SYSTEM DISORDERS

Botulism (BOCH-a-liz-em): Form of food poisoning in which a bacterial toxin prevents the release of acetylcholine at neuromuscular junctions, resulting in paralysis.

Muscular dystrophy (MUS-kyu-lar DIS-tro-fee): One of several inherited muscular diseases in which a person's muscles gradually and irreversibly deteriorate, causing weakness and eventually complete disability.

Myasthenia gravis (my-ass-THEH-nee-ah GRA-vis): Autoimmune disease in which antibodies attack acetylcholine, blocking the transmission of nerve impulses to muscle fibers.

Tetanus (TET-n-es): Bacterial disease in which a bacterial toxin causes the repetitive stimulation of muscle fibers, resulting in convulsive muscle spasms and rigidity.

Death usually occurs before adulthood because of a respiratory infection brought on by the weakness of respiratory or breathing muscles.

Another type of muscular dystrophy appears later in life and affects both sexes equally. The first signs appear in adolescence. The muscles affected are those in the face, shoulders, and upper arms. The hips and legs may also be affected. This type of muscular dystrophy occurs in about 1 out of every 20,000 people. Individuals afflicted with this disease may survive until middle age.

Currently, there is no known cure for any type of muscular dystrophy. Certain drugs have been developed that slow the progression of some types. Physical therapy involving regular, nonstrenuous exercise is often prescribed to help maintain general good health.

Myasthenia gravis

Myasthenia gravis is an autoimmune disease that causes muscle weakness. An autoimmune disease is one in which antibodies (proteins normally produced by the body to fight infection) attack and damage the body's own normal cells, causing tissue destruction. In myasthenia gravis, antibodies attack receptors on the membranes of muscle fibers that receive acetylcholine from motor neurons. Unable to receive acetylcholine, the muscle fibers cannot be stimulated to contract and weakness develops.

About 30,000 people in the United States are affected by myasthenia gravis. The disease can occur at any age, but it is most common in women between the ages of twenty and forty. The muscles of the neck, throat, lips, tongue, face, and eyes are primarily affected. Muscles of the arms, legs, and trunk may also be involved. Depending on the severity of the disease, a person may have difficulty moving their eyes, seeing clearly, walking, speaking clearly, chewing and swallowing, and even breathing. Physical exertion, heat from the Sun, hot showers, hot drinks, and stress may all increase symptoms.

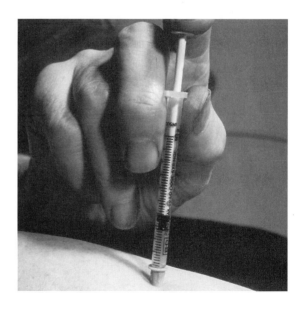

There is no cure for myasthenia gravis, but drugs have been developed that effectively control the symptoms in most people. The disease only causes early death if the respiratory muscles are affected and stop functioning properly.

Spasms and cramps

Muscle spasms and cramps are spontaneous, often painful muscle contractions. Cramps are

An intramuscular injection. Medication is injected into muscles when larger volumes of a drug are needed. (Reproduced by permission of Photo Researchers, Inc.)

usually defined as spasms that last over a period of time. Any muscle in the body may be affected, but spasms and cramps are most common in the calves, feet, and hands. While painful, spasms and cramps are harmless and are not related to any disorder, in most cases.

Spasms or cramps may be caused by abnormal activity at any stage in the muscle contraction process, from the brain sending an electrical signal to the muscle fiber relaxing. Prolonged exercise, where sensations of pain and fatigue are often ignored, can lead to such severe energy shortages that a muscle cannot relax, causing a spasm or cramp. Dehydration—the loss of fluids and salts through sweating, vomiting, or diarrhea—can disrupt ion balances in both muscles and nerves. This can prevent them from responding and recovering normally, which can lead to spasms and cramps.

> **SPASMS OR CRAMPS MAY BE CAUSED BY ABNORMAL ACTIVITY AT ANY STAGE IN THE MUSCULAR CONTRACTION PROCESS.**

Most simple spasms and cramps require no treatment other than patience and stretching. Gentle stretching and massaging of the affected muscle may ease the pain and hasten recovery.

Strains

Strains are tears in a muscle. Sometimes called pulled muscles, they usually occur because of overexertion (too much tension placed on a muscle) or improper lifting techniques. Strains are common and can affect anyone. Symptoms of strains range from mild muscle stiffness to great soreness.

Mild strains can be treated at home. Basic first aid consists of RICE: **R**est, **I**ce for forty-eight hours, **C**ompression (wrapping in an elastic bandage), and **E**levation. Strains can be prevented by stretching and warming up before exercising and using proper lifting techniques.

Tetanus

Like botulism, tetanus is also caused by a toxin released by a bacteria. This bacteria invades the body most often through deep puncture wounds exposed to contaminated soil. Many people associate tetanus with wounds from rusty nails or other dirty objects, but any wound can be a source. In the body, the tetanus bacteria releases its toxin, which affects motor neurons at neuromuscular junctions. Its effect, however, is opposite that of the botulism toxin. This toxin causes the repetitive stimulation of muscle fibers, resulting in convulsive muscle spasms and rigidity.

> **TETANUS IS OFTEN CALLED "LOCKJAW" BECAUSE ONE OF THE MOST COMMON SYMPTOMS IS A STIFF JAW.**

Tetanus is often called "lockjaw" because one of the most common symptoms is a stiff jaw, unable to be opened. The disease sometimes affects the body only at the site of infection. More often, it spreads to the entire body. The uncontrollable muscle spasms produced are sometimes severe enough to cause broken bones. Tetanus results in death when the muscles controlling breathing become "locked" and cannot function.

Up to 30 percent of tetanus victims in the United States die. Prompt medical attention is crucial in handling the disease. Treatment, which can take several weeks, includes antibiotics to kill the bacteria and shots of antitoxin to neutralize the toxin. Recovery can then take six or more weeks. Tetanus, however, is easily preventable through vaccination, which helps the body develop antibodies against the bacteria.

TAKING CARE: KEEPING THE MUSCULAR SYSTEM HEALTHY

As humans age, all muscle tissues decrease in size and power. Muscle fibers die and are replaced by fibrous connective tissue or by fatty tissue. The connective tissue makes the muscles less flexible. Movement is limited. Even muscles with normal tone will atrophy or waste away.

The effects of this eventual decline in the muscular system can be offset by regular exercise throughout an individual's life. Exercise helps control body weight, strengthens bones, tones and builds muscles, and generally improves the quality of life for people of all ages.

Some types of exercise help to strengthen the heart and lungs. These activities are called aerobic exercises. The American College of Sports Medicine and the Centers for Disease Control and Prevention recommend that people engage in moderate to intense aerobic activity four or more times per week for at least thirty minutes at a time. Walking, jogging, cycling, swimming, and climbing stairs are just a few examples of aerobic activity. These exercises also force the large muscles of the body to use oxygen more efficiently, as well as store greater amounts of ATP.

Exercises that increase the size and strength of muscles are called anaerobic exercises. These types of exercises require quick bursts of energy. Weight lifting (also known as strength training) and sprinting are just two examples anaerobic activity. As muscles grow larger, they require more energy to work, even when the body is at rest. To meet this increased need, the body is forced to use its stored nutrients more efficiently.

When combined with exercise, the following help keep the muscular system operating at peak efficiency: proper nutrition, healthy amounts of good-quality drinking water, adequate rest, and stress reduction.

The "Food Guide" Pyramid developed by the U.S. Departments of Agriculture and Health and Human Services provides easy-to-follow guidelines for a healthy diet. In general, foods that are low in fat (especially saturated fat), low in cholesterol, and high in fiber should be eaten. Fat should make up no more than 30 percent of a person's total daily calorie intake. Breads, cereals, pastas, fruits, and vegetables should form the bulk of a person's diet; meat, fish, nuts, and cheese and other dairy products should make up a lesser portion.

Stress taxes all body systems. Any condition that threatens the body's homeostasis or steady state is a form of stress. Conditions that cause stress may be physical, emotional, or environmental. When stress lasts longer than a few hours, higher energy demands are placed on the body. Combining exercise with proper amounts of sleep, relaxation techniques, and positive thinking will help reduce stress and keep the body in balance.

FOR MORE INFORMATION

Books

Avila, Victoria. *How Our Muscles Work*. New York: Chelsea House, 1995.

Ballard, Carol. *The Skeleton and Muscular System*. Austin, TX: Raintree/ Steck-Vaughn, 1997.

Feinberg, Brian. *The Musculoskeletal System*. New York: Chelsea House, 1993.

Llamas, Andreu. *Muscles and Bones*. Milwaukee, WI: Gareth Stevens, 1998.

Parker, Steve. *Muscles*. Brookfield, CT: Copper Beech Books, 1997.

Silverstein, Alvin, Virginia Silverstein, and Robert Silverstein. *The Muscular System*. New York: Twenty-First Century Books, 1994.

WWW Sites

Cyber Anatomy: Muscular System
http://tqd.advanced.org/11965/html/cyber-anatomy_musboth.html
Site provides detailed front and rear views of the human body with major muscle groups labeled. Also includes brief paragraph descriptions of the three types of muscle tissue.

Hosford Muscle Tables: Skeletal Muscles of the Human Body
http://www.ptcentral.com/muscles/
Web site is an index containing detailed information about the skeletal muscles of the human body. Included is each muscle's origin, insertion, action, blood supply, and innervation.

Muscular Dystrophy Association
http://www.mdausa.org
Homepage of the Muscular Dystrophy Association.

Muscular System
http://hyperion.advanced.org/2935/Natures_Best/Nat_Best_Low_Level/ Muscular_page.L.html

Site offers a description of cardiac, smooth, and skeletal muscle tissues and an investigation on how groups of muscles function in different areas of the body.

Muscular System

http://www.innerbody.com/image/musfov.html

Site includes large images of the human muscular system (front and rear views) with each major muscle linked to a paragraph explanation of its structure and function. Other links on the site feature a paragraph overview of the muscular system, an explanation of the muscle cell types, and nerve/muscle connections.

Bibliography

BOOKS

Arnau, Eduard, and Parramon Editorial Team. *The Human Body*. Hauppauge, NY: Barron's Educational Series, 1998.

Balkwill, Frances R. *The Incredible Human Body: A Book of Discovery and Learning*. New York: Sterling Publications, 1996.

Beckelman, Laurie. *The Human Body*. Pleasantville, NY: Reader's Digest, 1999.

Beres, Samantha. *101 Things Every Kid Should Know About the Human Body*. Los Angeles, CA: Lowell House, 1999.

Burnie, David. *Concise Encyclopedia of the Human Body*. London, England: DK Publishing, 1995.

Clayman, Charles. *Illustrated Guide to the Human Body*. London, England: DK Publishing, 1995.

Incredible Voyage: Exploring the Human Body. Washington, D.C.: National Geographic Society, 1998.

Marieb, Elaine N. *Anatomy and Physiology Coloring Book: A Complete Study Guide*. Fifth edition. Menlo Park, CA: Addison-Wesley, 1996.

Parker, Steve. *Body Atlas*. London, England: DK Publishing, 1993.

Parker, Steve. *How the Body Works*. Pleasantville, NY: Reader's Digest, 1999.

Parsons, Alexandra. *An Amazing Machine*. New York: Franklin Watts, 1997.

Rose, Marie, and Steve Parker. *The Human Body*. Alexandria, VA: Time-Life, 1997.

Rowan, Peter. *Some Body!* New York: Knopf, 1995.

Bibliography

Smith, Anthony. *Intimate Universe: The Human Body*. New York: Random House, 1999.

Suzuki, David. *Looking at the Body*. New York: John Wiley, 1991.

Walker, Richard. *3D: Human Body*. London, England: DK Publishing, 1999.

Walker, Richard. *The Children's Atlas of the Human Body: Actual Size Bones, Muscles, and Organs in Full Color*. Brookfield, CT: Millbrook Press, 1994.

Walker, Richard, ed. *The Visual Dictionary of Human Anatomy*. London, England: DK Publishing, 1996.

Weiner, Esther. *The Incredible Human Body: Great Projects and Activities that Teach about the Major Body Systems*. New York: Scholastic Trade, 1997.

Whitfield, Philip, ed. *The Human Body Explained: A Guide to Understanding the Incredible Living Machine*. New York: Henry Holt, 1995.

WWW SITES

Please note: Readers should be reminded that Internet addresses are subject to change. Some of the following web sites addresses (and those included at the end of each chapter) may have been removed and new ones added.

AMA Health Insights—Specific Conditions
   http://www.ama-assn.org/consumer/specond.htm
   Part of the American Medical Association's web site, this section provides in-depth information on a number of well known health conditions, focusing on what the condition is, symptoms, diagnosis, treatment, frequently asked questions, and support and information groups.

Anatomy and Physiology
   http://www.msms.doe.k12.ms.us/biology/anatomy/apmain.html
   Site provides varied information on nine human body systems. Although aimed at high school students, material also should be accessible to students in grades immediately below.

Atlas of the Human Body
   http://www.ama-assn.org/insight/gen_hlth/atlas/atlas.htm
   From the American Medical Association, an online atlas of the human body, including images and information on all major systems and organs.

BodyQuest
   http://library.advanced.org/10348/home.html
   Award-winning site is an exploration of human anatomy designed for students aged between eleven and sixteen. Information is present on

major body systems and parts. Site also includes experiments related to specific system or parts, a discussion board, and an interactive quiz section.

Explore the Human Body
http://www.eca.com.ve/wtutor/dani/introweb.htm
Site presents information (along with images) on the human body in seven lessons, each one focusing on a different body system.

How the Body Works
http://KidsHealth.org/parent/healthy/bodyworks.html
Information on certain major systems of the body is present on this site, along with information on topics ranging from nutrition to health problems (all with a focus on kids).

Human Anatomy Central
http://nurse-dk.com/anat/
Recommended site has a human anatomy links database that provides sixty-eight links to sites that provide information on certain body systems and on general anatomy and physiology.

Human Anatomy On-Line
http://www.innerbody.com/htm/body.html
Educational, interactive site presents information on the major systems of the human body with over 100 images and animations of the body.

Human Body
http://www.fcasd.edu/schools/dms/HBody.htm
Site, prepared by and geared toward middle school students, presents extensive information on seven major body systems: Circulatory, digestive, excretory, muscular, nervous, respiratory, and skeletal.

Human Body System Resources on the World Wide Web
http://www.stemnet.nf.ca/CITE/body.htm
Sponsored by Gander Academy of Gander, Newfoundland, Canada, this highly recommended, extensive site features links to ten body systems, each containing numerous links to information on that system and its parts. Site also provides links for general and teacher resources.

Mayo Clinic Health Oasis—Medical Reference Library
http://www.mayohealth.org/mayo/common/htm/library.htm
Site run by the renowned Mayo Clinic provides information on diseases and conditions ranging from arthritis to those affecting the skin.

NOAH: Health Topics and Resources
http://www.noah.cuny.edu/qksearch.html
Site run by the New York Online Access to Health (NOAH) presents extensive information on numerous health topics, from aging and Alzheimer's disease to tuberculosis.

Bibliography

Science Fact File: Inside the Human Body
http://www.imcpl.lib.in.us/nov_ind.htm
Images of and information on seven body systems is present on this site prepared by the Indianapolis-Marion County Public Library.

The Virtual Body
http://www.medtropolis.com/vbody/
Site is an interaction presentation of the human body, containing a series of elaborate displays of the various parts and functions of the human body using Shockwave technology.

United States National Library of Medicine
http://www.nlm.nih.gov/
Home page of the U.S. National Library of Medicine, the world's largest medical library.

Index

Italic type indicates volume number; **boldface** type indicates main entries and their page numbers; (ill.) indicates photos and illustrations.

Index

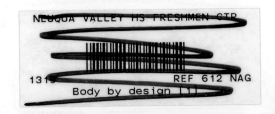